Best Wishes, Cindy.
I do hope that you enjoy
this "bit of history".
Bertha Boykin Todd
10 - 16 - 2019

P.S. It has been a pleasure
to meet you!

My Restless Journey

by

Bertha Boykin Todd

Edited by Rhonda Bellamy

A Publication of the
Ageless Foundation, Inc.

My Restless Journey

By Bertha Boykin Todd
Edited by Rhonda Bellamy

A Publication of the
Ageless Foundation, Inc.

Contact and ordering information:
The Ageless Foundation, Inc.
114 Mercer Street
Wilmington, NC 28403
910-367-5578
www.agelessfoundationinc.org

LIBRARY OF CONGRESS
CONTROL NUMBER: **2010917526**
Bertha Boykin Todd (author) and Rhonda Bellamy (editor)
My Restless Journey
Wilmington, NC, The Ageless Foundation, Inc.
243 pp.

Printing by:
Action Printing & Graphics
4852 Randall Parkway
Wilmington, NC 28403

First Printing: **November, 2010**
Copyright © 2010 – The Ageless Foundation, Inc.

International Standard Book Number
978-1-4507-4885-8

This book is dedicated to:

Edward Mack Todd
My spouse

Thomas J.L. Boykin
My father

Junious A. Boykin
My stepfather

Mallie Armona Farrior Boykin
My mother

Thomas Edison Boykin
My older brother

Ida Boykin Cooper
My older sister

(The aforementioned are deceased.)

Dr. Myrtle Boykin Sampson
My twin sister

Annie Boykin Carlton
My stepsister

All supported me in my numerous endeavors throughout the years.

Table of Contents

Foreword
by Rhonda Bellamy

"Father Time is not always a hard parent, and, though he tarries for none of his children, he often lays his hand lightly upon those who have used him well; making them old men and women inexorably enough, but leaving their hearts and spirits young and in full vigour. With such people the grey head is but the impression of the old fellow's hand in giving them his blessing, and every wrinkle but a notch in the quiet calendar of a well-spent life."

Charles Dickens could very well have been writing about Bertha Boykin Todd. With a physical and mental nimbleness that belies her years, the "old fellow" has indeed been kind. Some would credit genetics; I believe it is a well-spent life.

I don't recall being formally introduced to Bertha Todd; no introduction was necessary. She was, and is, as much a part of Wilmington's history as the river which runs through it. Natives will remember her largely singular role during New Hanover County schools' belated desegregation. Natives and newcomers will remember her leadership during the 1898 centennial effort.

"Each warrior wants to leave the mark of his will, his signature, on the important acts that he touches. This is not the voice of ego but of the human spirit, rising up and declaring that it has something to contribute to the solution of the hardest problems, no matter how vexing!" said basketball coach Pat Riley.

Such is the case with Bertha Todd, who simply wants to set the record straight for those who don't "get it". As we've sat around her kitchen table over the years, she has often told me about the restlessness that has gripped most of her adult life. She says she detects "it" in me.

The "it" is neither an action nor easily articulated. It's a knowing that history will show who stood up in times of struggle. But while history may speak for itself, Bertha Todd will speak for Bertha Todd...in her own words, in her own inimitable way!

Rhonda Bellamy
Editor

Introduction

It has been said that the most difficult language to communicate is the language of feelings. Sometimes it takes time to synthesize those feelings and even more time to see clearly the intricate pattern that is your purpose.

Everyone has a story to tell. My twin sister, Myrtle, professor emeritus at North Carolina A&T State University and clinicial psychologist, has talked about writing a book for almost 35 years, but I had neither the time nor the inclination.

When I first arrived in Wilmington in the fall of 1952, I had no idea that my entire 40 year career in education would take place in New Hanover County. Over the course of four decades, I served in six different capacities: Librarian/Media Specialist, Administrative Assistant in Human Relations, Assistant Principal in Human Relations, Assistant Principal/Graduation-Senior Certification, Principal of Secondary Summer School, Career Development Coordinator, and Director of Staff Development.

After my retirement in 1992, my late husband and I were working on the front lawn of our home when a retired educator stopped by the house to chat one day. The Wilmington native, who was advancing in years, greeted us and then made a statement that absolutely shocked me.

"Sister Todd, you know, during school desegregation, many of us were wondering what you were trying to prove," he said. I simply responded, "Oh, yes?" I too have wrestled with my restlessness, driven by an internal force that defies convention and sometimes common sense. While what I wanted to say has taken nearly 20 years, I am finally ready to tell *my* story.

My profound gratitude:

To my daughter, Rita Denise, who typed, edited, and offered suggestions throughout this entire process. She also encouraged me to continue with this effort when I would become discouraged and considered abandoning this project.

To my son, Brian Edward who, despite his busy schedule, offered support and even read a chapter, all the while reminding me not to become "consumed" by this project.

To my friend, Rosalind Moore Mosley, a former Williston student, graduate and a homeroom student of my spouse. Rosalind returned to Wilmington following her stay in Pittsburgh, PA. Her assistance has been invaluable.

To my niece, Laverne Midgette Leach, and her husband, Albert Leach, who provided significant assistance with their expert knowledge of photography.

To my editor, Rhonda Bellamy, who is one of the most creative individuals that I have ever met. Without Rhonda guiding me through the process and providing her extensive editorial experience, this book would not have become a reality. I am eternally grateful.

My Restless Journey

"The Early Years"
Chapter 1

"I used to be somebody if I ain't nobody now!"

My paternal grandmother, Tama Boykin, sang this ditty as she strutted around her Sampson County farm feeding chickens. Although she died before my twin sister Myrtle and I were born, I have often wondered why this became her familiar refrain. My father's parents were born in Wake County and later resettled in Sampson County, in a rural area defined by the Parkersburg post office and later the Garland post office.

Other than the fact that Tama was short in stature and had eventually lost her sight, I know little about the woman who gave birth to two daughters and four sons, including my father, Thomas Jefferson Lee Boykin, who was born May 17, 1883. His three brothers, Junious, James, and Benjamin, became full time farmers; while he and his two sisters, Frances and Maggie, studied to become teachers at Fayetteville State Normal (now Fayetteville State University).

It was at Fayetteville State Normal that my father met my mother, Mallie Armona Farrior of Duplin County, who was born October 19, 1896. Her mother's maiden name was Whitehead, and my maternal grandparents were both listed as mulatto. My grandfather was believed to have been sired by a white man who often took him fox hunting.

My mother was one of five girls and five boys born of the union. Her brothers were Elliott, John D., Mayloyd, Robert, and Booker. Her sisters were Mayonious, Thearthur, and Gladys and Thelma, who were my two favorite aunts.

Two of her brothers were said to be fair enough to be treated in the white section of the local hospital. My grandmother died when the youngest of her 10 children was nine months old, and my mother shared in raising Thelma. Elliott, the eldest male sibling, served in World War I and was not heard from for many years after the war. Family members believed he remained in France and probably passed as a Frenchman. Many years later, we learned that he died in New York City and chose not to maintain contact with the family. Another of the males, Mayloyd, lived to be 99 years of age. My mother and her nine siblings are all deceased, so little else is known about my maternal grandparents. But whenever I read about whites with the surname Whitehead or Farrior, I often wonder if we're related.

After marrying my parents settled in Sampson County where my father became principal of Garland Elementary School and my mother a third grade teacher. Four children were born of their union: Thomas Edison, Ida, my twin Myrtle and me, who were born on March 30, 1929, which happened to be Good Friday that year.

Myrtle and I were born in our rambling farmhouse, delivered by a midwife named Cornelius. I was named after the second wife of my father's youngest brother Ben. Myrtle, who was born 30 minutes later, was apparently a close enough rhyme with Bertha.

Though my mother left the classroom to become a full-time homemaker after Ida was born, she saw that our education was a top priority. Some of my earliest memories were of my mother reading to us – a duty later relegated to Ida who was two years older than Myrtle and me. My father would often bring us candy to be divided evenly among the three girls. Ida would wolf hers down, while Myrtle and I would enjoy ours at a slower pace. One day, just as Ida's reading of "The Little Match Girl" neared the climax, she stopped before we found out if The Little Match Girl died.

"I'm not going to read another line until you give me a piece of candy," she said.

Myrtle and I reluctantly forked over our treats. As a result we learned to read at four or five, motivated all the more by Ida's shenanigans.

My twin sister, Myrtle, and me at about three years of age with Model T Ford in left rear.

Our adopted godmother, Mabel Powell, worked at my father's school and encouraged our parents to enroll us in first grade at age 5 since there was no kindergarten at the time. On the first day, Myrtle and I cried so hard at having to leave the insulated confines of our home that we didn't return to school for a month. When we did return, we found we actually enjoyed school. By second grade we were doing so well that we "made two grades in one year", going from second to third grade in the middle of the semester. Consequently, we were always much younger than our classmates.

My mother, who was an avid reader, pianist, and soprano, was quite reserved in nature, offering balance to my father's more extroverted demeanor. Daddy was often away at meetings, either at Ingold Baptist Church, where he played piano, or leading a group of Sampson County citizens who wanted to establish a comprehensive high school in Garland for black students. At that time, black students in the Garland area could only complete the seventh grade unless their families could finance their studies at Sampson County Training School in neighboring Clinton. As was the custom, schools for blacks always included the words "colored" or "training" or "industrial". The high school for whites was just Garland High School. My father initially sought funding through the Rosenwald Foundation, established by Julius Rosenwald of Sears & Roebuck at the urging of Booker T. Washington. According to the National Trust for Historic Preservation, the program provided matching funds toward the construction of more than 5000 schools for blacks in the rural South from 1917 through 1932.

After being notified that the funds had been depleted, Daddy made a direct appeal to the local citizenry to contribute what small sums they could. Fortunately, state legislators made an appropriation, and he became the first principal of the newly-constructed Garland Colored High School in 1936.

His tenure would be short-lived. Plagued with heart problems and a stroke, he suffered frequent headaches and finally a bout of pneumonia for which he was prescribed penicillin. Our family doctor, Amos Neal Johnson, aptly cautioned that his heart was not strong enough to handle the penicillin. My father passed on April 7, 1937, just a few months after Garland Colored High School opened.

I can still remember the week when my father died. One of my mother's sisters, another favorite aunt, Gladys, lived in Montclair, New Jersey, and worked for a wealthy family as a governess. The family had two little girls about the same size and age as my twin sister and me and Aunt Gladys would send my mother boxes of the gently used clothing. In fact, Myrtle and I wore two of those dresses to my father's funeral. I still maintain contact with Aunt Gladys's daughter, Ida, who lives in Philadelphia, PA and continues to work for the federal government.

Only eight years old at the time, I did not know what "passed" meant. I soon learned that I would not hear Daddy's rich baritone voice singing "We Are Climbing Jacob's Ladder", and he would no longer ride us in his Model T Ford.

Daddy's dying left us destitute. To make matters worse, a man named Cromartie owed my father $300 at the time of his death and refused to honor the gentlemen's agreement, making it even harder for my mother to provide for us on our 50-acre farm.

A year after my father's death, my mother married my father's brother, who was 20 years her senior, and became stepmother to his two daughters and seven sons. Seemingly overnight our small family of five became a large family of 15. Because of the age disparity between my mother and stepfather/uncle, my stepbrothers and stepsisters were considerably older than my siblings and me. Some had already married and others were attending college. One or two remained on the farm. My stepbrother (and first cousin) Joseph Boykin, had already completed college and succeeded my father as principal of Garland Colored High School.

Of the nine siblings, my favorite was and still is Annie Boykin Carlton. Then a young teacher for the Sampson County Schools system, Annie also played the piano for our church. Our "big sister" taught Ida, Myrtle,

My father – Thomas JL Boykin

and me to play piano. At the time of this writing, she is the only living of the nine and is 103 years of age.

Despite our initial reluctance, my mother moved our family into our stepfather's house. Papa, as we called him, was a stern, hardworking middle-class farmer. We were all responsible for keeping the house clean, bringing in wood, and tending the farm, where we grew cotton, cucumbers, corn and the biggest cash crop, tobacco. Because Myrtle and I were the youngest of our extended family, we were sheltered. While we did have farm du-

My mother – Mallie Armona Farrior Boykin

ties, we mainly handled tobacco in the barn.

A family as large as ours never wanted for socialization. I remember big family dinners on the enclosed porch after church on Sundays. We would then retire to the living room, where we held debates on the issues of the day and sang and played the piano. We would meet on Wednesday nights to plan Saturday's social events for the densely populated neighborhood.

My stepfather ensured that the Sabbath was always strictly observed in his household. All of the children had to have good cause for not attending Sunday school and church. These rules were enforced until each child finished school, got a job, and moved out of the house or got married and built a home of his/her own.

My parents were also responsible for housing the itinerant pastors of Ingold Baptist Church when they preached on Sundays and were in town for monthly church meetings.

Our house was in an integrated neighborhood, and we were not unduly affected by the social dictates of the day. Contact with our white neighbors was generally limited to my stepfather's tobacco fields or under the shelter of the tobacco barn, where we conversed about any number of issues, though seldom about racial issues.

There were just a couple of instances that subtly reminded us of the differences. I remember a white couple in the neighborhood who called my father "Professor" rather than calling him Mister. When our mother remarried, this same couple called my stepfather Uncle Junious. When we asked "Papa," as we called him, if the white couple was related to us, he said, "Oh children, that's just the way it is."

We apparently didn't know how it was. When the white couple drove up one day and asked for our stepfather, we began calling the white man Uncle Jerry.

With the exception of my father's death, our childhood was uneventful. Thomas, Ida, Myrtle and I all attended Garland Colored High School. There was no 12th grade at the time, and Myrtle and I graduated in 1945 at the age of 16. Myrtle was valedictorian; I was salutatorian.

Thomas and Ida were already attending Shaw University in Raleigh. Because our mother couldn't afford to send all four of us to school at the same time, Myrtle and I stayed home for two years.

In the fall of 1947, we began our undergraduate studies at the North Carolina College at Durham, now named North Carolina Central University.

My brother, Edison, and older sister, Ida, while attending Shaw University.

My older brother, Thomas Edison.

My older sister, Ida, as an adult.

Ida Mae, the daughter of one of my favorite aunts, Aunt Gladys – then and now.

Thelma Farrior Boykin, one of my favorite aunts.

Lott Carey Family Picture - Back Row (from left to right)
Edward Todd, George T. Boykin, Aaron Boykin, Carolyn Boykin, Woodrow Carr, Livy J. Boykin.

Front Row (from left to right)
Bertha B. Todd, Annie B. Carlton, Lula Boykin, Blonnie R. Carr, Ida B. Cooper

In September, 1982, Aaron Boykin and the Boykin Family were selected as the Lott Carey Family of the Year. Dr. Wendell Sommerville, executive secretary/treasurer of the Lott Carey Convention, made the presentation. The Lott Carey Foreign Mission Convention is named after one of the first American and Baptist missionaries to West Africa. The former slave purchased his freedom in 1813 and later became the organizing pastor for the first Baptist Church in Monrovia. Each year the organization honors a family living in the city where its annual convention is held.

"Moving Toward Higher Ground"
Chapter 2

"The sloping hills, the verdant green.
The lovely blossoms beauteous sheen
Surround our college proud and gay,
Where wave our colors maroon and gray."

North Carolina College at Durham School Song

Our family's mantra has always been "Education is the key to a better life." In 1945 our brother Thomas and sister Ida, who were both attending Raleigh's Shaw University, were well on their way.

Myrtle and I continued to work on the family farm by day and we spent our evenings and break times reading and playing the piano. On occasion, Myrtle and I would travel to Norfolk and Portsmouth, Virginia for extended visits with our favorite aunt, Thelma, and her husband. Our stepbrother Joseph, who had been principal of Garland Colored High School, was now principal at Princess Ann High School at Virginia Beach. Our visits with Joseph included tours of Hampton Institute and Norfolk State University.

Thomas and Ida graduated from Shaw University in the spring of 1947, clearing the way for our chance at "a better life." Because Myrtle and I had to defer our collegiate plans, we thought the decision of which college we attended should be ours alone. After deciding that we wanted to attend Howard University in Washington, DC, we completed the entrance requirements, were assigned mentors, secured letters of recommendation, and made a deposit. We were accepted at Howard and had already received letters from our assigned mentors.

Imagine our disenchantment when Ida and our mother informed us that while we were making plans to attend Howard, Ida had enrolled us at North Carolina College at Durham, now North Carolina Central University. Their rationale was the fact that our mother would have to finance our college education from money acquired from the land she owned. They were also concerned about our limited socialization skills, since Myrtle and I had had little interaction with others beyond our large extended family.

Though our desire to attend Howard was dashed, we were happy that after two long years, we were finally going to college! In the fall of 1947, two shy, sheltered young females from Sampson County arrived on the campus of North Carolina College at Durham.

Judging from the stares of students and staff alike, it had been some time since the student body included twins. Incidences of multiple births seemed to be rarer at the time. The Dionne Quintuplets were an international phenomenon and we read everything we could about the only female identical set of five. But we weren't prepared for the intense scrutiny we faced on NCC's campus. We were no longer just Bertha and Myrtle, but "peat and repeat" and "double trouble." To this day, I detest being called any name other than my own. Even terms of endearment like "honey", and especially "baby", gall me.

Needless to say, this newfound attention exacerbated our already reserved demeanors. In addition to the stares, there were frequent requests for photographs and lots of questions about our obvious similarities. But while we still dressed alike, there was the dawning realization for us that we had separate personalities. For the first time, we had different schedules that forced us to

Myrtle (right) and me (left) sitting in front of B.N. Duke Auditorium on the campus of NCC during our freshman year.

interact with others on our own. Once weekly, alone in our dorm room, we made a ritual of paying three compliments to each other and listing three areas where improvement was needed. We also poked fun at the girls who cried and wanted to go back home. Sampson County held no such hopes for us. We were too happy to finally be in college!

Because of our two-year deferment, we were now 18 - the same age as the other members of our freshmen class. Our initial reticence quickly faded and we became actively involved in campus life. We joined the band as majorettes, sang in the college choir and became members of the YWCA and the NAACP. Myrtle and I were also selected to join the Alpha Chi chapter of Alpha Kappa Alpha sorority and the Beta Kappa Chi Scientific Honor Society. My schedule was full. Choir rehearsals on Mondays, Wednesdays, and Fridays and band rehearsals and science labs on Tuesdays and Thursdays. Dr. James E. Shepard, the founder of NCCU, passed away during our sophomore year and Myrtle and I were asked to serve as student flower girls for the memorial service held on campus.

Group picture of Alpha Chi chapter of Alpha Kappa Alpha Sorority following a reception.

Four years later, we graduated cum laude with B.S. degrees in biology. Our hopes of attending medical school were derailed with the realization that we had neither money nor scholarships for another four years of school. Still being supported by our mother, brother, and sister, we heeded their recommendation that we gain certification for a career in education.

We remained at North Carolina College for another year and a half, attaining master's degrees in Library Science. There was one problem. The college did not offer graduate housing at the time. Myrtle and I made an appointment with Chancellor Alfonso Elder and shared our concerns about the lack of graduate housing. Dr. Elder listened intently and stated that he would address the situation. The following year a residential facility for graduates was erected. It has always been my belief that going directly to the source when a matter needs to be resolved is much better than complaining to everyone else.

In the meantime Myrtle and I had finally found a room in a boarding house on a street facing campus. It was in this boarding house that I met a teacher from Williston Industrial School who informed me of an opening for a full time librarian in Wilmington, NC.

Our college life had been rewarding and we were both armed with two degrees. However, North Carolina College would be but the first of several institutions of higher learning that beckoned us both throughout our careers.

Myrtle (right) and me as majorettes.

Myrtle (right) and me crowned Kappa Sweethearts at the end of our junior year at North Carolina College at Durham.

Myrtle and me riding in the Homecoming Parade.

My undergraduate graduation picture.

My continuing quest for academic enrichment was colored by real-life interactions that forced me to face, for the first time, the fact that I was black.

UNIVERSITY OF NORTH CAROLINA AT GREENSBORO

The summer of 1973 saw me heading to Greensboro to spend the summer with Myrtle while I renewed my teaching certification at the University of North Carolina at Greensboro. This followed a Supreme Court ruling that schools of higher education in the South had to admit all citizens regardless of color. While I didn't expect the staff and students to enthusiastically embrace my presence, I did expect civility.

Several experiences that summer taught me more about human nature than about the intended subjects. In one incident a white, female professor required students in our mental health class to write one paper a week. In addition to gauging our writing skills, she thought the exercise would help her learn the students' names. The following week "Dr. Young" read excerpts from what she considered three exceptional papers, calling the names as she handed the three papers back to their authors. The look on her face as she called "Bertha Boykin Todd" told me what she could not. She had not expected the well-written paper to be authored by a black person.

A second incident involved a young white female student who suggested we continue our discussion on some topic at a nearby coffee shop. The shop was crowded as we entered, and I immediately began looking for a seat. When I turned around to look for her, she was nowhere to be found. I chalked up her vanishing act to the probability that she had recognized someone she knew and didn't want to be seen with a black person. Since that time I have become acutely attuned to a person's level of comfort when dealing with people of other ethnicities.

A third incident that summer occurred during final exams. "Dr. Young" gave us the test and instructions, informed us about the school's honor system, and left the room. About 10-15 minutes after her departure, a white female student entered the room and walked right over to me, the only person of color, and asked me to check the papers on the instructor's desk. I stared her straight in the face and informed her that if she wanted anything that had been placed on the instructor's desk, she would have to get it herself. I have always believed that she was sent to see if I would violate the honor system.

East Carolina University
Earning a 2ⁿᵈ Master's Degree and an Advanced Degree

It's widely known that twins tend to be competitive. Whether conscious or subconscious, that's certainly the case with my identical twin Myrtle and me. During my 17 years at John T. Hoggard High, she had earned a third master's degree and was working on her second doctoral degree. While I didn't feel the need to play catch up, she did awaken my desire to pursue additional degrees.

After passing the Miller Analogies Test, I decided to pursue a second master's degree in Educational Administration and Supervision. That summer found me heading to East Carolina University. My daughter, Rita, was attending UNC-Chapel Hill. My son, Brian, still in high school, remained at home with my husband Mack, who was working in administration at Roland Grise Junior High School. With my family able to manage on its own, I spent six weeks that restless summer immersing myself in ECU's campus life. I was well aware that this would likely be the last time that I stayed on a college campus.

I stayed in on-campus housing for the duration of the six-week program, leaving just once for the July 4th holiday. Weekends on campus included several watermelon socials that I could never bring myself to attend -- keenly aware of my being the only person of color in my program and the stigma attached to blacks eating watermelon. I remembered, as a child, seeing a card of a minstrel-like setting where one of several black people was eating watermelon. The caption read "Give us da rind" to which the watermelon eater replies, "Dar ain't gwine be no rind!" Thanks, but no watermelon socials for me!

During the second summer session, my final three weeks on campus began. Though the class was crowded, I finally found a seat located in the back of the large classroom and sat next to a white male student. The only reason this bothered me was because I realized that I probably would not be able to find a study partner. No one made overtures and I began to wonder if I should go it alone or drop out. I decided to remain – sink or swim.

Despite brief snippets of conversation with the young student about an upcoming test, he didn't suggest studying together and I certainly didn't broach the subject. Several days later when the professor brought the graded papers to class, he suggested that some of us might wish to consider dropping his class. I just knew he was speaking directly to me! By the time he

Myrtle talking with Mack, my late husband, after receiving her first doctoral degree from UNC- Greensboro in the 1970s. My back is to the camera.

had returned most of the test papers, I was beginning to slink down in my seat. Finally, the professor was holding the last two papers. I refused to even look at it until he announced that instead of passing his papers out with the highest grade first, he decided to reverse the order. Receiving one of the highest grades in this class was truly a proud moment for me!

The Final Graduate Course at UNC-Wilmington

I later learned that I needed an additional graduate course to complete my advanced degree. The course would be taught by a UNC-Chapel Hill professor at UNC-Wilmington. I had resumed my busy schedule at Hoggard High by then, but I was determined to take this last course. My husband and I enrolled, along with other educators, most of who were seeking certification renewal.

The assistant principal at Laney High (a white female) and I, who was then assistant principal at Hoggard, were very active in the class. We chaired committees, assisted other groups, and were eager to answer questions and make comments. The professor would begin his class by calling the roll. I noticed that he called the white students by their first names. With the three or four blacks in the class, he used courtesy titles. I was "Mrs. Todd" instead of "Bertha". Arriving early one afternoon, I informed "Dr. B" that I did not mind being called Bertha, and I was certain that the other blacks did not mind either. The professor accepted my suggestion -- or at least I thought he did.

Another time this same professor asked me how I was feeling. I responded that the school day had been demanding. When he began to trivialize my response, two of my white co-workers began to chide "Dr. B", much to his chagrin. Several sessions later, he said to me, "Bertha, I have just read about Idi Amin killing all of those people in Uganda. I'll bet you wish that they had been 'honkies.'" Bewildered by his comments, I replied, "I am shocked! The word 'honky' is not even in my vocabulary! After all, some of my best friends are white!"

I knew then that my hopes for an A or H (honors) in that course were doomed. During the last class session, the professor informed the group that he felt certain that some were going to be displeased with their final grade. He then cut his eyes at me. I found out why when I received my "B" in the mail. This professor was determined to teach me a lesson and "put me in my place". Later, in my office at Hoggard, I picked up the telephone to call him. Twice I returned the phone to its base. I just could not bring myself to "beg" for a grade that I knew I had earned. Several days later, one of my co-workers said, "Bertha, I thought that you knew that 'Dr. B' is a racist."

I have long wrestled with how this flagrant act of bigotry would mark my final attempt at formal education.

"Working Girl – Virginia Beach, Virginia"
Chapter 3

"Man may work from sun to sun, but woman's work is never done."
-Anonymous

With our mother, brother and sister footing the bill for our college education, Myrtle and I were often asked over a three-year period if we could find work on campus. We replied that we had not heard of any jobs, which was close to the truth. We had not *heard* of any jobs because we had not made an effort to *seek* any jobs. Both of us continued to believe we were due those college years, work-free, since we had to sit out two years while our older siblings completed their studies. Going back home to help out on the family farm was not an option for Myrtle and me as we became fully immersed in campus life.

During the spring of 1950, as we were completing our junior year, Myrtle spoke with a schoolmate who had worked on Virginia Beach during previous summers. Excited, Myrtle rushed into the dorm room to tell me about the possibilities. But we faced two challenges: getting our parents' permission and getting a job without having any skills.

Apart from our duties on the family farm, we had none of the marketable skills in demand in Virginia Beach. We could not cook well, nor had we babysat or cleaned house except for dormitory inspection. We certainly had not worked in a hotel, and there were many of those on the beach.

Well aware of the fact that our socialization was limited to band and choir activities, we knew we needed to broaden our horizons. We would be graduating the following year and needed to become better prepared for the real world of work.

Both of us wrestled with having to work with unfamiliar white people. Several of our professors were white, and we even square danced with white students from UNC- Chapel Hill and Duke University when the choir held socials on weekends. But that was the extent of our interactions with whites, except for our neighbors at home.

With our parents' permission, we boarded the bus to Virginia Beach in the summer of 1950. We had already contacted the Virginia Beach Employment Service for help in finding jobs. Although our stepbrother, Joseph, was the principal of Princess Anne County Training School and lived in Norfolk, Virginia, we wanted to be on our own.

Myrtle held two jobs that first summer with both ending just a few weeks before the season ended. Her first job was as a maid at the Sea Horse Hotel, which was owned by two white females. They knew Myrtle had no experience, so they taught her how to make up beds. Myrtle was a quick study and soon realized that she could hold a part-time job as well. The second job was for a family of three: a couple and the disabled sister of the wife. Myrtle told this family that she could cook and was hired to cook breakfast daily and clean the house periodically. Every day she would serve the same fare: eggs, bacon, and pancakes -- so much so that they began referring to her as "Pancake Myrtle."

My first working summer found me with *four* jobs, offering the first of many encounters with people of diverse backgrounds.

JOB #1

I was first hired as a maid/waitress at The Hilltop Inn owned by a Mr. Murray. Recently widowed, his lady friend managed the bed and bath establishment. Besides myself, there were two other black women from Washington, NC who had worked at The Hilltop for several years. I assume they made the beds, because I waited tables and assisted the cook.

The female manager would say to me: "Bertha, go upstairs and tell Mr. James that his breakfast is ready."

VIRGINIA BEACH EMPLOYMENT SERVICE
ROLAND COURT BUILDING
209 17TH STREET
VIRGINIA BEACH, VIRGINIA
PHONE 2598

REQUEST FOR INTERVIEW

DATE: JUN. -7 1950

MR. MURRAY

THE HILL TOP HOUSE, 40th STREET & OCEANFRONT

APPLICANT'S NAME: BERTHA B. BOYKIN

POSITION APPLYING FOR: MAID-WAITRESS

IMPORTANT: DO NOT INTERVIEW AN APPLICANT AS BEING FROM THIS OFFICE UNLESS THEY PRESENT THIS FORM PROPERLY SIGNED AND CURRENTLY DATED. THANK YOU.

VIRGINIA BEACH EMPLOYMENT SERVICE

PER:

My first job assignment with the Virginia Beach Employment Agency.

"Mr." James was the owner's young white son who was not as old as I was. While I would inform him that his breakfast was ready, I refused to call him "Mr." As business was slow that summer, I was eventually released. On my last day, the manager told me she wanted to speak with me regarding her perception of me. She then informed me that I had a "chip on my shoulder" and this wouldn't bode well in the working world. I thanked her for her advice, adding, "I guess I must have been born with a 'chip on my shoulder.'" I realized that I had not displayed the subservient demeanor expected of a person of my station.

JOB #2

I returned to the Virginia Beach Employment Service where the owner informed me of a good-paying job. The Perper household had a slight turnover problem. Apparently, people didn't work there longer than a week. I was to prepare breakfast and assist the regular housekeeper who reported to work later in the day. Myrtle and I could also stay in an upstairs room.

Mrs. Perper was not the most pleasant person, and she and Mr. Perper did not seem to get along very well. One day she asked me to bake two cakes: one using egg yolks and the other using egg whites. Not having baked cakes much since high school, my skills left much to be desired. I found two cookbooks and began to bake the cakes. Later in the day, Mrs. Perper walked into the kitchen and exclaimed, "Bertha, what in the world are you doing? The kitchen seems to have had a hurricane fly through it!" I replied calmly, "Mrs.

Perper, if you will just return to your bedroom, I shall clean up the kitchen when I have finished baking these two cakes."

Apparently that was the wrong thing to say to her. She later told me that I was asking her to leave her own kitchen. Maybe, I should have said, "Yes ma'am."

I knew my days in the Perper household were numbered. Though I felt she was going to fire me, I was planning to leave anyway. One day, before Mrs. Perper came down to breakfast, her spouse began eating his breakfast and asked me if I had ever been to the mountains. He said that he was taking his son to camp, and I was welcome to go along. My intentions were to invite my twin sister, Myrtle. It wasn't until I heard Mr. & Mrs. Perper discussing the matter at breakfast that I realized he had no plans to take his wife, meaning he and I would be driving back together. I became even more uncomfortable in the Perper house and left after one week.

JOB #3

The staff at the Virginia Beach Employment Service simply smiled when I returned for a third time seven days later. I told them I understood why most people remained in the Perper home for only a week. As the agency was getting a percentage of my pay for placing me, they were making money. I, however, was worried about whether I would have anything saved by the end of the summer.

I was sent to the exclusive Cavalier Hotel to work as a parlor maid, even though I didn't have a clue as to what parlor maids did. The Cavalier was absolutely gorgeous! Many blacks, both male and female, were employed at this posh hotel, which even provided living quarters for employees. Myrtle and I had already located a room for the remainder of the summer, so we stayed put. I was given a uniform and a white apron to wear. As a parlor maid my duties included making certain the ladies' restrooms were always clean, emptying ashtrays in the main lobby, and assisting guests as needed. This was light work and I did my job dutifully. I especially enjoyed hearing the musical performances in the lobby in the afternoons and evenings.

Right away the black employees began to tell me about the "boss's" likes and dislikes, including the need to braid my hair or be fired. Having tired of the braids I had worn in elementary and high school, I chose to wear my hair in a bun since it was quite lengthy.

The white female supervisor and I got along very well. She never even suggested how I should or should not wear my hair, nor did she mention my having "a chip on my shoulder." The summer season was winding down and the hotel released some workers, including me. Before I left the "boss" and I had a long conversation during which she wished me well as I prepared to return to college to complete my senior year. Myrtle's job had not yet ended, and I made my fourth and final trip that summer to the Virginia Beach Employment Service.

JOB #4

My fourth job in the summer of 1950 was with the Danziger family. Mrs. Danziger was an attractive woman who I learned years later was the same age as I was. She had been widowed or divorced, had a son and a daughter and was from a Protestant family of meager means. Mr. Danziger was Jewish and had acquired some wealth.

My job was to prepare breakfast for the children and tend to them during the day. My cooking skills had not improved, and I was thankful that Mrs. Danziger prepared the evening meal.

She and I hit it off well. On one occasion, Mrs. "D." asked me to help prepare dinner for unexpected guests of her husband. We managed to pull it off, and she was pleased, so much so that when it was time for me to return to school, she invited me to rejoin the family the following summer. Myrtle was also offered her job the next summer, so we returned to Virginia Beach in the summer of 1951 after graduating from North Carolina College at Durham.

Working at the Danziger's for a second summer was somewhat rewarding. I was already acquainted with the routine, and I wouldn't have to share a percentage of my salary with the employment service.

Mr. Danziger and I had many substantive conversations around the kitchen table. He liked to get my opinions on the issues of the day as he and his wife ate breakfast.

One morning during breakfast, Mr. "D." was argumentative and angry. He, his wife, and some friends were supposed to attend a social affair at the Cavalier Hotel. To his surprise, and certainly to mine, they were not permitted to enter because they were Jewish. I was flabbergasted when he asked me what I thought of the situation, but replied that I had become profoundly aware of Jim Crow practices while working at the Cavalier the previous summer, but I was not aware of discrimination against Jews.

I developed greater empathy for "Mr. D" as a result of this incident, and he became more interested in discrimination against Negroes -- the term used in the early 1950's for black people.

I shared with him one incident I observed at the Cavalier Hotel the previous summer.

Working in the lobby one afternoon, I noticed a foreign family of brown complexion who were staying at the hotel and being served in the dining room. When I noticed them moving freely about the hotel, I wondered to myself, "Just what is this management discriminating against – skin color, faith, or nationality?" After sharing this experience with Mr. "D." he calmed down a bit, and we continued discussing the negative impact of discrimination.

My first two summers as a "working girl" taught me a lot about human differences and similarities and laid the groundwork for future interactions with people of different beliefs and ethnicities.

"Family Matters"
Chapter 4

"The bond that links your true family is not one of blood,
but of respect and joy in each other's life."
-Richard Bach

Mack and me in the gazebo in the backyard of our home.

Early family portrait

met the man who would be-
come my husband during my
first year as librarian at Williston Industrial High School. Mack (as he was called)
attended Shaw University in Raleigh on
an athletic scholarship and was named
captain of the basketball team in his senior year. Mack was also a World War II
veteran who took advantage of the GI bill
to pursue an education. A few years later,
Mack earned a master's degree in Health
and Physical Education from North Carolina Central University. He joined the
New Hanover County school system a
year before I did.

Mack and I married in June of 1953. We
lost our first child. Our second child, Rita
Denise, was quite precocious. She was
keenly aware of being the only girl around
her brother and two male cousins, and
was extremely protective of her younger
brother. In the second grade she was
named Gregory Elementary School's "May
Queen", an honor she reveled in for the
rest of the year. By her third grade year,
she and several other children from our
neighborhood wanted to be able to bike
to school. Mack and I met with the other
parents and decided to request that our
children – three girls and one boy – be

allowed to attend the school closest to our home – the segregated Forest Hills Elementary School.

I will never forget the first PTA meeting at the newly desegregated Forest Hills School. The program went well, overall. However, at the social reception for parents, the white parents responded to us as if we were aliens from planet Mars. I recognized one gentleman at the gathering. He was one of the managers at Belk Berry department store who helped me find my son, Brian, who went missing in the store during the Christmas season. I recognized him, but as far as he was concerned, I was a complete stranger. And the principal was rumored to have stated that if a black child were to attend, she was going to resign.

Rita was always eager to embrace new experiences, including the world of work. One summer she got a job working with children in the City of Wilmington's public housing complexes. She would visit each center a day a week and read stories, play games, sing songs and make crafts with the children. In the afternoons, she would read and make crafts with the senior citizens in the centers. She found she liked working with people and the added incentive of earning her own money.

During the summer of 1972, my husband and I decided to send Rita on a six-week

Rita – then and now.

tour of Europe with a group of students through the American Institute for Foreign Study. She studied at the University of South Hampton in England for three weeks before touring the Mediterranean by sea for three weeks. Her tour took her to Turkey, Rome, Italy, Athens, Greece; and Jerusalem, where she swam in the Dead Sea and the Sea of Galilee. She said one of the highlights of the trip was visiting what is thought to be the location of Jesus' birth.

She was also active at New Hanover High School where she was a cheerleader, a member of the National Honor Society, Hanover Singers, Civinettes, and the student council. She was selected as one of two students in North Carolina to attend the Senate Youth Program sponsored by the William Randolph Hearst Foundation. Two students from each state and the District of Columbia were chosen for the weeklong, all-expenses paid trip to Washington, DC. During her senior year, she was crowned Alpha Psi Omega chapter of Alpha Kappa Alpha sorority's 25th Debutante Queen, another highlight of her high school years.

Upon graduation in 1975, she attended UNC-Chapel Hill and graduated from UNC-Chapel Hill with a degree in education. While at Carolina, she served as a "Sweet Caroline" during football season and sang in the Women's Glee Club. She later earned a master's degree and a principal's certificate from UNC-Wilmington.

Throughout her career in education, Rita committed herself to addressing the needs of the "whole" child, believing that "Students don't care how much you know until they know how much you care."

She retired in June of 2010 after serving 30 years in four North Carolina counties: Guilford County, Chapel Hill/Carrboro, New Hanover County, and Brunswick County.

A Young Entrepreneur?

Our son, Brian, began kindergarten at Forest Hills, a year after Rita began in the third grade. I was told that the same principal, who stated that she would resign or retire if black children every attended, was sometimes seen holding Brian by the hand as she visited classrooms. Brian may have developed an affinity for her because she so closely resembled his maternal grandmother.

At an early age, Brian told us he wanted to work in order to make his own money. His first stint delivering newspapers for the *Star News* really ended up being a family affair – even though the profits were his. Then, he decided to sell packets of seeds, which didn't prove to be profitable at all. In high school, he decided he wanted a car and said he was willing to work as a "bag boy" at a local grocery store to pay for it.

Mack wasn't crazy about the idea, but I was more amenable after explaining the pros and cons of car ownership. Brian had his sights set on a light blue Camero at a local dealership and knew how much it cost. I took him to Wachovia Bank and asked to speak with a loan officer with whom I had done business. Then I sent Brian in by himself so he would understand that the car was his responsibility – not ours. He got his Camero and proved to be industrious and responsible.

who then owned Eastern Delivery Service. Brian made many flights for Eastern Delivery. He also worked for Aeronautics, Inc. before he was hired by Delta Airlines, where he has been for 25 years, and 15 of

Brian – then and now.

In 1979 Brian graduated from New Hanover High School, where he had been a member of the marching band. During his senior year, he drove a school bus and even earned his private pilot's license. Upon graduation, he told his father and me that he wanted to be a truck driver or a pilot. He attended Embry Riddle Aeronautical University and later worked for Katherine Bell Moore, former Wilmington City Councilwoman and mayor pro-tem,

those years as a captain primarily piloting international flights.

Family Ties

Mack and I wanted to ensure that our family had the proper spiritual foundation. We joined Chestnut Street Presbyterian Church about 50 years ago when the Rev. B.H. Baskervill was pastor. The Rev. Perry D. Griffin is the current pastor of Chestnut Street. We also share strong bonds with the Griffin Todd, Sr. family and other Todd relatives from Zebulon, NC and surrounding areas.

Family Travels

Some of our fondest family memories are of our travels when Rita and Brian were growing up. I was the president of several organizations and served as a delegate to numerous national and international meetings. I would borrow money so the four of us could visitg locations like Boston, MA; Dallas, Houston, TX; Miami, FL; and New York, NY as well as the Bahamas, and other islands to name a few places.

One of our favorite trips was to Cherokee, where we stayed on the Native American reservation. Even though hotels and motels in other areas in North Carolina were closed to blacks, the Boundary Tree Lodge was open to everyone. Seeing another ethnic group in a different cultural setting was truly a learning experience. We made the trip with another family and the children enjoyed riding on the "Tweetsie Railroad" and taking the ski lifts up the mountain -- even though it was summer.

My Growing Family

My notion of family is not limited to blood ties. Several students became a part of our family during my working years at Williston and Hoggard high schools.

"B" and "G" were both intelligent and helpful as library assistants during my years as a Media Specialist at Williston. During the summer of their junior year, neither was able to find a job. This particular summer, I was working in the library on a federal grant

and shared my salary with them. It wasn't much, but it was better than nothing. The three of us worked diligently to get the library in order for the upcoming school year.

I began to ask the young ladies about their plans after graduation. Since neither had close relatives who had attended an institution of higher learning, neither had seriously considered going to college. I began to talk with them about the value of furthering their education beyond high school and even visited their homes to speak with their mothers. The visits and motivation paid off. When I told my sister Ida about their desire to attend college, she gave them watches, luggage, clothes and other items needed for college life. Of course, both of us supported them financially as much as we could.

One of the young ladies graduated from Winston-Salem State University and is currently employed in a government position. The other completed three years at Fayetteville State University. I am not certain if she ever completed her fourth year. The last time I conversed with her, she had to return home due to illness in her family.

A third young lady, "M", moved to Wilmington from upstate New York before graduating from high school. I was in administration at Hoggard when a male friend of hers came to my office and asked me to look out for her, which I did. She completed her high school requirements in New Hanover County's alternative school and enrolled at UNC-Wilmington.

I worked with her to keep her vehicle from being repossessed and guided her through setting up the first student undergraduate chapter of the NAACP. She was intelligent, vivacious and wanted to achieve. "M" completed three years at UNC-W before relocating to another area. She is currently working with a major airline. Although I never confronted her about my suspicions, I had a strong feeling that she had run away from home. Years later I had an opportunity to meet her mother after the two had reunited.

There were two young black males that we also adopted into our family. My first protégé was "LT", who was a junior when Williston was dissolved in 1968-69. When "LT" was assigned to Hoggard, he immediately began to make a place for himself. Outgoing, LT was determined to make his high school days count. He mixed well with all of the students and he and I developed a bond. One day when he went to the home he shared with his mother in the Jervay public housing complex, he discovered that his mother had passed. I began to serve as a surrogate mother for "LT", who moved in with his sister. I purchased a used car so he could help take members of his football team home after practice. "LT" was encouraged to attend UNCW after he graduated and talked my sister Ida into letting him stay rent-free in a home she owned. A friend of mine who was a professor in the philosophy department at UNC-W, a fellow Family Services/ Travelers Aid board member, agreed to become his mentor.

"LT" graduated from UNC-W, joined the Air Force, and married. He pursued a master's degree during his tour of duty in the Air Force, from which he retired as a lieutenant colonel after 24 years of service.

"LT" then became a special investigator at U.S. Investigation Services for several years. The last time I spoke with "LT", he was an Air Force Junior ROTC Commander.

Another protégé was Stephen McCary-Henderson, who was referred to me by a former Hoggard student. We didn't connect until one day when I was in the school's infirmary and learned that a female student had been in a fight on campus. When the student told me her name, I asked her if she was related to Stephen. When she said he was her brother, I asked her to tell Stephen to come to my office for a visit.

In December of that year, Stephen came to see me. I immediately felt compassion for this skinny, disheveled young man as he sat down on a couch. He was one of five children whose mother had passed the year before. His aunts had split the siblings among them. Stephen was having trouble with his aunt's boyfriend and decided that he was going to run away from home. By this time, I had decided that I was not going to bring another student into my family and not bond too much with them at school, having already "adopted" four other students. Yet, Stephen's story tugged at my heart and I wanted to help him find a better life.

He was a fairly good student, but was quite sullen in nature and only spoke when he was asked a question. During this second visit I gave him money to buy a pair of pants and asked him to come back to my office to show me the purchase, which he did.

Stephen would come to my office often during his years at Hoggard. When he informed me again that he was planning to run away from home, I knew that I needed to act quickly. I prayed on it and decided to write a note to Stephen's aunt offering to serve as his guardian at Hoggard while she maintained her official guardianship. She readily agreed to the offer. A few months later I called his aunt to inform her that I had located a room for Stephen across the street from my house, in the same rental house where the young lady was living and whom at the time; I was assisting financially since she was a student at UNC-Wilmington. Much to my surprise, his aunt readily agreed to the arrangement and even moved him into the house for me. He would ride to school with me each day and I would check in with his teachers regularly. Domestic tensions between Stephen and "M", the female student, often required weekend communication sessions that I moderated.

Financially Stephen's paternal aunt, who lived in Detroit, MI, assisted me as much as she could. The rest was left up to me

Stephen McCary-Henderson then and now.

and my family. He began to refer to me as "mom" and ate in our home most of the time. When Stephen wanted to take Driver's Education, I readily consented and gave him permission to practice with my car -- even teaching him a few driving tips. He passed the test and is now one of the best drivers in the world – at least in my eyes.

I promised Stephen that if he did well in high school, my husband and I would send him to A & T State University in Greensboro. We suggested A &T because my twin sister, Myrtle, was a professor there and would be able to monitor him in college as I had done at Hoggard. Stephen was accepted at A&T State University and preparations were made for his official enrollment. We traveled to Greensboro and left my socially adopted son in the care of my twin sister. My daughter, Rita, was teaching in Greensboro at the time and was also available to assist him. Stephen graduated with honors from A & T with a double major in mathematics and computer science. How proud we all were on commencement day!

Stephen went on to earn a master's degree from the University of Mississippi and a doctorate a few years later. My son, Brian, and I flew to Cleveland to attend his graduation. Currently, Dr. Stephen McCary-Henderson is a tenured professor at A & T State University in the education department where he has served for several years.

Assisting these five high school students was a rewarding challenge. My family always welcomed these new additions and we openly shared family meals, activities and programs with them from the 1960s through the early 1980s.

My husband Mack also mentored many young males as a coach and health and physical education teacher at Williston. His form of discipline when students acted out was thumping them on the head. Although most of the head-thumped males probably resented his approach at the time, many of them have since expressed to me how his disciplinary tactics helped them to improve their behavior, which led to improved academics.

Mack also spoke with his college coach to see that two young males received four year basketball scholarships: Lee Monroe sent to Shaw University and Clarence Stewart went to Morgan State. Both excelled in undergraduate school, continued their studies, and earned doctorates in education. Dr. Monroe and Dr. Stewart have both made impressive contributions in the field of education in several states and internationally.

Having grown up in a close knit family, I have always felt that a secure family environment, whether by birth or choice, has a direct effect on a person's well-being. It is my hope that these seven continue to be solid citizens and lend a hand to others as they have been assisted. Pay it forward!

*Mack and me with a foreign student in December, 1973
at Winter Park Presbyterian Church.*

Home Away From Home on Christmas Day

From 1976-1984, Winter Park Presbyterian Church sponsored a special program for foreign students who were attending colleges and universities in the United States. During the Christmas holiday, many of these students did not have the funds or chose not to go to their homelands. Organizers at Winter Park asked local citizens to host Christmas Dinner for these students. I relished the opportunity to participate and encouraged my sister and neighbors to participate as well.

Early on Christmas Day my spouse would make his way to Winter Park Presbyterian to pick up our guests. While Mack, Rita, and Brian entertained our guests, my sister and I would finish cooking the meal, which usually took a few days to prepare. The Christmas Day experience, which included anywhere from two to eight students, featured lively conversations about the customs in our respective cultures. What a rewarding experience – to know that we had served as an extended family for students from as far away as Iran, Iraq, Zaire, South Africa, China, Japan, Indonesia, Chile, Turkey, Israel, and Thailand.

All pictures courtesy of Winter Park Presbyterian Church. (Ms. Charlotte Rochelle)

"Williston, Williston, Williston – Go Tigers!"
Chapter 5

"Our voices we raise in a song of thy praise
The greatest school under the sun."

from Williston School Song

Shopping on Front Street my first year in Wilmington.

Armed with undergraduate and master's degrees from North Carolina College, Myrtle and I began to earnestly pursue employment as librarians, often referred to today as media specialists. I was primarily interested in working at a junior college or college, but was belatedly offered a position at Barber-Scotia College in Concord. But, I had already signed a contract with New Hanover County Schools and was told by the superintendent that if I broke the contract, he would see to it that I did not get a job anywhere in the state of North Carolina. Fearing that I did not have time to find work outside the state, I became one of two librarians at Williston Industrial High School in the fall of 1952. Following one year of employment at Williston Industrial High School, I was transferred to the newly constructed Williston Senior High School. At the time there were only two high schools in New Hanover County: the all-black Williston Senior High School and the all-white New Hanover High School. I would serve as librarian at Williston for the next 14 years. I was determined to establish a library that was second to none.

At our first faculty meeting, a number of the new teachers introduced were former Williston graduates who had earned their college degrees and were returning home to teach. Two educators, Jeanne Barksdale (Jeanne Barksdale Keith Harris, former classroom teacher) and George L. Tally, Williston's assistant principal, had attended North Carolina College at Durham while Myrtle and I were there. I was happy to recognize at least two familiar faces.

New faculty members were introduced, but few made comments. When I was introduced, however, I felt compelled to tell the group about the importance of libraries. After noticing the stares, I began to wonder if these faculty members were unaccustomed to speaking out.

That thought was confirmed a few months later when an elderly, male native Wilmingtonian came to me during lunch and asked, "How did you get here? Did you come on the train?"

I replied, "No, my brother brought me by car." A few weeks later, I was told that such a question was reserved for "outsiders" who were not born and bred in Wilmington.

While working at Williston Senior High School, I also became an employee of Williston College, an extension of Wilmington College sponsored and supported by Fayetteville State University. After my regular school day at Williston, I would order and process library books for Williston College, which was run by F.J. Rogers, a former Williston Industrial High School principal.

First Countywide Book Fair in New Hanover County

In the fall of 1960, I coordinated the first countywide book fair. With Principal Booker T. Washington's endorsement, I convened a meeting of principals and department heads of all the elementary, junior high and senior high schools in the county. With my colleague, Anna Gardner Burnett, who taught typing and shorthand, we worked to develop "A Library of Your Own" theme.

With a family setting as the background, we used an eight track tape recording with a message about the importance of reading at home. The schools were still

Booklet I ordered on "How to Run a Book Fair". Read booklet many, many times!!!! Organized 1st countywide book fair held in November of 1958.

segregated and only the central office staff visited the 35 exhibits set up in the Williston gymnasium. Those that did visit were impressed with the promotion and asked if I would become one of the county's storytellers to be featured on the educational television channel stationed at Hemenway Hall, where the central office was then located.

Having no broadcast experience, this was no small feat. After much thought and prayer, I took them up on the offer. A tape recorder was borrowed from the county audio/visual office, and my first story, "The Littlest Angel", was broadcast in November of 1968. This storytelling stint lasted for two years, with positive feedback from some of the students and teachers in the elementary, junior high and high schools.

New Hanover County Schools
WILMINGTON, NORTH CAROLINA

MAY 23, 1968

MRS. BERTHA TODD
LIBRARIAN
WILLISTON SENIOR HIGH SCHOOL
WILMINGTON, N. C.

DEAR BERTHA:

PLEASE ACCEPT OUR SINCERE THANKS FOR ALL THE WORK YOU HAVE DONE THIS YEAR TO HELP US HAVE A "STORY TIME" FOR THE CHILDREN IN THE NEW HANOVER COUNTY SCHOOLS.

YOUR STORIES ARE ALWAYS A SUCCESS AND WE KNOW THAT YOU SPEND MANY HOURS PREPARING THEM FOR US.

IF YOU WOULD LIKE TO HELP US AGAIN NEXT FALL, PLEASE CALL US. WE KNOW YOU WORK HARD AND WE HATE TO FEEL THAT WE WERE ADDING TO YOUR WORK LOAD.

SINCERELY,

CLAUDE H. MCALLISTER
DIRECTOR, TELEVISION EDUCATION

DWP

MB Interactions with Supervisors

It became increasingly clear that no degree of professionalism or commitment to one's work could ameliorate the deeply entrenched views held by some in the school system.

In my first year at Williston Senior High School, I became a bit wary of the county's media supervisor, who I'll refer to as "MB". While white librarians were afforded courtesy titles, she addressed blacks by their first names. This didn't sit well with me. So when she visited me at Williston, I asked her if we could talk in the library conference room. After three separate discussions on the issue, I informed her that since she would rather our professional relationship remain on a more informal basis, she could feel free to call me "Bertha", and I would refer to her by her "first name". I did this until her retirement from the school system.

Book Order Denied

My supervisor also refused to place a book order that I had painstakingly compiled using all of the professional catalogs that I could locate. The book order was given to her in the fall of the school year but had not arrived by mid-year. When I asked why, she informed me that it included too many titles on desegregation and the integration of schools. Therefore, she and the superintendent decided not to place the order. I was incensed. I replied that if she and the superintendent had other catalogs from which I could order, please send the catalogs to me. Williston never received the catalogues or the book order.

The Testing Dilemma

Williston students had pride in their school and respect for and confidence in their teachers. A spirit of excellence permeated Williston and most students felt they needed to perform "doubly well" in order to be recognized.

One of my saddest moments at Williston came when a senior class took the Standard Achievement Test (SAT) and made outstanding scores. The students did so well that Superintendent H.M. Roland informed Principal B.T. Washington that these seniors would need to retake the test because their scores were too high. The test was re-administered and the scores remained high, but the incident grieved me greatly.

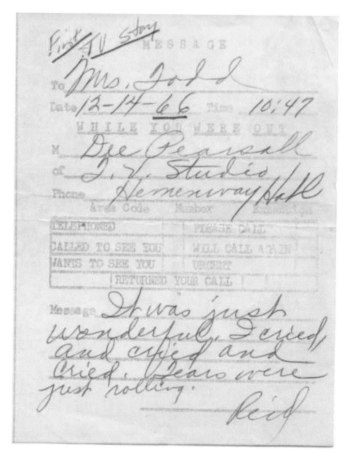

Response to 1st story told on T.V.

William G. Lowe and Bertha B. Todd – Under Scrutiny

Williston's respected government teacher William G. Lowe came to the library one Monday morning to inform me that he and I had been placed under surveillance. He thought he was being targeted because he taught students about their rights and privileges as U.S. citizens – what they could and could not do. I felt I had been placed under surveillance because of my book order and the messages that I was sending to the superintendent. When Superintendent Roland visited the newly built school with some representatives from the state Department of Public Instruction, he asked if I did not think that this was the best library in North Carolina. I replied that I could not agree to such a statement since I had not visited that many new libraries in the state of North Carolina. I quickly ascertained that he did not think very well of my response.

Remembering Lowe
Notes from one of the "Greensboro 4", Joseph McNeill in the Star News November 11, 2009. In speech delivered to the class of 1959.

"Remembering Government teacher, William Grady Lowe, McNeill said he 'made sure all of us left Williston High School knowing who we were, proud of who we were, to stand up for our rights no matter where we were, and to carry ourselves like men.' McNeill recollected the Williston experience leading up to his own political actions.

People like William Grady Lowe prepared us, teaching us how to stand up for our rights. We knew that one day it would come and it came when we finally made up our minds to put an end to it."

Permission Slips for Use of Public Library

Another issue concerned Williston students using the main public library. I was provided with a pack of permission slips that had already been signed by Principal Booker T. Washington. He asked that I also sign these slips for students to use only after they had checked Williston's book collection and the collection of books at the segregated public library on Red Cross Street. I had already heard that some citizens had challenged the use of the main library by students from Williston. So each time I gave a student a slip to use at the main public library, I would stress the need for them to be on their best behavior. I'm sure that had they not behaved, I would have gotten instant feedback. This process continued until Williston Senior High School was dissolved in 1968.

Traveling with the Library Club

Williston also had a very active Library Club and some of its members even held state offices. When the group attended state and regional meetings, we traveled by activity bus. Once, when returning home, we stopped at a restaurant with a busload of hungry students, but the manager refused to serve us. As chaperone and advisor of the group, I became frustrated and angry. The bus driver apologized, but the blame was not his. During the 1960's, segregation and discrimination were blatant and widespread.

Catherine Howze Robinson (Copeland) Drama Teacher, Composer, Exceptional English Teacher

A bright light during my tenure at Williston was Catherine Howze Robinson (Copeland), who became my role model of sorts. Catherine had moved to Wilmington when her father became the minister of First Baptist Church.

She taught drama at Williston and Wilmington College (now UNC-Wilmington) before moving to Greensboro to teach at A & T State University. Her energetic teaching style and great sense of humor endeared her to students and staff alike. In the early 1950s, Catherine directed three plays in the community, casting me in the lead role each time. The only title I can recall is "The Path Across the Hill".

The school song composed by Catherine impressed me the very first time the students sang it. The line "the greatest school under the sun" was especially meaningful, aptly capturing the pride exhibited by the staff and students.

The Williston Glee Club

Williston's Glee Club made a name for itself across the state. The first director was the late James Thompson, one of my classmates at North Carolina College at Durham. We met while he was working toward a bachelor's degree in music. During our four years of undergraduate study, Myrtle and I sang in the college choir and James served as accompanist. After earning additional degrees, he served as music director for several colleges and universities.

Later, the Williston Glee Club thrived under

> **"Dear Williston"**
> Down deep in our hearts lies a love so strong and true
> A love for thee, Dear Williston
> We cherish thy name and thy precepts too;
> All our loyalty we give, Dear School, to you.
> If ever we falter or if we ever fail,
> From thee we new courage shall gain;
> Thy standards uphold when ordeals assail;
> For we love and honor Williston's dear name.
> **CHORUS**
> Our voices we raise in a song of thy praise
> The greatest school under the sun.
> We'll ever adore Alma, Dear,
> Ever lift our praise to you, Dear Williston.

the masterful direction of B. Constance O'Dell. "Connie", as she is referred to by many, is also the godmother of my son, Brian. Her late husband, Howard, was also a former principal in the New Hanover County Schools system.

Connie later became a school counselor, serving at Hoggard High School following the dissolution of Williston Senior High School in the summer of 1968.

As a fitting footnote, the Williston Alumni Glee Club, under Connie's direction, was invited to perform at The White House in December of 1992 during the administration of former president William Jefferson Clinton.

The Williston Marching Band
Another cultural institution was the Williston Marching Band. Director Robert J. Floyd's distinctive beat and rhythm was known statewide. Crowds at large events like the Azalea Festival were dazzled by the spirited music and choreographed routines. In my first year at Williston, I agreed to work with the majorettes since I had been a majorette in college for two years. When I'd enter the teachers' lounge at the end of the school day, to change my clothes for majorette practice, the older teachers would laugh at me. Some, I'm sure, thought I was a bit "off" to spend such a long day at school – without pay! I just wanted the majorettes to be the best they could be.

Athletics
Williston functioned as a major social center for Wilmington's black community, as William M. Reaves noted in his exhaustive encyclopedia "Strength Through Struggle". Many public concerts, lectures and other programs were held at the school. Its mascot was the Tiger and its

football, basketball and baseball teams won numerous state titles among African-American schools — notably, a hard-fought state football championship in the 1955-56 seasons, according to Star News columnist Ben Steelman. (April 23, 2010)

**Two white teacher interns
1967 – 1968**

Although the Supreme Court ruling on school desegregation was made on May 17, 1954, it was years later before the public schools in New Hanover County were fully desegregated. Two white interns, Dennis Brandon and Tony Ivins, were assigned to Williston from 1967-1968. Though I was not officially designated to mentor them, having an office in the library made me more accessible than classroom teachers. They often sought me out as they struggled to understand the unfamiliar culture at the all-black school.

In one instance, Dennis was teaching his class about the flag and citizen responsibilities. After the class was over, he asked me why the students had no sparkle in their eyes. After patiently listening to him, I responded, "Mr. Brandon, you are teaching students – some below the poverty level, all of whom have experienced discrimination, and most of whom have had no dealings with white people and have not been able to trust white people. These students are probably thinking about all of these things while you are enthusiastically teaching about the U.S. flag and the respect that it warrants.

Dennis looked at me and said, "You know, what you said makes a whole lot of sense!"

Tony, the other intern, had a more reserved manner. I recall working with him on lesson plans, taking into account his inexperience with cultural peculiarities. Despite the differences, both interns completed this special year without incident.

Jean Taylor, a white math teacher, transferred to Williston in 1968. She related well to students and faculty members and was among a group of students and faculty members who marched from Williston to the courthouse following the assassination of Dr. Martin Luther King, Jr. on April 4, 1968. Jean and I would later become co-workers at Hoggard High School.

The Reaction to the Assassination of Dr. Martin Luther King, Jr.

While at Williston in 1968, I heard rumors about an impending visit from Dr. Martin Luther King, Jr. As history would record, Dr. King instead traveled to Memphis, TN to assist sanitation workers who were seeking union representation and a salary hike. That fateful trip would lead to his assassination.

As I grappled with my own emotions, I began to wonder how the Williston students were going to react. When I arrived at school the following day, I could sense the tension. After checking with some of the teachers on the second floor hall, I knew that the day would be challenging.

My initiation into riot management actually began at Williston when I learned that a group of students wanted to go to New Hanover High School and demand that the principal lower the flag to half mast.

The classroom teachers were trying hard to keep their students in their respective rooms but they were fighting a losing battle. Since I was the librarian without a homeroom class, I walked the halls pleading with students who had walked out of class to return or come to the library and sit. These students were not violent, but they were hurt, frustrated and angry.

the gym if the principal agreed.

Principal Booker T. Washington did agree and an announcement was made over the PA system. After everyone was settled in the gym, the principal called on me to introduce Mr. Clemmons, who made an impassioned speech that resonated with the visibly upset student body.

> **Taken from the Negro Almanac: (page 296)**
>
> "King's death caused a wave of violence in such major cities as Washington, DC (11 dead; 24 million dollars property damage, over 8, 000 arrests, over 1, 000 injuries); Chicago (nine dead, 11 million dollars property damage, nearly 3, 000 arrests, 500 injured) and Baltimore (6 dead, 14 million dollars property damage, 5800 arrests, and 900 injured). Without restraint against looters, death tolls would have been even higher. Both grief and anger suffused the black community. The anger was assuredly all the more fanatic precisely because King had been so irretrievably dedicated to nonviolence."

Due to the violence that occurred in Wilmington following Dr. King's assassination, the National Guard was called in to assist with the unrest and a curfew was imposed.

Two young black teachers, a male and a female, had joined the Williston faculty in the past year. Since some of the students regarded the more seasoned faculty members as the "establishment", I felt the students would listen to the two young teachers. I sought out Mr. Clemmons, an intelligent, articulate young man, and begged him to speak with the students in

The school administration then decided to get the buses ready to return the students to their homes. However, a group of teachers and students were permitted to walk downtown to the courthouse. When we arrived, we simply stood there and sang, "We Shall Overcome". There were no speeches and no violence. After singing and some crying, we marched back to school.

Little did I know that within two months, Williston Senior High School would close for good. The graduating class of 1968 would be the last.

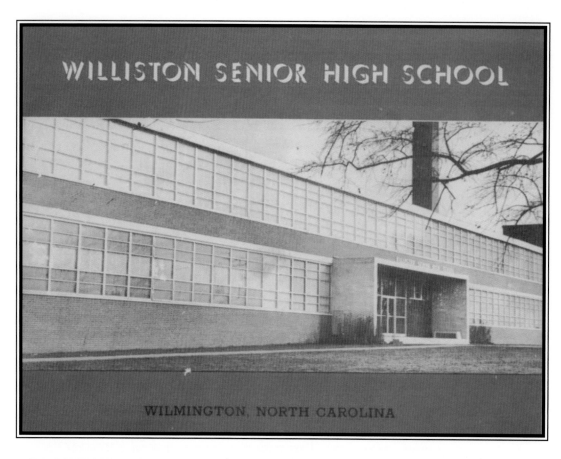

WILLISTON SENIOR HIGH SCHOOL

WILMINGTON, NORTH CAROLINA

The History of Williston

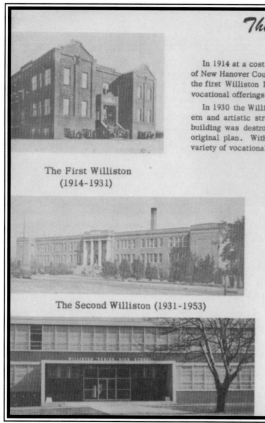

The First Williston
(1914-1931)

The Second Williston (1931-1953)

The New Williston

In 1914 at a cost of little less than $20,000 dollars, the Board of Education of New Hanover County erected, on a tract of land deeded to the Board in 1912, the first Williston Industrial School with D. C. Virgo as principal. The first vocational offerings were agriculture and home economics.

In 1930 the Williston Industrial High School moved into a larger, more modern and artistic structure with F. J. Rogers as principal. Unfortunately the building was destroyed by fire in 1935 but was rebuilt almost according to the original plan. With the new building came an expanded program and a wide variety of vocational offerings.

In September of 1953, the new million dollar Williston Senior High School, located on South Tenth Street between Nun and Church Streets, was occupied.

The present plant consists of five units. The class room unit contains 17 class rooms, offices, health room, library and college lounge. The auditorium section contains an auditorium having a seating capacity of 672, three special laboratory rooms for art, music, and dramatics; a class room and a student activity room. The gymnasium unit contains a modern gymnasium that can also be used as an auditorium, seating about 3,000; two class rooms, coaches offices, and two special rooms. The vocational building houses a band room, a D.O. room, and five shops. The East Wilmington unit houses two shops - Tailoring and Agriculture.

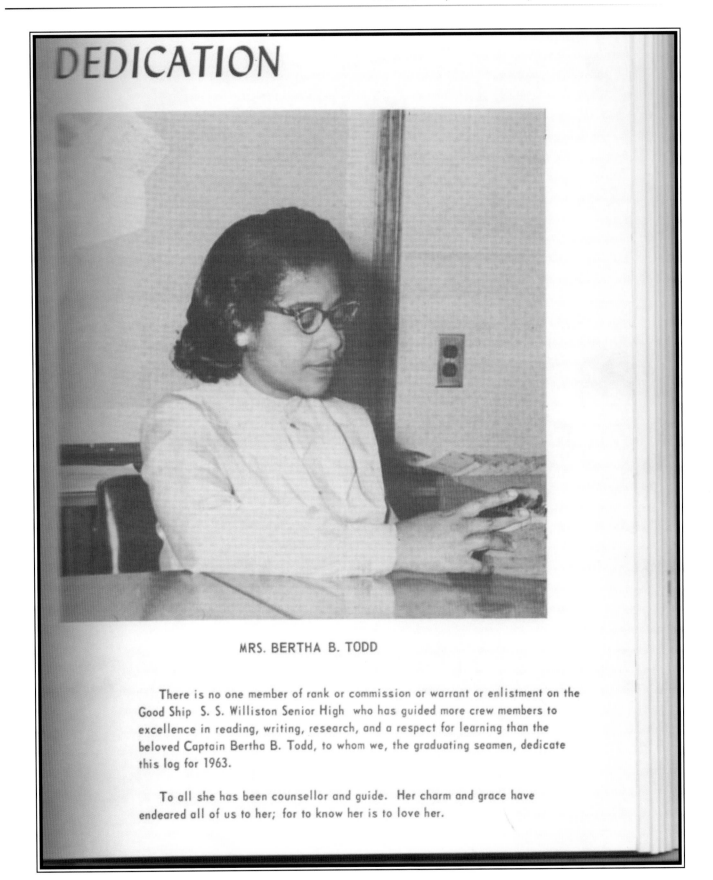

DEDICATION

MRS. BERTHA B. TODD

There is no one member of rank or commission or warrant or enlistment on the Good Ship S. S. Williston Senior High who has guided more crew members to excellence in reading, writing, research, and a respect for learning than the beloved Captain Bertha B. Todd, to whom we, the graduating seamen, dedicate this log for 1963.

To all she has been counsellor and guide. Her charm and grace have endeared all of us to her; for to know her is to love her.

1963 Willistonian Dedication Page

"The Viking Ship in Stormy Weather"
(J.T. Hoggard High)
Chapter 6

"A smooth sea never made a skillful sailor."
– English proverb

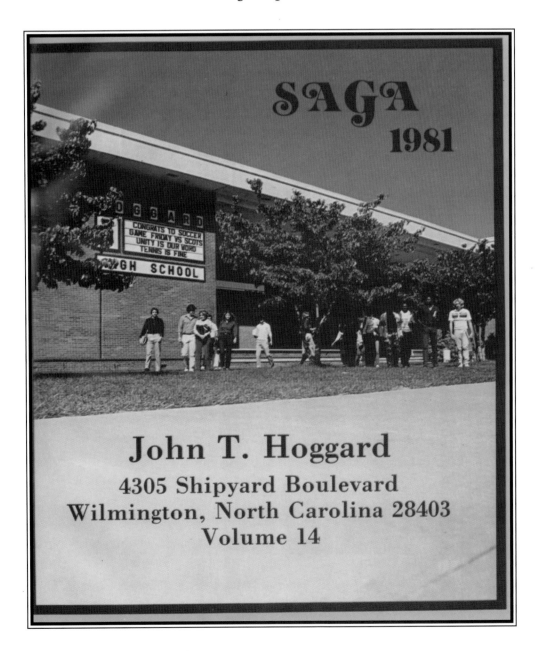

SAGA
1981

John T. Hoggard

4305 Shipyard Boulevard
Wilmington, North Carolina 28403
Volume 14

More than a decade passed between the 1954 Supreme Court ruling ending school segregation and 1968, when black students made up roughly one-third of the county's student population. Williston, the county's historically black high school, had a few white teachers, but no white students.

With relatively little public discussion, the Board of Education voted in 1968 to convert Williston Senior High School into a junior high school, with all high school students transferring to New Hanover and Hoggard High Schools, as noted in *Dixie Rising* by Peter Applebome.

I first heard news of Williston Senior High's closing from my sister Ida. A few days later, I went to the school library to retrieve my personal belongings, not wanting them to become mixed up with the school's property. A few weeks later some of the teachers began to receive school assignment letters. But two weeks before the start of school, no one had contacted me about my school assignment for the 1968–1969 school year.

Here I was with fifteen years of experience as a librarian and no school assignment. Needless to say, I was becoming quite anxious. I finally received the letter stating that I had been assigned to John T. Hoggard High School. I had read that the school opened in the fall of 1967, but did not have the slightest idea where Shipyard Boulevard was. Half of Williston's faculty was being transferred to Hoggard, so at least there would be some familiar faces.

The first faculty meeting was a bit strained, but I was impressed with the principal, Dr. C.D. Gurganus, when he placed the reading, "Children Live What They Learn" in the school's handbook. This reading is a favorite of mine. The meeting went well, but when it ended very few returning teachers remained to welcome those of us who were there for the first time. My first thought was, "If this is the welcome that the Williston faculty members get, just how will the black students be treated?" Well, the worst was yet to come. The "Viking Ship" was about to enter extremely stormy weather.

Children Learn What They Live
By Dorothy Law Nolte, Ph.D.

If children live with criticism,
they learn to condemn.

If children live with hostility,
they learn to fight.

If children live with fear,
they learn to be apprehensive.

If children live with pity,
they learn to feel sorry for themselves.

If children live with ridicule,
they learn to feel shy.

If children live with jealousy,
they learn to feel envy.

If children live with shame,
they learn to feel guilty.

If children live with encouragement,
they learn confidence.

If children live with tolerance,
they learn patience.

If children live with praise,
they learn appreciation.

If children live with acceptance,
they learn to love.

If children live with approval,
they learn to like themselves.

If children live with recognition,
they learn it is good to have a goal.

If children live with sharing,
they learn generosity.

If children live with honesty,
they learn truthfulness.

If children live with fairness,
they learn justice.

If children live with kindness and
consideration, they learn respect.

If children live with security,
they learn to have faith in themselves
and in those about them.

If children live with friendliness,
they learn the world is a nice place
in which to live.

Fellow librarian "DN" was friendly and helpful. There was only one office in the library, but she helped me carve out a little space in the audiovisual room, which I really did not mind. Since I had more experience as a librarian, we decided that "DN" would do most of the office work and I would remain on the floor to assist the students.

I usually sat at a table near the office that became a gathering spot for white students who, after some initial hesitation, liked to talk with me about any number of issues. So much so that I had to stay late to complete my library duties.

The black students were becoming a bit jealous of my growing relationship with the white students. When heated discussions ensued months later, some of the black students exclaimed, "Mrs. Todd, you belong to us!" I replied, "No, I belong to all of the students at Hoggard."

When racial tensions between the students began to mount, "walking the floor" became an advantage for me. I knew where the "hotspots" were as black and white students, in the informal setting of the library, would talk to me or near me. I often overheard plans devised by students against the administration, teachers or other students. When I got wind of anything serious, I would immediately inform the administration and staff. That's when I began to feel like a "double agent", of sorts.

Cheerleaders & Majorettes

Every facet of school life revealed how differently blacks and whites viewed their academic experience. From the selection process for cheerleaders and majorettes to the Student Council, race was a factor.

It was spring and time for cheerleader tryouts. I had heard some students saying among themselves that if no black cheerleaders were selected, there would be a riot the next day. I informed Principal Gurganus and prayed that at least one cheerleader would be selected. The next day I learned that, indeed, no black cheerleaders had been selected, so I stood in the hall to see if anything was happening or going to happen.

When I looked to my right, I saw a rather large group of students marching down the hall. When they neared me, I asked where they were headed since it was time for them to report to their classrooms. A few looked at me and made some smart remarks. Of course, I became peeved. The group then went to the first and third floors encouraging other black students to come out of their classrooms and join them. I felt certain the group of angry black students would return.

Hastily, I went to the gym and asked Coach Jim Hebbe to pull out the bleachers. He stopped all classes in the gym and did as I requested. I immediately returned to my post in front of the library doors where a much larger crowd of students began approaching me. I yelled as loudly as I could, "Students, we are going to the gym."

Some of the students repeated the directive and began heading to the gym. Soon some 300-400 students filled the bleachers. I thought, "What in the world am I going to do with all of these students?" By this time, a few of the coaches began entering the gym and one rushed to hand me a bullhorn. Of course, I began to speak as if I knew exactly what I was doing. I told the students that they must have some serious concerns since they did not go to their classes or had been persuaded to leave their classes.

The students became quiet and attentive, and I asked them to tell me their grievances, which I began to write out. Finally, two assistant principals came to the gym and took turns talking into the bullhorn, handing it back to me while they went to talk with the principal. Dr. Gurganus had informed central office about the situation and was advised to make plans for the students to go home. Many objected, saying they wanted to remain atschool. We agreed not to send them home but, in the interest of crowd control, kept them in the gym for more than four hours before releasing them.

When Coach "Spike" Corbin told me that I had done a good job with the students, I became hysterical due to the nervous energy that I had expended for more than four hours. Following this outburst, I retreated to the infirmary to recuperate for a couple of hours before returning to the library.

When the next tryout for majorettes was held, the bandmaster wanted to play it safe by asking me to serve as a judge since I had been a majorette in college. Many times I suggested to the band director that a percentage formula be used to reflect the school's diverse population.

A New Position at JTH
During the 1970-1971 school year, North Carolina received $7.7 million from the federal government to help ease the transition from segregation to desegregation, according to a March 17, 1971 article in the *News & Observer*.

I suspect that New Hanover County schools received an allotment since we were one of the school systems receiving quite a bit of negative press. A new position, administrative assistant in human relations, was created at each of the high schools. The title was later changed to assistant principal of human relations then to assistant principal.

During the 1970 – 1971 school year, I was hospitalized and was recuperating at home for a couple of weeks. Principal C.D. Gurganus visited me and informed me that the school board had funded a new position in both high schools. I recommended four teachers on Hoggard's faculty (two blacks and two whites) for consideration. Much to my chagrin, I had been recommended to serve in the new position. I told him that I really enjoyed my work in the library, was not interested in a position with no guidelines,

and would need to talk with my husband before responding. A few days later, C.D. informed me that he would need my answer by a certain date.

I spoke with my husband, Mack, who immediately said, "No!" He was well aware of the long days that I was already putting in, as well as the summers I had worked without compensation. I then contacted a close friend, Dr. Leroy Upperman, and explained my dilemma. He said, "Bert, suppose you refuse the position? What do you think your role at Hoggard would be?"

I answered, "To assist the person hired in order to tell him/her about the activities that I have been coordinating to help quell the violence and improve the communication between the faculty and students." As soon as the words were out of my mouth, I knew I was going to accept the position.

Setting up Office and Setting Up Guidelines

After I informed C.D. that I would accept the position, he told me there were no funds to set up my new office, which would be housed in a former teachers' lounge on the second floor of the main building.

A number of questions swirled in my head. What was my day going to be like now? Where was I going to find furniture to make this place attractive? Where could I locate information that would help to steer me in the right direction for this new position that I was reluctant to accept in the first place?

First things first. I had to set up my office. I contacted Sutton Council Furniture Store to request leftover carpet and solicited lumber for a chest from Godwin Lumber & Building Supplies (now E.W. Godwin's), one of the largest businesses operating in the area in the 1970's. Other items were bought using my personal funds. Principal Gurganus ultimately located a small sum of money that I used to purchase a few other items. My goal was to make the office as inviting for students as possible.

After setting up my office, I ordered several books that I thought would help me to establish guidelines for the new position. I knew school board members expected me to develop programs and activities that would curtail the riots and improve communication among students and faculty.

The "Viking 16"

As the school disturbances continued, I thought about engaging some unofficial student leaders: those who had a "following" but weren't affiliated with the student council. Since the "Viking" had been selected as the school's mascot, I selected 16 males: eight whites and eight blacks to comprise the "The Viking 16". The idea worked.

The "Viking 16" Commands/ Resolutions

1. That we make a special effort to respect each other.

2. That we try to understand why the other person has a difference of opinion.

3. That we make a great effort to stop using abusive language and ask other students to do the same.

4. That we have the courage to stop name calling.

5. That we get down to settling our differences in a better way.

6. That we try to see each person as a member of the human race instead of black and white.

7. That we leave all badges, symbols etc. that might increase negative feelings at home.

8. That, if two students engage in a conflict, we are to discourage the conflict rather than encourage it.

9. That we make a special effort to provide a calm atmosphere for the benefit of everyone.

10. That we work for the betterment of John T. Hoggard High School.

In my office

Miss John T. Hoggard

When I assumed the Administrative Assistant in Human Relations position, my goal was to establish new organizations, awards, and other forms of positive recognition that were not at Hoggard when former Williston students and teachers arrived. I vividly recalled the displays of school spirit during Williston's Homecoming Week celebration. I also knew that since black students now comprised roughly 30% of Hoggard's student population, a black female student would be unlikely to be voted homecoming queen.

It then occurred to me to create a new "Miss John T. Hoggard" position. I discussed the idea with my co-worker, social studies teacher, Student Council Advisory

—Blacks and whites work for amity—
Hoggard students begin movement for friendship

By LOUISE LAMICA
Education Editor

Sixteen students at John T. Hoggard High School began a movement this week aimed at "providing that both black and white students can get along as friends and work together in making John T. Hoggard the best school in the city, where education is available to anyone who wants it."

The sixteen — eight black and eight white students, are Easley Abraham, Michael Baldwin, Michael Bethea, Donnie Bridges, Anthony Brinkley, Nathan Davis, Barry Doyle, Gregg Ellison, Shawn Flewwellin, Billy Futch, Danny Henderson, Eddie Huft, Samuel Kirby, Donald Manpon, Ronald Mapson and Rich Marston.

Working with assistant principal Mrs. Bertha Todd as their advisor and coordinator, the 16 paired off during specially scheduled sessions and visited classrooms in the school, reading each class 10 "commandments" drawn up by Mrs. Todd and approved by the group.

Copies of the "commands" with the students signatures have also been posted around the school for students to observe and study at their leisure.

Calling themselves "the true Vikings of John T. Hoggard High School," the students read the commands to the classes they visited, emphasizing that each would make a special personal effort to obey them in the interest of harmony and understanding: They read:

1. That we make a special effort to respect each other.
2. That we try to understand why the other person has a difference of opinion.
3. That we make a great effort to stop using abusive language and ask other students to do the same.
4. That we have the courage to stop name calling.
5. That we get down to the business of settling our differences in a better way.
6. That we try to see each person as a member of the human race instead of black and white.
7. That we leave all badges, symbols, etc. that might increase negative feelings at

VIKING MOVEMENT — Tired of racial disturbances, 16 Hoggard High School students began a special movement to improve human relations at the high school this week. They are, clockwise, Easley Abraham, Michael Baldwin, Michael Bethea, Donnie Bridges, Anthony Brinkley, Nathan Davis, Barry Doyle, Gregg Ellison, Shawn Flewwellin, Billy Futch, Danny Henderson, Eddie Huft, Samuel Kirby, Donald Mapson, Ronald Mapson and Rich Marston. (SECO Photo)

home.

8. That if two students engage in a conflict, we are to discourage the conflict rather than encourage it.
9. That we make a special effort to provide a calm atmosphere for the benefit of everyone.
10. That we work for the betterment of John T. Hoggard High School.

The students, who prepared statements on their reasons for launching such a movement, were unanimous in expressing their hope to see racial disharmony at the school ended, some to the point of weariness at all the turmoil that has occurred there.

"I can't wait to see the day when students at Hoggard will be considered as human beings instead of black and white," commented Shawn Flewwellin.

"Together we hope to accomplish a great deal, but together only," wrote Anthony Brinkley. "Not as black and white but as young people of today."

"There's a way to do everything and I am concerned with my school," noted Michael Bethea. "I want to have something to contribute to all the students. I don't see any use of fighting when we all can learn to get along."

Nathan Davis wrote that "we want the schools to be safe in later years. The seniors will soon be gone. We want the way to be better for our sisters, brothers and friends and relatives. That way they won't have to call policemen on the school grounds to hurt both races."

"I hope that we, who are only a few, have shown to the school and the community that we can come together and work together and that we can take responsibility," Easley Abraham said.

"Our group is trying to show the Board of Education and our principle that we can act our age," declared Greg Ellison. "But most of all, we the Vikings of Hoggard are qualified to do what we are supposed to do.

"This school is built to work on the basis of student government," he continued." Hoggard mostly runs on self-responsibility of students. And it is about time that each student at John T. Hoggard realizes that this is what they have to do."

Principal C. D. Gurganus said Thursday that many students at Hoggard were showing interest and enthusiasm for the new movement, and that he was "extremely proud" of what the 16 students have done.

"I feel these 16 who have worked with Mrs. Bertha Todd have in fact helped to improve our human relations as school," he said.

The administrator also praised Mrs. Todd in her constant efforts to work with students of both races at the school to improve human relations and iron out personal grievances.

"The Viking 16"

Board chair and friend, Carole Whebee Ellis, who supported the idea. I implemented several other awards program to provide more opportunities for students to be recognized, including the service organization "Order of the Vikings" and the merit-based "A True Viking" Award for outstanding students.

Hoggard's Vikettes

Two female students visited me in my office one day with the idea for an all-girl chorus, later called the "The Vikettes". Impressed with their proposal, I secured two advisors (initially one white and one black) and began developing criteria. The group was formed and rehearsals began. The Vikettes' debut was a splash and similar groups were established at New Hanover and Laney high schools a few years later.

The Vikettes became so popular that two black females came to my office a few years later to request that the group become 50% black and 50% white since there was very little opportunity for black students to become involved in a number of other activities. I told the girls I would pray and meditate on their request.

A few days later, I sent for the two young ladies and informed them that making this popular group 50/50 would be reverse discrimination. I also informed the advisor of my decision.

Although the Hoggard Vikettes began with two advisors (1 black and 1 white), Vivian Yates Crosby served as the primary advisor from its inception. By the time she retired in July 2010, she had worked with the Vikettes for more than 30 years.

Athletics

Since Hoggard was located a good distance from the homes of most of the black students, remaining after school to participate in sporting events was out of the question. There were few, if any, cars available to transport them. The use of activity buses had not been considered. Several of the coaches had good relationships with the black athletes, but many were reluctant to take them home after games and practices. So I purchased a used car for a football player who promised to transport his fellow student athletes.

Student Council

The student council was another sticky issue. During the 1967-1968 school year, student council officers had already been elected at their respective Williston and Hoggard high schools. Hoggard principal C.D. Gurganus assigned me to serve as one of the student council advisors and we decided that, for this first year, Hoggard would have co-positions for each office. During my entire 17-year tenure at Hoggard, I continued to serve as a student council advisor, working with other advisors to sponsor district and state conventions.

A very sensitive student council issue occurred during the 1968–1969 school year. The Williston co-president decided not to salute the U.S. flag during a school ceremony. When one of the white, male student council officers saw this, he reported this to the entire student body and recommended the black co-student body president be impeached. With enough riots stemming from other issues, we couldn't have the student leadership going at it, too.

I summoned the black male co-president to the library conference room and asked why he refused to salute the flag. "DJ", I'll call him, informed me that he was angry about being co-president, felt he was in "alien territory" at Hoggard, and felt disrespected by the teachers and the students in his role as co-president. Furthermore, he did not like saluting a flag that symbolized so much discrimination. "DJ" looked at me, with tears running down his cheeks, and said, "Mrs. Todd, I have never met a white person I can trust".

I listened to his litany and then asked him if he trusted me. He replied, "Yes, ma'am." I said, "Well, since I have met some whites whom I can trust, you will have to take my word that there are some whites whom you can trust!" "DJ" looked at me and said, "Mrs. Todd, I will trust your word on this."

It saddened me that this young black male with so much potential felt this way. Even sadder was the fact that many of the black students from Williston shared his sentiments. Nevertheless, the impeachment and another riot were averted -- at least for a while.

Due to the merging of the two schools, the respective student councils spent the summer of 1970 revising the constitution to provide for more equitable representation.

SEPT. 10, 1970　　Wilmington, N. C.　　ONE-B

A labor of summer-long love

John T. Hoggard students revise school constitution

By LOUISE LAMICA
Education Editor

Many students who attended John T. Hoggard High School on Shipyard Boulevard never really had a summer vacation in the strictest sense of the word this past summer.

They spent hour after hour, week in and week out, revising their school constitution, which they call "our constitutional Revision."

These students are members of the Student Body, their president in senior Stephany Points. And they are still meeting twice a week to work on the revisions, which they expected to be completed by mid-fall.

One of the basic reasons for such a project was to amend any part of the constitution which might lead to such incidents as the racial tensions and violence which broke out last school year at Hoggard and New Hanover High School.

Working with this Student Body in such a major undertaking are faculty advisors and Principal C. D. Gurganus and his associate principals.

Need for such a revision is one of the most important projects the Student Body has ever undertaken, according to Stephany Points.

"The present homeroom representative system," she explains, "has proved ineffective in a school of 2,200 students for several reasons."

She lists them as 1) the large number of homeroom representatives attending each meeting, and 2) a lack of representation from a cross section of the student body.

Proposed revisions the Student Body is now working on include: 1) electing a total of 30 representatives, 10 from each of the 10th, 11th and 12th grades; and 2) representatives to be elected by residential precincts, thereby allowing for a more fair representation.

Other changes include a Review Board and a Critic Board. The Review Board was formed in order to strengthen Student Government. It is headed by the vice-president of the Student Body, and four alternating members of an Executive Board, equivalent to a president's cabinet.

These individuals discuss any suggestions they have for the betterment of Student Council, or any problems they may be having as representatives.

"This board should prove particularly effective this semester while we are still operating under our present Constitution," Stephany continues. "It creates a more personal atmosphere in such a large Student Council."

The purpose of the Critic Board is to give each candidate, during a Student Council election, an opportunity to express his views on various issues. It is felt that by doing this the students will be better informed on the qualifications of the candidates.

Special effort is also being made to have a greater representation of black students on the election committee, which is in charge of all elections at Hoggard.

According to Mrs. Bertha Todd, student Council faculty advisor, many steps have been taken at the school for the purpose of creating a wholesome feeling among all students. She also feels that students at Hoggard are becoming more aware of each others as individuals.

These changes — plus what the school calls "Hoggard's philosophy" — are believed by school personnel and students to guarantee individual equality to the 2,200 students enrolled there.

The "Hoggard Philosophy" stresses the development of the individual with a learning toward increased self discipline and a greater amount of responsibility, school educators explain.

The school offers many opportunities for this to be exercised. A lack of bells for class changes offers the opportunity for a student to practice self discipline, and at the same time provides a more relaxed atmosphere within the school. A designated smoking area for students is designed to help him become more aware of the importance of assuming responsibility.

Many of the students feel these privileges enable them to develop a greater sense of maturity, both as students and as future citizens.

"We realize that to keep these privileges calls for a good deal of responsibility on our part," one said.

Another such facet is the Department of Order, the judicial branch of Hoggard, a board composed of two sophomores, three juniors and four senior assemblymen.

The board is moderated by Jane Noffsinger, secretary of Order, who feels that such a program has a good chance to be effective this year—"but only with the help of the students," she added.

Miss Noffsinger explained that students responsibility and their individual development is the primary purpose of such a department.

For example, if a student is not complying with the guidelines as set up, such as skipping class, his name may be given to faculty advisors, the Secretary of Order, or any assemblymen.

When a student is requested to come before the board, he is given a chance to explain the situation presented. The offense is discussed at great length, and the student is given every possible chance to explain his actions regarding the incident.

"So actually," Miss Noffsinger continued, "the Department of Order is a group of students, each elected by the entire student body, each concerned with keeping their school in order — and giving each one a chance to be responsible along with that challenge of freedom."

CONFERENCE—Hoggard High School's Student Government Body has been hard at work this summer revising the school's Constitution, designed to offer equality to the 2,200 students enrolled there. Conferring here are Doug Odell, Stephany Points, Russell Davis, and Principal C. D. Gurganus. (SECO Photo by Herman Benton)

Speakouts, Rap Sessions, and Discussion Groups

I suggested to Principal Gurganus that a room be designated during fourth and fifth lunch periods for students to express their feelings freely. He agreed and asked some teachers who had these periods available to assist me with executing the idea. Since all students were taking English classes, we relayed information about the sessions through those teachers. Speakouts were held the first year, rap sessions the second year and discussion groups the third and final year. The Hoggard teachers who assisted me were dedicated and, slowly but surely, black and white students began to learn more about each other. The sessions had the intended effect and there was a measurable difference in relations between the students.

I was still working in the library at the time, which I'm sure is one of the reasons the school board recruited me for the new position. I coordinated the project from 1968-1971, and my fellow librarian became understandably impatient with the amount of time I was devoting to the sessions. She finally went to Dr. Gurganus and told him that my library duties were suffering because of my newly acquired responsibilities.

Assemblies, Assemblies, Assemblies

Carole Whebee Ellis and I worked closely with the student body. We could sense when the "natives were getting restless" and would ask the principal to schedule an assembly, a pep rally or just a "talk rally". Our strategy for engaging students in dialogue to diffuse tensions appeared to be working.

Many times Carole suggested contacting a young, white attorney who was quite articulate and would command the students' attention. George Rountree, III would select a topic like citizenship or behavior and pace back and forth in front of the captivated students. His presence was a blessing during those assemblies in the 1970s. We would meet again years later when I served as co-chair of the 1898 Centennial Foundation in 1997.

Because the 1970 – 1971 school year had been so difficult, I felt a burning desire to personally thank certain black and white students who had exhibited much courage in the face of chaos. They, along with many other students, teachers, and administrators, worked hard at creating a positive, stable, and balanced environment at Hoggard.

Changing of the Guard
From Principal C.D. Gurganus to
Principal Michael J. Saus

Just as I was settling into my new position assisting Principal Gurganus with the student disturbances, he called me to his office one morning to inform me that he would be leaving Hoggard. I began crying and the tears would not stop. Realizing I had no prior knowledge of this impending change, he informed me that the principal from D.C. Virgo would succeed him. I had heard of Michael Saus, but had never talked with him personally. Shortly thereafter, Principal Saus came to Hoggard and called for an administrative staff meeting. Of all things, the lock on my office door jammed and I could not get out of my office. I thought, this man will think that I am so

JOHN T. HOGGARD HIGH SCHOOL
4305 SHIPYARD BOULEVARD
WILMINGTON, NORTH CAROLINA 28401

June 7, 1971

Dear _____ :

All of us are aware of the fact that this year at John T. Hoggard High School has definitely been a challenging one. During the periods of unrest at our school many of the students lost faith, lost hope and resigned themselves to a remaining dark and gloomy year at Hoggard.

You were among the few who persevered and continued to work in the interest of rebuilding positive relations within our school—whether by thinking up new projects, giving a smile or helping hand to someone else, or by continuing to work on previously organized activities.

Please accept my sincere thanks to you for contributing so much to our school in the area of human relations.

Sincerely,

Bertha B. Todd
Administrative Assistant
of Human Relations

This is a copy of a letter that was sent to seventy-five students who attended John T. Hoggard High School during the 1970-71 school year. Each letter was individually typed in order to give it a personal touch. I heard that some students framed their letters. Others had additional copies made to send to relatives.

loyal to C.D. that I am simply refusing to attend his first meeting.

Though C.D.'s departure was difficult for, especially after the long, hard hours we had put in at Hoggard, I had to accept this "changing of the guard".

Activity Periods

Another idea that occurred to me was to hold a school-wide activity period at least once weekly until the disturbances abated. Once the atmosphere improved, these activity periods were held bimonthly, and eventually monthly until the early 1980's. This mammoth undertaking for a 2200-student population would require precise organization and the cooperation of the entire faculty and staff. I discussed the plan with principal Michael J. Saus who gave his stamp of approval to implement the following strategy:

1. Determine the number of clubs that we could sponsor by polling 115 to 120 teachers.

2. Have as many co-advisors as possible – one white and one black.

3. Determine the most effective period of the day to schedule these activity sessions.

4. Provide "holding rooms" for those students who did not wish to join any of the clubs.

5. Provide rooms for "study hall" areas.

6. Locate teachers and teacher assistants to monitor the halls during these activity periods.

The first school-wide activity period proved to be successful. Disturbances began to abate as students, black and white, began to request new clubs and activities. Once again, the students' focus shifted from fighting with each other to collaborating to ensure the success of their clubs. The students were excited about their new informal activities and shared news of their interests and progress with me. Without the cooperation and support of the teachers and administration, this project would not have been successful. The endeavor proved to be quite time-consuming, given my other duties at school and my rounds on the community circuit in the afternoons and evenings.

Sponsoring Human Relation Workshops – Teachers and Students

Wilmington Mayor B.D. Schwartz appointed me to the countywide Human Relations Commission in 1971. Meanwhile, those of us at Hoggard organized a Faculty Human Relations Committee and a Student Human Relations Committee. Both groups planned numerous programs and activities to foster better understanding among the ethnic groups.

"The Wilmington-New Hanover Human Relations Commission was reorganized during the weekend and according to the Port City Mayor BD Swartz and commission chairman Bill Cullom, the first meeting of the group will be at 5 PM December 5th at a place yet to be determined."

"Members of the Human Relations Commission included members of both races, and are from almost every part of our community, Mayor Swartz said."

'By having representatives of organizations present their viewpoints, perhaps we can establish good relationships between the black and white communities,' Swartz said.

Swartz said, 'We want to hear both black and white grievances, anytime they have a grievance.' He added that the purpose would be to correct rumors."

'I'd rather everyone be vocal rather than violent,' Swartz said. 'Maybe together we can solve our problems, be it in schools, employment, or government."

-The Sunday Star-News, November 21, 1971

NEWLY-REORGANIZED HUMAN RELATIONS COMMISSION IN SESSION
First meeting of group Monday centered around need for more understanding

Dec. 7, 197_

New Human Relations group holds 1st meet

By MILTON JORDAN
Staff Writer

"I don't think we could have gotten into the mess we are in accidentally; we were steered here. That took a lot of work, and it is going to take a lot of hard work for us to get ourselves out of this mess," declared O. Kelly Lawson, a member of the newly organized Human Relations Commission which held its first meeting Monday.

Meeting in the conference room of the County Commission Building, the 27 members, representing a broad area of opinions on local conditions, assessment of the two or three major problems facing Wilmington and New Hanover County.

Lawson's comments summed up briefly the consensus of the group which indicated that the basis of the area's problem is a lack of understanding, patience, tolerance, and involvement.

Some 54 problems were specifically mentioned, covering a spectrum that included inadequate employment and employment opportunity, a lack of peace and too much violence in the community, polarization of the races by minority groups in both races, housing, wrong attitudes, and a host of others that though stated in slightly different terminology all came out meaning that there is a lot wrong here, and it is robbing citizens of this area of the right to peaceful and productive lives.

Also on hand for the meeting was Mayor B.D. Schwartz and County Commission Chairman Meares Harriss.

"Let's forget the past," Schwartz said in his introductory remarks. Let's work on the present and the future," he challenged while thanking the new slated in slightly different terminology all came out meaning that there is a lot wrong here, and it is robbing citizens of this area of the right to peaceful and productive lives.

Also on hand for the meeting was Mayor B.D. Schwartz and County Commission Chairman Meares Harriss.

"Let's forget the past," Schwartz said in his introductory remarks. Let's work on the present and the future," he challenged while thanking the new members for accepting the call to service and pledging the city's support in the commission's effort.

Harriss also pledged the county's support, and added that he hoped everyone would be able to work together for the better of the area.

Aaron Johnson, representing the State Human Relations Commission, offered that

group's assistance, and Doug Curley, vice-chairman of the commission observed that never in his memory had so many people gathered around one table with one thought in mind—a better Wilmington.

Just before the group began offering their assessments of the problems, T.C. Jervay, publisher of The Wilmington Journal, pointed out that the composition of the new commission—22 whites and 15 blacks—did not truly reflect the 50-50 ratio that had been pledged when this movement for change got underway.

Both Bill Cullom, chairman of the commission, who helped to spearhead the drive for a new group, explained that a diligent effort for a 50-50 ratio was made, but because some groups did not respond to a call for representation, this was not possible.

They both also said all effort will be made to keep the ratio close, while Jervay noted that the difference did not speak well for the cultivation of trust among the races.

In other comments before opening the floor for review of the problems, Cullom charged the commission that, "We must always be honest and straightforward with each other."

Though there was absolutely no debate or discussion of the problems listed, one problem did generate a unanimous vote, the only vote taken during the meeting. It was mentioned that often the news media, local, state and national, tended to play up negative incidents in Wilmington, but did not give similar publicity to positive actions.

Jervay moved that the commission request the members of the local news media with state and national contact through wire services to circulate the forming of the new commission, and the initial steps being taken to solve some of the problems here. The motion was seconded and carried unanimously.

Wilmington City Manager John A. Jones in comments near the tail end of the meeting observed that a newcomer to Wilmington notices four basic problem areas: unpaved streets in certain districts, the lack of black faces in government, the lack of black involvement in civic organizations, and the lack of opportunity for blacks and whites to sit down and talk over problems.

On the first two observations, Jones announced: "Those are my problems." On the third, he said he felt this was a symptom of the lack of communications between the races, and he vouchsafed the hope that the

fourth observation is now a thing of the past.

Before closing the meeting, Cullom told the group that these 54 problems mentioned would be compiled and a list would be sent to each commission member and that they could compile a priority list of these problems for discussion during the next meeting, slated for Dec. 20th at 5 p.m.

There was one protest lodged during the meeting, and it came from a citizen in the audience, Bruce Sandy who said he felt that those persons who have lived in Wilmington less than a year should not serve on the commission because "they don't know what our problems down here are." He also said he felt there are both too many professional people on the commission and too many old faces from the Good Neighbor Council.

Sandy said he felt there should be more of the hard working class on the commission, causing G.D. (Tex) Gross, of the United Klan of America, to quip: "U there's anyone on this commission who doesn't work, I want them to meet me outside and tell me how they do it."

David Massey, student representative on the commission, immediately asked if there was anyway for Sandy to be made a member of the commission.

Cullom replied that the official quota was filled, and promised to consider Sandy's request in making future appointments.

Cullom and Jones reported that the city is moving forthwith to hire a new Human Relations Director. The post has been vacant since Robert T. Nicholas resigned back in September.

Special Appointment of the Mayor and BBT

North Carolina Governor Bob Scott appointed Mayor Schwartz and me to a special state committee. Neither of us knew why we were chosen, but we graciously accepted the appointments.

ROWP vs Church of the Black Messiah

During this period of unrest, two adult groups formed in the community: Rights of White People (ROWP) and Church of the Black Messiah. Both groups had student members and most of the student members seemed to attend Hoggard. One school day a student member of ROWP came to my office and complained about the fact that black students were able to meet with the schools superintendent and board members; he wanted the same courtesy extended to his group. From the time I accepted the new position, I was determined to assist *all* students, regardless of ethnicity. This student was no exception.

When we concluded our discussion, he informed me that he would bring me some written concerns. When he returned a few days later with the grievances, he asked if I could have copies made for his group and for myself, and if I would contact the superintendent and board members, which I did. The superintendent also

STATE OF NORTH CAROLINA
GOVERNOR'S OFFICE
RALEIGH 27611

ROBERT W. SCOTT
GOVERNOR

December 10, 1971

Mrs. Bertha Todd
Assistant Principal
Hoggard High School
Wilmington, North Carolina

Dear Mrs. Todd:

In order to alleviate the tensions and unrest within many of the public schools of our State, I am forming a citizens task force to look into this troublesome problem and to come up with recommendations.

I would like for you to serve as a member of this task force, which will hold its initial meeting on December 17 in the Conference Room of the State Administration Building here in Raleigh. Registration will begin at 10:15 a.m. at the conference site, with the meeting to start at 11:00 a.m.

I plan to open the meeting by speaking to the problem and to the work of the task force. After this, we plan to have brief preliminary remarks among members of the task force and then to recess for lunch. No provisions for lunch have been made, so you will be on your own. After the lunch break, we plan to reassemble and to divide into a number of workshop or seminar groupings, concluding later in the afternoon with a brief summary session.

I feel that you can provide input into this effort to maintain a proper climate of learning within our schools and to assure continuing public support for them.

I would appreciate a reply from you at your earliest convenience.

Cordially,

Robert W. Scott

Letter from Governor Bob Scott

asked that I forward a copy of the written concerns, which I sent by courier. With the concerns duly noted and a date set, I thought my duties were fulfilled and I could move on to the next situation.

The morning of the scheduled meeting, the ROWP student came to my office again and informed me that he had another request -- would I accompany him

and the group to the scheduled meeting? It was then that I knew that the students knew I was there to assist all groups. I agreed to serve as the advisor for the group during the meeting, which went well. I was the only black person in the room and simply listened to the students, Dr. Bellamy and the board members. When one particular question was asked, board member Vera Shands offered an

Staff photo by Ken Cooke

AT SESSION — Wilmington Mayor B. O. Schwartz and Bertha Toddy, administrative assistant at Hoggard High School in Wilmington, at school unrest session.

Mayor BD Swartz and Me

even-handed response to their inquiry that caused me to hold her in high esteem ever since. What a meeting!

In all of the responsibilities assigned to me during my 17 years at Hoggard, I made a very special effort to remain objective and view concerns through the eyes of the students, and sometimes the adults, regardless of ethnicity.

A Call for Black Studies

Black students at Hoggard and New Hanover High asked several times for a course in Black Studies. Following the dissolution of Williston Senior High School, all funds were divided equally between New Hanover and Hoggard, with the principals given the discretion of using the funds as they saw fit. Dr. Gurganus gave the funds to the Hoggard library, with the stipulation that books written by and about African-Americans be ordered. When the first book order arrived, they were catalogued and placed on the shelves, much to the delight of the black students. At the end of the school year, when my colleague and I took inventory of the books, not only had the books been read, most of them had been taken. The following year, I ordered additional books written by and about blacks. They too were taken. It occurred to me that I didn't have that problem at Williston because the students were getting their "fill" about their heritage from their teachers and had no need to hoard the resources. I ordered as many books as possible at Hoggard until the funds were depleted.

In the 1970-1971 school year, when the county's curriculum bulletin was distributed for the next school year, I checked my copy immediately, certain that after the many boycotts by black students at Hoggard and New Hanover, the repeated requests for a class in Black Studies would be granted. No such class was listed.

I contacted the superintendent at once and asked why such a needed course had been omitted. He replied that no one had officially requested the course. I informed Dr. Bellamy that I would be happy to do so if that's what it took. The following letter was hastily composed and taken to central office by a courier.

Following receipt of the letter, Dr. Bellamy, school board member and attorney George Clark, and I had lunch at the Boucan Room, a local restaurant and motel at Third & Walnut streets owned by the Saffo family, to discuss the course in detail. Minority Cultures was approved by the Board of Education and added to the 1971 – 1972 high school curriculum. Following the vote, I quickly developed the requested course syllabus.

Two Hoggard Assemblies Etched in My Memory Forever
Assembly #1

A colleague told me of a film titled "Black History: Lost, Stolen or Strayed" that was available through the North Carolina Department of Public Instruction. Nancy Thompson (Beane), a social studies teacher, student council advisor and friend had shown the film to her classes. She said the film had been well-received, so I decided to re-order the film for use by other

Copy

February 24, 1971

Dr. Heywood Bellamy, Superintendent
New Hanover County Board of Education
Hememway Hall
Wilmington, N. C.

Dear Dr. Bellamy:

During the discussion of item 19 (changes - Curriculum
Bulletin) February 23 agenda of the New Hanover County Board
of Education, I felt an urgent need to offer some suggestions
and opinions. However, I failed to do this since I wanted
additional time to evaluate my thoughts.

In my present position at Hoggard I feel that it is
necessary to be in close contact and communication with black
and white citizens of Wilmington. A special effort is made
to do this-contacting on an extensive basis.

I am aware of the changes that have been proposed for
the two high schools in the areas of English and Social
Studies. These changes are good. However, due to continued
unrest, I feel an urgent need for those in the administrative
unit of New Hanover County to consider and approve a separate
elective course in the culture and heritage of minority groups.

I have previously felt (and advocated) that such information should be included in the proper courses (U.S. history,
English, science, etc.) At this time, however, I feel as if
the need for this information is far too urgent to wait for
such inclusions in the types of courses previously mentioned.

A separate elective course at this time plus minority-
group information included in proper courses being taught
will help to intensify an effort to disseminate information
designed to develop and encourage racial pride. Such deve-
lpped pride should help to provide an atmosphere of harmony
and understanding--thereby creating an atmosphere that is
conducive to greater educational efforts.

Your understanding and consideration of this request will
be appreciated.

Sincerely,

(Mrs.) Bertha B. Todd
Administrative Assistant of
Human Relations

Letter to Dr. Bellamy requesting a Black Studies Course.

social studies teachers. My decision, however well-intentioned, resulted in a fiasco.

On the day of the screening, an announcement was made directing teachers to bring their classes to the gym. I soon discovered that some teachers who had study halls were also among the classes coming to view the film. Since they were already entering the gym, I thought that turning them away would cause an unnecessary disturbance.

As the students began to view the film, I became aware of restlessness among some of the students from the study halls. Should I stop the film or allow it to continue? I decided to let the film continue and pray that a major disturbance would not ensue. The students filed out of the gym without incident. However, violence did erupt the next day, and the film was blamed for inciting the disturbance.

Since I had made the decision to show the film, I had to make things right. Some parents contact several school board members and, soon after, Dr. Bellamy called me for a detailed explanation of the uproar. I submitted the following information.

POINTS TO BE CONSIDERED BEFORE THE FILM IN QUESTION IS TO BE VIEWED
FILM TITLE – "Black History: Lost, Stolen, or Strayed"

1. The film should not be viewed at two separate viewings. Parts I and II should be viewed consecutively.
2. An introduction (sheet enclosed) and a follow up make the film much more effective.
3. The film was shown 3 times to groups larger than classroom size.
   a. Twice in the library on Wednesday, February 17th. There were approximately 100 – 150 students in the library for each showing.
   b. Once in the gym, on Thursday, February 18th. This group numbered between 900 – 1, 000. Comment: I have heard since that this group included some of the same students who saw the film in the library.
4. The film was scheduled to be viewed on a voluntary basis. Students from study halls were the persons to be considered.
5. The film was shown one week and one day before the trouble erupted at Hoggard.
6. The film was also shown to students at New Hanover High School. The number of students viewing the film is not known at this time. (approximately 360)
7. The film was shown in both schools without a reaction in one school. Why?
8. An introduction and follow up make viewing the film more effective.
9. Teachers who expressed a desire to view the film were supposed to have been cleared through the librarians.
10. The film was checked out from the public library. Since then I have

received a brochure from my church with a description of the film. This brochure is enclosed for your reading.

11. This film came from the NC State Board of Education. It is recommended for the following grade levels: Junior High/Senior High/College/Adult

12. No individuals made any expressions concerning the showing of this film at the time the film was being shown. No public comments were made prior to today's discussions. This seems to indicate a lack of communication on the part of faculty members. Any complaints would have been considered had they been made public.

COMMENTS

I am sorry that the implication was made by some parents that the showing of this film tended to create undue tension at Hoggard. There may have been some feeling created on the parts of some teachers and students. I do not feel that the majority of the students felt negatively toward the viewing. I feel that some type of follow up should have been done by each teacher who chose to bring (his) her class to the library or the gym. However, since certain teachers were not expected to view the film, no effort was made by the program planner to make such a suggestion.

Another point to be considered: Hoggard is a school that was affected during a disturbance that began at New Hanover High School. A great effort has been made to create harmony within Hoggard. Although this has been done, most of the black students were absent from Hoggard ... during the boycotting period. This absence created a somewhat negative feeling on the part of white students toward black students who chose to be absent in support of grievances voiced by students at New Hanover High rather than come to school and indicate a loyalty to Hoggard.

Personally, I feel that the adult black and white communities have tended to create greater tension because of comments that have been made in the homes during and after the period of turmoil in Wilmington. From the meetings that I have attended the feelings are very strong.

I shall be grateful to you for any comments you might offer concerning the film and the viewing by the students.

Assembly #2

Things appeared to be settling down two to three years after the schools were merged. Students began requesting an assembly during Black History Month. Still smarting from the actions of the students following the film, I had no intentions of acting on their requests.

Finally, in February of 1976, I felt that the entire student body was ready for a Black History Month assembly. Some of our Hoggard alumni were attending UNC-Chapel Hill and told me about a group called the "Ebony Readers" who recited contemporary poetry. Since Angela Wright, a former Miss John T. Hoggard was in this group, I thought they would be an appropriate choice for a Black History Month assembly. I had also invited a group of dancers from North Carolina A & T State University. Since my twin sister, Myrtle, was teaching at A & T, I asked her to take care of any arrangements that the dancers would need.

Some Hoggard students were also participating in the assembly, and the faculty and student body were excited. On the day of the assembly, I informed Principal Saus that we were ready for students, who were given the option to attend, to begin moving into the gym. The students were quiet and respectful as they proceeded into the crowded gymnasium. A few administrators and faculty members were standing and Principal Saus was near the stage preparing to give the greeting.

My anxiety began to rise when I noticed that all of the contemporary readers from UNC-Chapel Hill were dressed in black and wore armbands. I thought since our former Miss John T. Hoggard is in the group, I am sure that everything will be fine. I looked toward the stage and one of the Chapel Hill students was refusing to hand the microphone to Mr. Saus. One or two of the readers had already read their poetry and neither reading was what I expected. I glanced at the student body and they were beginning to look bewildered. Finally, Principal Saus took the microphone and asked the students to return to their classes immediately.

The teachers and students began to file out. The poor dancers from A & T moved to the stage and began to perform as the students left the gym. What a mess!

After all of that detailed planning for the very first Black History Month assembly, I was forced into damage control mode. I couldn't decide whether to scream or cry! Fortunately, no disturbances ensued among the large gathering of students.

I went to the athletic area near the gym and just sat to decide what my next step should be. But rumors began flying: "Mrs. Todd has gone to hide somewhere!" Of course, that was not the case. I had to wait for the A & T dancers to prepare to leave and see them off to Greensboro. As far as the Ebony Readers from UNC-Chapel Hill were concerned, I did not want to see them at all. I was going to contact Chancellor William Friday to inform him about how his students had completely messed up my program!

I contacted Dr. Bellamy and informed him of how well Principal Saus had handled the situation. I also told him that I was going to contact Chancellor Friday the next morning. The following letter is the response to my complaint regarding these students.

**Unforgettable Events
While Sailing on the Viking Ship
First Faculty Social**

In the mid-1970's, the Hoggard faculty expressed a desire to host a weekend social, which members of the Human Relations Committee began planning. Each person was assessed a small fee to cover the cost of food and other refreshments at a motel on Market Street. It was the first time most faculty members felt comfortable enough to mingle on an informal basis away from school. The social was an overwhelming

March 24, 1976

Mrs. Bertha Todd
Assistant Principal
John T. Hoggard High School
Wilmington, N.C. 28401

Dear Mrs. Todd:

It is my understanding that you were the official at John T. Hoggard High School which worked out the details of the Ebony Readers' performance during the Black Culture Week of February 1976. I also understand that Mr. William Pass was the contact person for the Ebony Readers.

As Chairperson of the Black Student Movement, I deeply regret that the Ebony Readers did not adhere to the previously agreed upon format and content for the presentation. And I apologize for the disruption which was caused by the selections read during the program.

Please be assured that the content of the materials presented were not intended to reflect any attitude towards your student body or faculty. A discussion has been held and an understanding with the Ebony Readers has been reached. There should be no misunderstanding or similar occurrences in the future.

Please know that the Black Student Movement does value its relationship with other institutions within the state and we do regret that this occurred.

Sincerely,

Gloria Carney
Gloria Carney
BSM Chairperson

cc
Harold Wallace, Faculty Advisor

Letter from UNC-Chapel Hill regarding inappropriate behavior during an assembly.

Gregory Congregational Church and the Student Boycott

In 1971, I began to hear rumors among Hoggard students that black students from New Hanover and Hoggard had been given permission to meet at Gregory Congregational Church. I quickly sent for some key black male students and urged them to continue to work out their problems at Hoggard. One of the students promised me he would talk with the others to dissuade them from going to the church. Whether he did or did not, the students ended up at Gregory Congregational the following morning.

When I discovered a majority of Hoggard's black students were absent the next day, I contacted John Beane, my white male counterpart at New Hanover, who accompanied me to the church. The adults present when we arrived seemed unconcerned about the students being at the church instead of in school. John and I sat in the back. The students thought we were there to take roll until I stood up to speak and found myself suddenly cast in the role of community leader rather than an employee of the New Hanover County Board of Education. The students wanted Mr. Beane to leave, but I informed them that if he goes, I go. They agreed to allow John to stay.

When John, Rev. Templeton, and I were the only adults left in the church, I knew some action had to be taken to get the students to return to their respective schools. I told the group of about 100 students that we needed someone to take notes.

One student found paper and a pencil and said she was ready. I explained that this meeting was going to be conducted in an orderly fashion, that they were to raise their hands to be recognized, and each should express the concerns serious enough to warrant a boycott. Each concern had to be verbalized so it could be prioritized. We continued until noon and their agitation seemed to be abating.

Much to my surprise, someone had called the news media. I informed Rev. Templeton and the students that, "I am not the community leader for this group, I did not call this boycott, and I did not call the news media." I made similar comments to the editor of the *Hanover Sun*, who had entered the church by that time. I was totally unaware that he was taping my comments. I realized then that I had become the leader of this student group by default.

Although their grievances were aired many times, the students would not return to school. I really began to feel sorry for Rev. Templeton. No other minister would allow the students to meet in their church. I also wondered why adults from the black community were conspicuously absent from the boycott.

The following week I returned to the church -- this time alone. I had already informed Dr. Bellamy of my intention to

-------------- 'No one has heard our side' -------------- 1971
Boycott's

Black student group to boycott schools

By LOUISE LAMICA
Education Editor

Declaring that "no one has heard our side of the school disturbances," around 100 black students representing New Hanover and John T. Hoggard high schools gathered in Gregory Congregational Church at 6th and Nun streets Thursday and vowed they would not attend school again "until we get our rights back."

"We're not getting an education anyway," said one of the students, "so why shouldn't we stay out?"

Connie Tindall, one of the spokesmen for the group and a student from Hoggard, said the group was declaring Friday "Liberation Day" and called on other black students to join their boycott.

Among their complaints were charges that white students have attacked black students, with the black student sent home and the white one allowed to remain on campus; that students were not allowed to give their side of the story when involved in a school disturbance, and that many white groups were attacking blacks at both high schools.

The students, who remained orderly throughout the day in the church, called on various news media to hear their complaints in an effort to make their side of the disturbances known.

Spokesmen for the gathering had a list of complaints drawn up to present to news media. Point by point the list read:

1. Black students have been suspended without cause.
2. Mr. Scott (NHHS Principal John J. Scott) allowed white non-students to come on the NHHS campus.
3. Black students want black studies included in the school curriculum.

4. Black students want January 15 (Dr. Martin Luther King's birthday) set aside as a day of mourning.
5. Black students have been harasssed by male faculty members.
6. Mr. Scott only gets one side of a story when two students are involved in a fight.
7. Mr. Scott did not investigate the Barbara Swain case, a black sophomore who was attacked by white students at the Wildcat.

One student explained that Barbara Swain was attacked last Friday at the Wildcat near 13th and Dock Street, a black from New Hanover, and that she received a cut in the affray.

Another student charged that whites had attacked him at New Hanover, and in fighting back, he received a suspension and refused the opportunity to explain his side of the fight to school principals.

"Black students are always sent home," the entire group agreed, "with the whites allowed to remain at school."

"We're told we have equal rights," Tindall told news media, "but when push comes to shove we don't have the same ones.

"If I'm in the wrong I expect to get sent home," he continued, "but if I'm defending myself I don't think I deserve it."

"Anywhere we go we're outnumbered," another student charged. "We're supposed to be integrated, but integrated means unity, and there's none between the races at either high school."

Some students charged that they were being harassed by male faculty members at New Hanover, and that on one occasion a black student was beaten around the head and shoulders by one.

Another charged that white students were attacking black ones "because we're in their school. They don't like it because it's their school and we had to join it. But our school was taken away from us."

Many other charges of unfairness were listed by the students, who emphasized over and over that they did not intend to go back to school until these things are righted.

"We can't win because of our color," Tindall said, "and we want an education. But I don't feel like I have to get run over to get one."

Principal John J. Scott said Thursday night that he had heard the list of complaints drawn up by the group, and was ready, willing and most anxious to answer the allegations point by point.

Mrs. Bertha Todd, assistant principal at Hoggard High School, met with the students during the day and took their complaints to Dr. Heyward C. Bellamy, school superintendent. Mrs. Todd said Dr. Bellamy was studying the list, and would call a meeting of the Adult Advisory Committee of the Board of Education either Friday or Monday to assess the situation.

During the school day Thursday, no further incidents were reported by either Scott, Gurganus, or Police Chief H. E. Williamson. "As far as we were concerned it was a normal working day," Williamson said Thursday night.

Student boycott article

assess the boycott situation. He approved my second visit and requested that I find a minister, an adult community citizen or an educator who had flexible hours to accompany me.

No one accepted my invitation. When I arrived at Gregory Congregational, Rev. Templeton informed me that the young Rev. Ben Chavis would be visiting the church that afternoon. In fact, I had never heard of him. But he would become a household name as a member of the "Wilmington 10".

Secondary Summer School
Serving as the first female principal of secondary summer school in New Hanover County was both challenging and rewarding. In the 1970s, it was a rarity for women (black or white) to serve in this capacity. When Superintendent Heyward Bellamy extended the offer, my initial thought was, "Just how will white males respond to working under the leadership of a black female?"

After accepting the position, I called the man who had served in summers past and he basically said, "Bertha, all you need to do is have the students meet in the gym and send them to a classroom according to their desired subject."

Reflecting on my own undergraduate registration at North Carolina College, I devised another process. Registration would be held in the Hoggard

cafeteria, and I would ask those teachers who were at the top of the summer school lottery list to volunteer two days of their

time to take care of registration. Teachers were contacted, and all agreed to work with this new method.

Summer school went well for both summers. In fact, attendance doubled during the second summer, requiring the need for an additional secretary.

When Dr. Bellamy asked if I would be willing to serve on a regular basis, I declined. Though I felt honored at breaking the gender barrier, I was ready to pursue other goals.

Seining in tidal marshes is fun as well as educational for students in oceanography classes

[handwritten] First year Bertha Todd served as Principal of Secondary Summer School

Can this be
summer school?

By MARJORIE SMITH
Staff Writer

Drive by Hoggard High School any day of the week, and you will find it hard to believe summer vacation is in full swing.

The place is alive with activity, and students are spilling from every doorway, sitting on the stone balustrades in the sunshine, with arms full of something that looks remarkably like school books.

After nine months of required schooling, and with the long lazy beach days stretching ahead, a goodly number of high school students have chosen summer school as part of their vacation picture.

There are more summer students than last year, according to Bertha Todd, director of the two summer sessions, with over 400 enrollment spanning both sessions for full-unit courses. This is almost double last year's figures.

Mrs. Todd, guidance counselor at Hoggard during the academic year, is the first woman ever chosen to direct this summer activity, and has enjoyed it as "a real change of pace and less hectic" than her regular role.

Mrs. Todd said there is no predominant reason why so many enroll in summer school, but at least three of equivalent value.

A good many students who have failed one or more semesters in a required course can make up this deficiency during the summer.

Others want to get certain requirements out of the way in summer school to enable them to enjoy some extracurricular activities or special electives available in the regular school year.

Still others simply want enrichment...more of their special interests than there is time for in nine month.

Then, of course, there are particular courses taken just for fun. Take oceanography, for example, and lots of kids are doing that, with field trips at the beach, perfect weather for marine life study, and a week-long trip down the Florida coast all part of the curriculum.

Tennis is a popular summer class, too, as well as driver's education, both for obvious reasons. Strangely enough, the most popular class of all, according to Mrs. Todd, is mass media, one of the new communications half-unit classes.

History and government, said Mrs. Todd, are the required courses students choose most often to tackle during the summer just for expediency.

Role of the Family is another favorite, and a down-to-earth look at family relationships it is, too. Every week, "Ann Landers Day" spices this class with an opportunity for students to submit anonymously their own family problems for class discussion.

There are 19 teachers in the summer faculty, each handling a class load of about 22 students. Every student can take a maximum of two full units during the summer, or four half-unit classes. The day's scheduling from 8 a.m. till 3:45 p.m. makes a full day's work for those who want the maximum load.

With a $45 fee for every full unit course, and with some of the above-mentioned reasons for tackling summer school, Mrs. Todd says there are virtually no drop-outs or attendance problems. Those who are enrolled have every inclination to give it serious attention.

"There is even a parolee enrolled for the second session," Mrs. Todd said, "which is a first time for this situation. I expect this student to be a good one, because the summer session will help him with admission to school in the fall."

The six-week school, in two separate terms, is scheduled from June 19 to August 9, with the second session beginning Wednesday. Scheduled courses are general math, algebra I and II, geometry, physical science, chemistry, biology, oceanography, basic composition, advanced composition, science fiction, mass media, sports literature, word power, history, government, and tennis.

Tennis a favorite in summer curriculum

Sunday Star-News

feature page

one-d

July 14, 1974

Music hath charms to cool the savage heat

Secondary Summer School

"An Unofficial Board Member"
Chapter 7

"Expectations, unofficial ones, tend to get much higher."
-Jeetil Patel

several times in the 1970's, one or two members of the New Hanover County Board of Education would introduce me as a board member. When I corrected them, one replied, "Well, Bertha, you meet with us so often that I simply forgot."

That wasn't far from the truth. Though I was in administration at Hoggard, I often met with board members in their executive meetings as we strategized to bring balance back to the school system. The school board formed an Adult Advisory Committee, of which I served as second vice chair, to explore the sensitive issues it grappled with during the 1970's. Some of the issues were so sensitive that I choose not to discuss some details. Generally, the board members readily accepted our recommendations.

1970-1971 school Org (Adults)

SEPT. 5, 1970   Wilmington, N. C.   FIVE

Citizens form advisory committee to New Hanover Board of Education

A Citizens Advisory committee to the New Hanover Board of Education was formed this week, composed of 25 local citizens from a cross-section of this community.

Organization of such a committee followed months of consultations and discussion on the effectiveness of such a group to assist the Board of Education in community communications and advisory service.

Composed of members of both races, the Advisory Committee's basic objectives are improved communications between the public and the Board of Education, which is composed of only six members.

At its organization meeting this week, attended by members of the Board of Education and Dr. Heyward Bellamy, superintendent of New Hanover County schools, officers were elected and the function of such a committee discussed.

Elected as permanent chairman of the group was F. Quintel Smith, manager of a production unit at General Electric.

Other officers elected were Mrs. Marianne Yarboro, vice chairman; Mrs. Bertha B. Todd, second vice chairman, and Mrs. Gerald Points II, recording secretary.

Meetings of the Advisory Committee will be held once a month at Hemenway Hall, the next meeting to be held Sept. 17.

In forming such a committee,

the School Board sought a cross-section of interested people representing both races and all occupations.

Among them are factory employees, PTA presidents, school teachers, machinists, engineers, mechanics, supervisors, a building inspector and a former member of the Board of Education.

Each will work with the school board, the Board of Education and with concerned parents and interested citizens to strive for improving education in this school system.

Members of the committee and their avocations are:

James M. Goodrum, machinist at Babcock and Wilcox; John A. Mitchell, also with Babcock and Wilcox; B. E. Kirkendall, General Electric; James M. Motsinger, engineer with Hercules; Mrs. Carol J. Sterling a clerk at Hercules; Jesse Rollinson, mechanic at Timme; Samuel Bryant of

Allied Chemical; Robert J. Floyd, 1970-71 vice president of PSTA- New Hanover High School; L. M. Newsome, an insurance representative and former member of the Board of Education.

Howard Carter, city building inspector; Mrs. Mamie Robinson, center supervisor for the Parks and Recreation Department; Mrs. Betty B. Chinnis, a supervisor at France Neckware; Edward Evans, supervisor at France Neckware; Mrs. Rosa Sloan of Garver; Richard E. Barker, official at Heide and Company;

Robert J. Hazlegrove, designs supervisor at DuPont; W. G. Moore of DuPont; Mrs. Bertha B. Todd, a teacher at New Hanover county schools.

Bill Huffine, real estate; Mrs. Martha Huffine, a parent, and

Ballet dancer defects

LONDON (UPI) — Russian ballerina Natalaia Makarova, in England on tour with the Leningrad Kirov Ballet, Friday requested political asylum in Britain. The British Home Office said it had granted her request.

active in PTA and James B. Wilson, executive editor of the Star-News Newspapers.

Mrs. Points, recording secretary, is the 1970-71

president of John T. Hoggard High School. Mrs. Marianne Yarboro, vice chairman, is a parent and active in PTA and other school affairs.

Formation of Advisory Committee

New Hanover County Schools
Wilmington, North Carolina

MRS. BERTHA B. TODD
114 MERCER AVENUE
WILMINGTON, N. C.

DEAR MRS. TODD:

YOU ARE INVITED AND REQUESTED TO SERVE AS A MEMBER OF THE ADULT ADVISORY COMMITTEE ON SCHOOL AND COMMUNITY RELATIONS. YOU WERE RECOMMENDED AND SELECTED AS A CITIZEN WHO IS INTERESTED IN SCHOOL AND CIVIC MATTERS AND IT IS HOPED YOU WILL ACCEPT THIS INVITATION AND ACTIVELY SERVE.

AS INDICATED BY ITS NAME, THIS COMMITTEE WILL ACT IN AN ADVISORY CAPACITY TO THE NEW HANOVER COUNTY BOARD OF EDUCATION AND WILL SERVE AS A LAISON LINK BETWEEN THE BOARD AND THE ADULT POPULATION OF OUR AREA. WE ALL KNOW THERE ARE MANY PROBLEMS TO BE SOLVED IN THE IMMEDIATE FUTURE AND HOPEFULLY THIS COMMITTEE WILL AID TREMENDOUSLY IN SOLVING THESE PROBLEMS BY KEEPING ABREAST OF THE ACTIONS OF THE BOARD, BY DISSEMINATING CORRECT INFORMATION, BY HELPING ELIMINATE HALF-TRUTHS AND FALSE RUMORS THAT SO OFTEN CAUSE A GREAT DEAL OF TROUBLE AMONG BOTH STUDENTS AND PARENTS, AND BY DOING EVERYTHING POSSIBLE TO PROMOTE THE ORDERLY OPERATIONS OF OUR SCHOOLS OVER THE ENTIRE COUNTY.

THIS COMMITTEE WILL BE COMPOSED OF APPROXIMATELY 25 FINE CITIZENS, INCLUDING YOURSELF, AND WE SHOULD LIKE TO HAVE YOU MEET IN THE IMMEDIATE FUTURE IN PREPARATION FOR THE OPENING OF SCHOOL ON SEPTEMBER 1, 1970.

WILL YOU PLEASE INDICATE YOUR ACCEPTANCE OF COMMITTEE MEMBERSHIP BY WRITING ME IN CARE OF NEW HANOVER COUNTY BOARD OF EDUCATION, P.O. BOX 390, HEMENWAY HALL, WILMINGTON, NORTH CAROLINA, OR CALLING THE OFFICE OF DR. HEYWARD C. BELLAMY, SUPERINTENDENT OF SCHOOLS, TELEPHONE NUMBER 763-5431.

SINCERELY,

E. A. LANEY, CHAIRMAN
NEW HANOVER COUNTY
BOARD OF EDUCATION

EAL:DWP

Invitation from E.A. Laney to sit on Advisory Committee

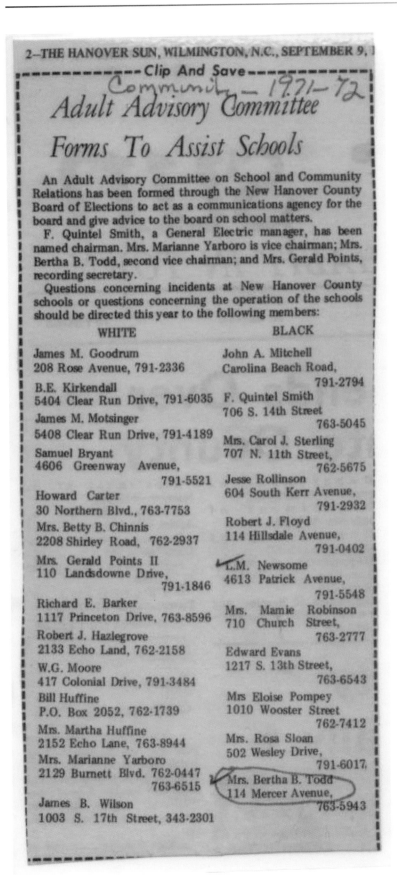

Community — 1971-72

----- Clip And Save -----

Adult Advisory Committee Forms To Assist Schools

An Adult Advisory Committee on School and Community Relations has been formed through the New Hanover County Board of Elections to act as a communications agency for the board and give advice to the board on school matters.

F. Quintel Smith, a General Electric manager, has been named chairman. Mrs. Marianne Yarboro is vice chairman; Mrs. Bertha B. Todd, second vice chairman; and Mrs. Gerald Points, recording secretary.

Questions concerning incidents at New Hanover County schools or questions concerning the operation of the schools should be directed this year to the following members:

WHITE	BLACK
James M. Goodrum 208 Rose Avenue, 791-2336	John A. Mitchell Carolina Beach Road, 791-2794
B.E. Kirkendall 5404 Clear Run Drive, 791-6035	F. Quintel Smith 706 S. 14th Street 763-5045
James M. Motsinger 5408 Clear Run Drive, 791-4189	Mrs. Carol J. Sterling 707 N. 11th Street, 762-5675
Samuel Bryant 4606 Greenway Avenue, 791-5521	Jesse Rollinson 604 South Kerr Avenue, 791-2932
Howard Carter 30 Northern Blvd., 763-7753	Robert J. Floyd 114 Hillsdale Avenue, 791-0402
Mrs. Betty B. Chinnis 2208 Shirley Road, 762-2937	L.M. Newsome 4613 Patrick Avenue, 791-5548
Mrs. Gerald Points II 110 Landsdowne Drive, 791-1846	Mrs. Mamie Robinson 710 Church Street, 763-2777
Richard E. Barker 1117 Princeton Drive, 763-8596	Edward Evans 1217 S. 13th Street, 763-6543
Robert J. Hazlegrove 2133 Echo Land, 762-2158	Mrs Eloise Pompey 1010 Wooster Street 762-7412
W.G. Moore 417 Colonial Drive, 791-3484	Mrs. Rosa Sloan 502 Wesley Drive, 791-6017
Bill Huffine P.O. Box 2052, 762-1739	Mrs. Bertha B. Todd 114 Mercer Avenue, 763-5943
Mrs. Martha Huffine 2152 Echo Lane, 763-8944	
Mrs. Marianne Yarboro 2129 Burnett Blvd. 762-0447 763-6515	
James B. Wilson 1003 S. 17th Street, 343-2301	

Members of Advisory Committee

Only two of us served in dual roles as administrators and community leaders: Anna G. Burnett and me. I was truly beginning to feel as if I was a "double agent", even enlisting two white male colleagues at Hoggard to attend Klan meetings at Hugh MacRae Park. They would bring back information so I would have a broader perspective when dealing with these sensitive situations. Later, one of the Klan members, "TG", was invited to become a member of the Human Relations Commission established by Mayor B.D. Schwartz. "TG" and I became pretty good friends and even voted together on several issues, including renaming the former Eighth Street Center to the Martin Luther King, Jr. Center.

I maintained communication with the central office administrative staff, offering suggestions and providing information culled from community meetings. Sometimes, I would attend as many as four meetings a day to provide board members with as many perspectives as possible.

I remember associate superintendent Dale K. Spencer calling my home one night to make a special request regarding a rather "sticky" community issue. Dr. Bellamy was out of town at the time. After apologizing for the lateness of his

Weather

Mostly sunny and cool
HIGH: upper 50's
LOW: low 30's
Wrightsville water
temp: 57

Wilmington Morning S[

My telephone an

VOL. 104. — NO. 130. PRICE 10 CENTS WILMINGTON, N. C., SATURDAY, MARCH 20, 1971 32 PAGES — TWO SECTIO[

'. . . we've got to turn back before we can go forward'

Frinks: Blacks need 'crash program' of e[

By JOHN SIKES
Editor of Editorial Page

The blacks have got to have "a crash program of education among our people so that we will be educationally qualified to move ahead on equal terms with anybody in anybody's school anywhere".

Thus, Golden Frinks of the Southern Christian Leadership Conference at once highlighted his reason for wanting Williston High School reinstated here as a predominantly Negro high school and sounded a new note in the black man's equality-educational demands.

Frinks was invited here to put the SCLC formally into the present debates (and confrontations) about the New Hanover County school system. He is also here to spearhead the scheduled March 30 "repression march", as he calls it, from Wilmington to Raleigh.

He sounded his views, freely and easily, in an informal and exclusive conversation Friday at SCLC's temporary headquarters in Longshoreman's (ILA) Hall on S. Sixth Street.

In Frinks' thinking, there would be enough white students enrolled in Williston High — if the school were to be reinstated — to meet the ratio requirements of the Health, Education and Welfare and Justice Departments regulating the racial make-up of schools.

When asked if it wasn't somewhat retrogressive for the blacks to want Williston High reopened as chiefly a Negro school (Williston once was New Hanover County's Negro high school) when blacks had fought for so long to attend integrated so-called white schools, he said:

"We've come to the view (in the SCLC) that we've got to turn back before we can go forward in education."

The suggestion that he might be going in for sloganeering on this point brought this reply:

"Not at all. We now know that we are

not prepared — we haven't had the opportunities — educationally at this point for equal education in the so-called white schools.

"We've got to catch up educationally with the whites before we can achieve equal schooling.

"We've got to have a crash program of education among our people so that we will be educationally qualified to move ahead on equal terms with anybody in anybody's school anywhere."

Frinks feels strongly that if his SCLC's influence could have been brought to bear early enough that horrible shambling at Williston Junior High last week would never have happened. Also, that much of the physical encounters, perhaps all of them, last month between whites and blacks would not have occurred if the SCLC had been operating here.

"We are against violence," he said.
"Don't get me wrong. We know our

people are repressed economically, educationally, socially and politically. But we want to change all this for the better through non-violent methods.

"We want to understand the whites and we want the whites to understand us. There's no way for us to understand each other as long as we call each other 'whitey' and 'honkie' and 'pig' and 'nigger' and 'coon'.

"There's no way for us to understand each other if we shoot at each other and throw bricks at school buildings and beat each other up.

"The only way we can understand each other and find that peaceful co-existence both blacks and whites — the good blacks and whites — so earnestly want is by reasoning with each other.

"We want to be treated as human beings, and we want to treat whites as human beings."

What about the march coming up?

"Our march to Raleigh is a symbol. It

symbolizes our non-violent at[
Those two coffins, representi[
deaths of two of our people here, a[
the symbol of futility of the killi[
ween the races. The overall symbo[
the march is to be our non-violent [
against repression."

In times of trouble, racial or oth[
there's strong talk here, and els[
that the communists are at the bo[
it all; thus, last month's strife her[
the Williston incident was char[
some as a part of a large com[
conspiracy. What about that?

"I can't spell communism," [
said.

That was his expression to me [
communism had nothing at all to [
the trouble.

There's been a lot of talk that [
Panthers had formented last [
trouble, although Chief of Police [
Williamson and Captain of Det[

(See 2 On Page 2)

All-black schools not a solution, says Dr. Eaton

DR. H. A. EATON
'No future in going back'

By LYNDAL WARREN
Staff Writer

Dr. Hubert A. Eaton, the black community leader whose 1964 court action led to desegregated schools in New Hanover County, said Friday the return of previously all-black schools to the black community is not the solution to racial disturbances.

"I think problems in the schools are not school problems, but community

problems," Eaton said. "It is too much to expect students to do what the community won't do."

Eaton explained, "Our schools have been desegregated, but there has been no distinct policy of integration — and there is definitely a difference between desegregation and integration."

"There has been insufficient effort on the part of the community to take steps to integrate at all levels."

Golden Frinks of the Southern Christian Leadership Conference said Thursday the present education system is repressive against blacks and that Williston Junior High School should be returned to the black community as a high school.

At the time, Frinks described the closing of Williston as an act of destruction against the black community, removing an institution blacks could identify with.

Eaton, vice chairman of the N. C. Advisory Committee on Public Education, said Friday, "I don't think Mr. Frinks has the background or the feel of the community to the extent he can come into a community and advocate changes in the school system, whether it's opening Williston or any other policy change.

"It has been my belief the black people should continue to make efforts to move into the mainstream of American life, and Williston School is not a prime issue in the controversy.

"I won't say there are no students, no

(See 3 On Page 2)

Living costs inch up

WASHINGTON (UPI) — The cost of living rose at a markedly slower pace in February for the second consecutive month despite a continuing spiral in prices for food and clothing, the Labor Department reported Friday.

The moderate 0.2 per cent increase following a 0.1 per cent climb in January indicated possible easing of the pains of inflation that have wracked the nation for the past several years.

Labor Secretary James D. Hodgson cited the latest statistics as evidence that the Nixon Administration is "clearly headed in the right direction" in its fight to stabilize prices.

The February increase put the Consumer Price Index at 119.4 per cent of the 1967 base period, meaning that it cost $11.94 last month to buy the same assortment of goods and services that could have been obtained for $10 just over three years ago.

With adjustment for seasonal factors, the February increase remained at 0.2 per cent. If that rate prevailed for a year, the annual increase would be about 2.5 per cent, a figure considered most acceptable by Nixon Administration economic strategists.

But wholesale prices soared 0.9 per cent last month, the sharpest increase in more than 17 years ·

City police seek killer of Wright

Wilmington Police Chief H. E.
Williamson said Friday night

50 highway pat[ordered to dut[

By JOHN HENDRIX
Staff Writer

A group of 50 state highway patrolmen, specially trained to handle civil disorders, were alerted for duty in Wilmington Friday.

Gov. Bob Scott's aide, David Murray, announced the troopers, headed by Capt. Bill Sherrill, were assigned to the area following a request from Wilmington Mayor Luther Cromartie.

Police Chief H. E. Williamson termed the situation very explosive and said the request for assistance from the state patrol was made in order to prepare for any trouble that might arise.

Earlier in the week three schools were closed and a funeral scheduled Saturday for a black youth shotgunned to death last Saturday night combined to increase the tense situation which has not completely relaxed since 10 days of turmoil early in February.

"Tension is running very high," Williamson said. "The situation is very explosive."

CHIEF WILLIAMSON
'Tension high'

During the disorders in February, more than $500,000 in property was destroyed by fire bombings, a black and a white

were killed, [
wounded an[
people suffer[
Williamson [
for the state p[
Scott despite [
tivities of the [
were no more [
occur on a ne[

"As you all [
said, "Mr. B[
North Carolin[
Racial Justic[
Frinks Mr. M[
Southern Chri[
Conference an[
the city.

"The office[
police, the cit[
mayor are [
making nec[
secure add[
equipment to [
situation that [

Already on [
additional tr[
dered into the [
men from the [
Tobacco and S[
and State [
vestigation ap[

S. Viet t[dwindle

Golden Frinks visit to Wilmington

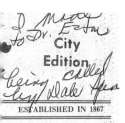

ESTABLISHED IN 1867

cation

SECO Photo
GOLDEN FRINKS
SCLC representative

men

ere

Also arriving Friday was Col. Arthur S. Bouchard from the state adjutant general's office.

During the February disorders, a battalion of National Guard were called out and served on active duty from Sunday Feb. 7 to Friday, Feb. 12.

"We just never got it straight from the last time," Williamson said.

Frinks who had led civil disorders in other parts of the state has been busy with meetings with members of the black community since his arrival on Thursday. Chavis, a key figure in the Feburary racial disorders, has announced his group will back up whatever plans Frinks and the SCLC have in mind.

Friday's police blotter showed officers arrested one person for disorderly conduct in the 2000 block of Chestnut Street; bomb threats were made at Chestnut Street School and Lake Forest School and a window was broken at Chestnut Street School by a thrown rock.

ps

Laos

call, he informed me that Golden Frinks intended to come to Wilmington because of a presumed lack of black leadership.

Frinks intended to disrupt the Azalea Festival parade to draw attention to the plight of African-Americans who felt shut out from the annual festivities. With the exception of the Williston High School, band, there was little representation from ethnic groups.

A native of Horry County, SC, Frinks grew up in Tabor City before moving to Edenton. After active duty service during World War II as a staff sergeant at Fort McCullough, Alabama, Frinks returned to North Carolina and began efforts to end segregation and discrimination. He would later become known as "The Great Agitator" and "Mr. Civil Rights."

Mr. Spencer wanted me to contact Dr. Hubert A. Eaton, Sr. and ask him to make some comments to the Wilmington Morning Star. I don't recall if Mr. Spencer had called Dr. Eaton and been rebuffed or

just thought that I should mediate. I reluctantly agreed to call Dr. Eaton, who I knew was growing tired of trying to seek justice while most African-Americans complained about his efforts. In other words, he was bitter and frustrated.

After praying, I made the call to Dr. Eaton and soon found that I had aptly predicted his reaction – a tirade of angry words as he complained about African-American hostility toward him. I knew this to be true because I had heard some of the comments circulating in the community. When Dr. Eaton ran for the New Hanover County Board of Education, many said, "Who does he think he is? He won't even speak to me!"

Within the black community, there seemed to be a great disconnect between the courageous stances Dr. Eaton took and the personality and class clashes with those he was trying to help.

We talked for about two hours, or rather Dr. Eaton talked and I listened, interjecting my thoughts now and then. Finally, I asked him to pray about the request and either contact Mr. Spencer or the news media. I was pleased to see the following comments in the Star News.

Just Who Was Dr. Hubert A. Eaton, Sr.?

A longtime Wilmington physician, Hubert A. Eaton (1916 – 1991) was the point man for most of the civil rights battles in New Hanover County for more than three decades.

With his daughter, Carolyn, Eaton was the lead plaintiff in a 1964 federal lawsuit that led to desegregation of New Hanover County Schools in 1971. Eaton also joined other black doctors in suing for equal staff privileges at the former James Walker Memorial Hospital, and he led efforts to desegregate Wilmington College (now the University of North Carolina at Wilmington), the Wilmington YMCA, the Municipal Golf Course and the New Hanover County Public Library.

A nationally ranked amateur in the old American Tennis Association, Eaton also served as guardian and mentor to Althea Gibson, while the future tennis star was attending Williston High School. Gibson would go on to win both the women's Wimbledon title and the US Open in 1957 and 1958.

Born December 3, 1916, in Fayetteville, NC, the son of a doctor, Hubert Arthur Eaton graduated from Johnson C. Smith University in 1937. At the time, African-Americans were not admitted to any of North Carolina's medical schools so, with some state assistance, Eaton studied medicine at the University of Michigan, earning his MD in 1942.

Eaton married Celeste Burnett, the daughter of Dr. Foster F. Burnett of Wilmington, and after completing his internship in Winston-Salem, he entered partnership with his father-in-law in 1943.

In his 1984 autobiography, *Every Man Should Try*, Eaton wrote that he became a civil rights activist when he was called to testify at a trial – and realized that the county courts maintained separate Bibles to swear in black and white witnesses.

In 1951, Eaton and Dr. Daniel C. Roane sued the county school system under the Supreme Court's "separate but equal" ruling in Plessy vs. Ferguson. Using side-by-side photographs and statistics, the doctors argued successfully that black-only schools in New Hanover County were dramatically inferior to those of whites. The suit forced the county into a massive building program to improve school facilities.

Eaton ran for a seat on the New Hanover County Board of Education in 1952, 1954, and 1956, the first African-American to seek public office in New Hanover County since the 1890s. He lost all three races, but paved the way for other black political leaders in the 1970s. Later Eaton would serve on the board of trustees of Cape Fear Technical Institute (now Cape Fear Community College) from 1963 – 1973, and on the board of trustees of the University of North Carolina at Wilmington from 1977 – 1985, becoming chairman of the board in 1981.

Eaton was chief of staff for Community Hospital, the county's black hospital under segregation from 1948 – 1949. He was president of the Old North State Medical Society, the organization of the state's black physicians from 1964 – 1965.

Eaton died in Wilmington on September 4, 1991. In 1996, Eaton Elementary School located at 6701 Gordon Road in Wilmington, NC was named in his memory.

Board Signs Off on Sock Hops

Golden Frinks had threatened to "let the chickens loose" during the Azalea Festival Parade. In an effort to provide post-parade activities for black students, I asked the Central Office and the Board of Education to allow one of the organizations to which I belong to sponsor sock hops in the gym of the former Williston Senior High School. After explaining my rationale, my request was granted. Sock hops were held for several years after the Azalea Festival Parade and were sponsored by local chapters of Jack & Jill of America or Alpha Kappa Alpha Sorority. For a nominal entry fee, students could enjoy clean fun and stay off the streets.

Fired?

I had an opportunity to meet with the New Hanover County Board of Education many times during the 1970's, sometimes as a member of the Adult Advisory Committee and sometimes alone.

I remember one executive committee meeting when board members were discussing the percentage of black students who were members of school groups and clubs at New Hanover and Hoggard high schools. At the time, the percentage of black students in groups and clubs at New Hanover was extremely low. One board member then turned to me and asked, "Bertha, you have blacks in most of the clubs and groups at Hoggard, don't you?" Realizing how difficult it had been to get black students to participate, I lost my composure. I informed the board members that they simply had no idea how difficult being a member of these groups was. The black students (one or two) were usually ignored, not given an opportunity to become involved and, for the most part, were simply names on membership rolls. I said much more than that, but that's all I care to mention.

Returning home in my car that night, I thought to myself, "Well, I really blew it this time." I just knew that I would be asked to resign immediately or maybe they would allow me to stay through the end of the school year. Fortunately, I was not fired for my outburst at that executive session.

This "double agent" role was beginning to wear me down. Between all the meetings and strategy sessions and raising my children, my plate was full. Had it not been for the support of my husband, older sister, and mother, I could not have been as involved as I was.

One time, Dr. Bellamy called a special meeting, but gave no reason. When I arrived, Dr. Bellamy, the county's guidance supervisor and another person were already there. I kept waiting to find out the reason for the meeting. After some time, the school system's guidance supervisor, Ethel Booth, asked me how I felt about the dual role I had assumed during this period of school desegregation. After making a few comments, my tears began to flow. I sobbed uncontrollably. Then all was quiet.

The meeting ended and, to this day, I believe that the purpose of the meeting was for me to ventilate. I was becoming weary while hoping and praying for improvement in the schools and the community. At the end of the 1970's my role as an unofficial board member ended.

"A Superintendent for All Seasons"
Chapter 8

*"You can easily judge the character of a man by
how he treats those who can do nothing for him."
-James D. Miles*

*Dr. Heyward C. Bellamy
Former Superintendent of New Hanover County Schools*

Born in Horry County, SC, Heyward Bellamy and his family moved to Wilmington in 1935. After graduating from New Hanover High School, he continued his education at the University of North Carolina at Chapel Hill. He also served in the Air Force for several years before joining New Hanover County Schools, where he quickly moved up the ranks from teacher to assistant principal to principal.

I first met Dr. Heyward C. Bellamy when he was serving as the New Hanover County Schools system's Supervisor of Secondary Education beginning in 1960.

During a 1965 visit to Williston Senior High School, Dr. Bellamy met with me to discuss plans to expand the school library to an extra room across the hall. He began suggesting which library books should be placed in the new location. Having done my research, I disagreed with his suggestions and asked the first-year superintendent if he had ever worked in a school library. He enthusiastically replied that he had been a page or library assistant in high school and college.

"I am certain that you had a good experience assisting in the library during those years. However, since I am the librarian here at Williston and have been since 1952 and have a master's degree in the same area, I would be most appreciative if you would permit me to make this decision about which books are to be placed in the extra room", I responded. Dr. Bellamy looked at me and said, "The decision is yours."

Of course, I didn't know at the time that the Board of Education would select him to become superintendent in July of 1968. I also didn't realize that circumstances would forge a professional relationship as we worked closely toward a very challenging goal – school desegregation.

Final Commencement at Williston

The mounting tensions within the student body at Williston from April through June of the spring of 1968 was evidenced by William G. Lowe, a respected government teacher, who had difficulty getting the top students to tone down the rhetoric in their graduation speeches. Some teachers were becoming anxious about commencement night due to the disturbances that marred the normally tranquil school environment following Dr. King's assassination.

My husband and I attended the crowded commencement ceremony. When the time came for seniors to give their speeches, you could hear an audible sigh of relief from faculty and staff as each speaker left the podium. As soon as the final student speaker, an intelligent, articulate, and physically imposing young man, began his speech, I knew we were in trouble. "CS", I will call him, finished his provocative speech by giving the black power symbol. When he finished, the audience became strangely quiet, and Dr. Bellamy looked at him as if to say, "What next?"

The principal continued with the commencement exercises as if nothing had happened. When it was time for the students to receive their diplomas, some of the students refused to shake Dr. Bellamy's hand. What a night! None of us knew then that that would be the last commencement at the all-black high school.

Before school closed that year, Dr. Bellamy called me and asked if I knew the name of the student who had spoken at commencement. I did not, but I soon learned that William G. Lowe was this student's senior class advisor. When I asked the unsuspecting Lowe if he had read the student's speech prior to the ceremonies, he replied that he had sent for the student many times, to no avail.

Williston Senior High School was dissolved in late summer of 1968. However, I would have many more conversations and meetings with Dr. Bellamy during the turbulent 1970s through his retirement in 1981.

When I moved to John T. Hoggard High School, I am certain that Principal C.D. Gurganus informed Dr. Bellamy of our efforts to break up the school riots during the transition from segregation to desegregation.

In his annual Christmas greeting, Dr. Bellamy expressed his appreciation to all employees. This Christmas greeting capped a tumultuous year for the New Hanover County Schools system, and it helped make school employees more aware of his appreciation for the efforts of many in the system to promote peace on earth, goodwill toward men.

I maintained open lines of communication with the superintendent, informing him about individuals who might help stem the violence. Leo Shepard, a young,

black male, was one of the people whom I recommended.

Sensitivity Sessions

After the interracial dialogue sessions at the YWCA, several of us met with Dr. Bellamy to recommend that the employees in the New Hanover County School system participate in similar dialogues. I am not sure if Dr. Bellamy was swayed by the apparent camaraderie between Betty Cameron, Alice von Oesen, and me or if he was already planning sensitivity sessions. The following school year, all county employees were required to attend a week-long session conducted by professional facilitators.

Dr. Bellamy was praised by some and vilified by others for advocating for these dialogue sessions. In fact, he and his family received many threats and his daughter, Mary, required a "shadow" during some of her years at Hoggard. But I believe those sessions helped our diverse student body to be better understood by their teachers during this crucial period.

Dr. Bellamy and I regularly debated school and community issues, either face to face in his office or by telephone. After one such heated discussion, I realized that our discussion was going in circles. In exasperation, I threw up my hands and said quite loudly, "Yessah, Boss!" Well, that broke the ice. We both laughed at this mock deference to his role as superintendent. Though we didn't agree on all issues, we both wanted to maintain a peaceful, orderly school system in an accepting community.

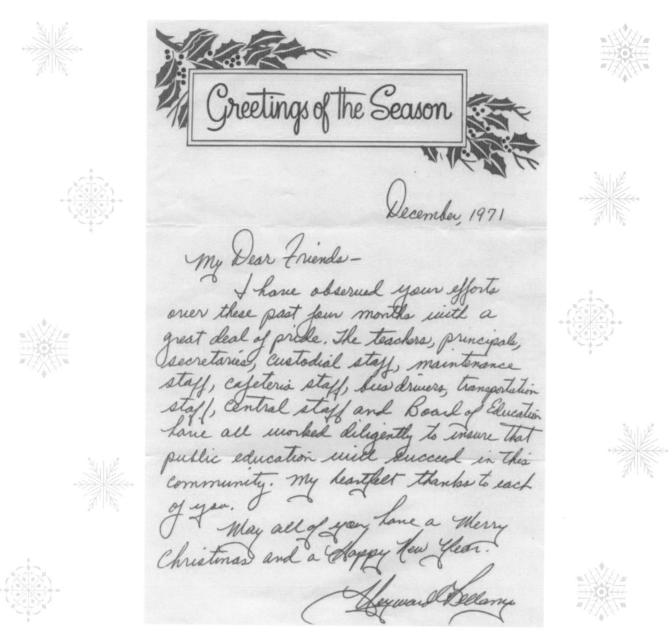

Holliday Greeting from Dr. Bellamy

In the early 1970's, a committee developed a survey to gauge student sentiment during the period of transition. I was responsible for coordinating the administration of the survey at Hoggard. When Dr. Bellamy learned this, he asked to see the packet of responses that I brought home one Saturday. Early Sunday morning, as my family and I were preparing for church, his wife, Mary Bellamy, came by our home to pick up the package containing the surveys, which indicated to me that getting through this uneasy period had become a family affair.

New Hanover County was one of the last counties in the state to desegregate, and Dr. Heyward Bellamy served the school system well during that turbulent time. He retired in 1981.

"The Final Seven"
Chapter 9

*"In the last analysis, what we are communicates far more eloquently
than anything we say or do."*
-Stephen Covey

I often think of the thousands of students I interacted with between 1952 and 1984. My tenures at Williston Industrial, Williston Senior High and Hoggard high schools totaled 32 years, or nearly two generations. I had served as a librarian/media specialist, administrative assistant/human relations specialist, and principal of secondary summer school, et al.

But the 17 years at John T. Hoggard High School had taken their toll. I had worked day and night, summer and winter, with and without pay to broker fragile relations in our school and in our community. It was time for a change.

Since joining the New Hanover County school system in 1952, I had acquired two additional degrees -- neither of which I felt was being put to good use. "Restless" and not quite ready for retirement, I applied for several central office positions that would allow me to make greater use of the second master's degree and Ed.S. from East Carolina University. Despite several rejections, I relied on my belief in divine guidance, knowing that my working life was not yet over.

When the position of Career Development Coordinator was advertised, I applied immediately and was selected for the position. For the next five years, I had the pleasure of working with some of the brightest and most effective teachers in New Hanover County. The Career Development Program began with 14 educators, male and female, black and white. In the first year (1984-1985), approximately 200 teachers applied for the 14 available slots.

The Career Ladder Program, one of 16 pilot programs implemented throughout the state, began in 1984 and continued for a decade. The merit pay based program provided incentives to teachers who progressed "up the rings" by reaching increasingly complex levels of professional performance. Coordinating this special program with top educators in New Hanover County was one of the highlights in my 39-year career.

My last two years at the New Hanover County Central Office were spent as Director of Staff Development, which included overseeing the new teacher certification, the wellness programs and coordinating workshops. The school assignment responsibility will forever hold a special place in my career memories.

While serving as the Wellness Coordinator, I coined a phrase that I thought was quite catchy – "Our first wealth is good

Sunday Star-News / Sunday, November 24, 1985

Local/Region/State

1C

Boone won't vote on liquor, 2C

County watches teachers as test begins

By Cathy Gant
Staff Writer

The classroom performance of some New Hanover County teachers has been observed all week by other teachers as testing of a career development program begins action.

New Hanover County is one of 16 school systems chosen by the state to test the legislature-mandated pay plan, which aims to pay teachers according to their advancement up a five-step career ladder. The pilot period is four years, and teachers are not required to participate.

As part of the pilot procedure, 14 teachers and other school employees were hired as evaluators to observe how well other teachers do their jobs. The evaluators were specially trained in a variety of techniques during a four-day workshop in Jacksonville. They have also attended additional workshops, classes and seminars in Wilmington.

The evaluators will observe each teacher twice a year, and principals will also make two annual observations, Career Development Coordinator Bertha Todd said.

The evaluators are Vickie Brown, Yvonne C. Marshburn, LaDonna Hauser, Michael Zentmeyer and Mary Q. Moore, from elementary schools; Veronica McLaurin and Ruthy Davis from junior high schools; Elizabeth B. Davis, Cynthia P. Henry, Nancy S. Horton, Shirley Prince and Jacqueline F. O'Grady from senior high schools; Susan Mintzes from the exceptional children's department and Lurlene Alston from the guidance program.

Because of the reputations of the 14 educators who were hired as evaluators, there is some concern among the community that the pilot program has taken the best teachers out of the classroom. Mrs. Todd said that isn't so.

"Let me say right now that all the best teachers have not been taken from the classroom," Mrs. Todd said. "New Hanover County has many effective teachers. This program is just one that has 14 of those effective teachers."

Those teachers will return to the classroom in one or two years anyway, which is a condition of their job. The pilot program is designed to limit the term of the positions to one or two years, Mrs. Todd said. The evaluators are paid at the supervisory level and, when returning to the classroom, will return to teaching salaries. Mrs. Todd said those teachers were aware of the jobs' limitations when they were hired.

Mrs. Todd is developing a slide presentation to give non-teachers more information about the career development program.

In another phase of the plan, New Hanover County's 30 school principals participated in a performance appraisal training program last week at the school administration building. The appraisal techniques will be used in accordance with the career development plan.

Similar training will also be available to assistant principals, supervisers and directors during December, Assistant Superintendent for Personnel El Clark said.

Ms. Clark, who is responsible for implementing the local career development plan, also meets regularly with school officials from the other 15 school systems. Although training for the evaluators started later than local school officials wanted, Ms. Clark said the rate of progress on the local career plan "is right where we want to be."

Career Development Program

health." Even now, though many years have passed, this phrase has even greater meaning.

As staff development director, I was responsible for coordinating numerous workshops, both within individual schools and at central office. One program of which I am especially proud was the Teacher Expectations Student Achievement Program (TESA). In the behavior change program, educators learn 15 interactions to improve three main areas of teaching behaviors: questioning, feedback, and student self-esteem. Results included improved student academic performance, increased attendance, a decrease in disciplinary problems, and an improved classroom climate.

"Our First Wealth is Good Health"
EMPLOYEE WELLNESS PROGRAM
New Hanover County Schools

After gaining the support of then Superintendent Tom McNeel, the program was mandated for *all* educators – principals and teachers alike – for more than five years. When I retired in June of 1992, the program was still being used by some educators.

TESA Program Results

*Improves interactions between educators and students by raising awareness of how teacher's expectations affect student's performance.

*Builds collegial team partnerships by providing peer support for participants.

TESA is designed to modify the way teachers interact with students through heightened awareness of how perceptions affect their expectations. Results of classroom research show that the users of TESA interactions improve student academic performance, gender and diversity awareness, attendance, classroom climate, and reduce student discipline problems.

Journal of Personality and Social Psychology, 1992, Vol. 63, No. 6, 947-961. Copyright 1992 by the American Psychological Association, Inc. 0022-3314/92/53.00

SCHOOL ASSIGNMENTS

Of the many programs for which I was responsible, the most challenging was the school assignment program. Some students wanted a special subject or program not offered at their assigned school; some desired to be closer to where they lived. Still others wanted a "fresh start" because they were experiencing problems at their school they were attending.

This duty required me to meet with parents and guardians to discuss their requests, consult with the principal, and make recommendations in each case. The Board of Education would ultimately render the final decision. Though I was supposed to give my recommendations to the superintendent and the assistant superintendent of personnel, they decided that I should make the presentations directly to the school board since I was more intimately involved in the process and made the initial decisions regarding the school assignment requests.

I performed this time-consuming task to the best of my ability, all the while having to stay on top of all my other duties. For some reason, this particular responsibility reminded me of the old song "My Last Affair" -- so much so that at the retirement social of the Principals'/Assistant Principals' Association, I wrote lyrics penned to the tune of "My Last Affair".

"My Last Affair"
Dedicated to the Principals and Assistant Principals of New Hanover County

Can't you see what school assignments have done to me?
I'm not the same as I used to be
This is my last affair!

Tales of woe – parents and children all told me more
They told much more than I cared to know
This is my last affair!

Forms to complete; appeals to the Board
They sought to bend my ear
Stole my time away; changed my schedules, too

All came to me in dismay!
So I've taken a vow; no more school assignments will I process now!
I'll cross my heart and I'll take a bow.
THIS IS MY LAST AFFAIR!!!

**Words by
Bertha Boykin Todd, Director
Staff Development
New Hanover County School System
June 11, 1992
Tune: "My Last Affair"**

My last seven years were spent in the Department of Personnel under the supervision of El N. Clark, former assistant superintendent of personnel. Dr. Clark is an intelligent, meticulous professional who called the shots as she saw fit. Though we disagreed on several issues I respected her professionalism. I will always be grateful for the loyal support of my secretary, Dorothy Doak-Hill, who assisted me in fulfilling my responsibilities.

While my duties were challenging, my final seven years were also rewarding. My "restless" spirit obliged me to continue working in the community, where I gained further insight into the relationship between the school system and the community.

These seven years concluded my 39 years of official service to the New Hanover County Schools system. Since 1952 I had worked in six different capacities under six superintendents: Herrick M. Roland, E.C. Funderburk, William H. Wagoner, Heyward C. Bellamy, Richard F. Flynn, and W. Thomas McNeel.

I retired in June of 1992. However, I was still restless. Little did I know that I would become intensely involved in yet another controversial community project several years later.

Mack and I attending NHCS Central Office Retirement Dinner. Taken by John Bryan, Head of NHCS Audio/Visual Department

"Bertha – An Activist?"
Chapter 10

"The pursuit of goals gives meaning to life."
-Bertha Boykin Todd

I have never considered myself an activist, though several reporters over the years have conferred the moniker, which to me connotes a militancy that I have never possessed. Rather, I have become a leader by default, stepping up to the plate as circumstances demanded.

Over the course of about 50 years, I have been intensely involved in two controversial projects: school desegregation and the 1898 commemoration. In both efforts, I sought to bridge gaps through mediation and effective communication, whether one-on-one or in group settings.

During the 1970's and 1980's, I coined the phrase "individual of distinction" to denote my being the only African-American on various boards and committees. For ten consecutive years, I either chaired or served as president of one organization or another: chairing the Human Relations Commission for one year; the Wilmington Chapter of The Links, Inc. for three years in the 1970's and two years in the 1990's; the Wilmington Chapter of Jack & Jill of America, Inc. for three years; and the Alpha Psi Omega Chapter of Alpha Kappa Alpha Sorority, Inc.

It was a daunting decade and I actually had to set up an office in my home, complete with a copy machine, a new typewriter, and a legal size file cabinet, to better manage my commitments. Of course, I continued to spend long hours on my "day job" while simultaneously trying to help raise my children. Needless to say, I wouldn't have been able to fulfill any of those obligations were it not for the support of my husband, Mack, who was attentive to our family's needs.

Family Services/Travelers' Aid
I served two terms on the board of directors of Family Services/Travelers' Aid, which provided counseling and travel aid for families in crisis. In addition to serving as a regional member-at-large, I edited the regional newsletter.

I attended several of the organization's national meetings in Atlanta, Boston and California and conducted workshops.

Department of Social Services
I was one of the first African-Americans to serve on the board of directors of the New Hanover County Department of Social Services, where I served two terms. Another board member, Karen Gottovi, former New Hanover County Commissioner and state chair of the Department of Aging, and I advocated for more African-Americans to serve in administrative roles.

Cape Fear Museum Board of Trustees

I was tapped to fill the unexpired term of a board member who resigned and went on to serve two full terms of my own. During my tenure, I approached the Williston Alumni Association about the possibility of equipping a meeting room at the museum, which is now the Williston Auditorium.

YWCA

One of my most rewarding involvements has been with the YWCA, which constructed the first agency in New Hanover County to accept people of all ethnicities. In the 1970s, one of the YWCA's national mandates was "to eliminate racism".

In the early years of volunteering with the YWCA, I worked closely with Bessie Faye Hunt, Louise MacRae, and Bobbie Jo Lineberger at the Phyllis Wheatley Branch (black) of the "Y" which was then located at 110 S. 7th Street. The main branch (white) was located at 708 Market Street.

During this time, I was asked to travel to Winston-Salem to seek a sizable grant from the Z. Smith Reynolds Foundation for the purpose of building an integrated YWCA on South College Road. Accompanied by Bessie Faye Hunt (YWCA staff member and later executive director), Pickett Taylor (late board member and sister of Betty Cameron), and Carter Mebane, we spent the night and prepared for our meeting the next morning.

Following a lengthy discussion, the Reynolds representative informed us that the grant proposal would be denied if submitted in its current form. He informed us that given the violence surrounding school desegregation in New Hanover County, we stood a better chance if our narrative was revised. Bessie Faye and Pickett Taylor immediately decided that I should rewrite the narrative for this important grant.

On the trip back to Wilmington, we began discussing the revision. The only paper we could locate in the car was an empty grocery bag, which I used to begin reformulating the narrative.

This writing was submitted as a part of a YWCA packet to the Z. Smith Reynolds Foundation for grant consideration.

Miss Bessie Faye Hunt, Carter Mebane, Mrs. Pickett Taylor, and I traveled to Winston Salem in order to meet with a representative from the foundation. After studying the materials orginally submitted the representative asked the group to resubmit information slanted toward a reflection of the current times (1971).

I was chosen to do the special writing.

As a result of information resubmitted by the YWCA a considerable amount of money was given to the local building fund for the YWCA.

This visit to Winston Salem was made before work on the building was actually begun.

YWCA grant documentation

YOUNG WOMEN'S CHRISTIAN ASSOCIATION
WILMINGTON, NORTH CAROLINA 28401

708 MARKET STREET   119 SOUTH SEVENTH STREET

December 10, 1971

Z. Smith Reynolds Foundation
Wachovia Building
Winston-Salem, N. C. 27102

Ladies and Gentlemen:

The Wilmington YWCA in January, 1970, had a local capital funds
campaign to build a much-needed interracial facility in the county's
geographic and population center.

The drive fell far short of our expectations partly because of the
general economic conditions and the drop in the stock market at the time
we were moving into the solicitation period of the campaign. We raised
$150,000, and of this amount $58,758 was pledged by the "Y" Family —
those closely associated with and involved in its work.

We have been beset with many problems in our efforts — many are a
result of our plans to build a facility for use by ALL women and girls.
We are the first volunteer agency to seek capital funds in the community
on a totally integrated basis. At this time, when strife is great and
the rifts between blacks and whites are widening, our building program
has been caught in the middle. Many individuals and groups capable of
making substantial gifts have refused our requests. This is a part of
the white backlash and a renewal of black distrust our community has
experienced in the last year or two.

Presently we are operating programs in two very inadequate and
dilapidated frame houses. Both are located in a section of town where
our members (both black and white) are afraid to come at night. Night
programs have dropped from four nights weekly to one. As you can see
from the enclosed statistics, both buildings are really just holding
their own at a time when, with the rapid community growth, participation
should be growing. Dedicated volunteers and professional staff are
determined to keep the YWCA alive and functioning until the move can be
made to a better location.

YWCA grant documentation

Z. Smith Reynolds Foundation
Page 2
December 10, 1971

We have worked hard with the architect in reducing our plans to provide a basic building in which to carry on a worthwhile program in the immediate future. The revised plan will require a minimum of $250,000 plus the outdoor pool and cabana for showers and dressing rooms. The map included indicates the location of schools in the county as well as the present and proposed location of the YWCA and the location of the other social and recreational agencies such as the YMCA, Girls' Club, Boys' Club, etc. As you can see, we are moving to the area where the greatest growth will be experienced in the next twenty years.

We are very hopeful that your foundation will be interested in helping us complete this building program. Your favorable consideration of this request will mean much in the lives of the women and girls of this community.

Sincerely,

W. Carter Mebane, III
General Chairman, Building Fund

Mrs. L. A. Taylor
Chairman, Building Committee

M/T/bjl

YWCA grant documentation

EXCERPTS FROM A LETTER FROM <u>MRS. BERTHA B. TODD</u>, Administrative Assistant in
Human Relations of John T. Hoggard High School; concerning YWCA Dialogue Group

"These comments, I hope, will serve to indicate to you the major role that
YWCA members have played in a city beset by racial turmoil and disturbances.

"....Approximately four years ago, Wilmington's only black senior high school
was closed abruptly as a senior high....Meanwhile the community's citizens (parents,
students, teachers, Board of Education) failed to do any pre-planning to facilitate
smoothly operated schools on an integrated basis....As a result, tensions and
communication gaps were becoming quite evident between the two races.

"A group of six (black and white) YWCA women decided to take a stand in
attempting to bridge this communication gap. This group sent letters to all
PTA presidents, urging them to make a special effort to prepare their school,
parents and children for the integrating process. This small YWCA nucleus invited
other community citizens to meet with them for dialogue before the opening of
school. They held several conferences with the superintendent of Schools, urging
him to go on television in order to ease the tensions that were continuing to
build prior to schools' opening. I feel that the schools were opened with less
tension than there would have been had not the YWCA chosen to take a strong stand.

"....One recommendation (from the Education Committee of the Human Relations
Commission chaired by the writer) - human relations workshops for all teachers
in New Hanover County — has proved to be quite effective thus far. Last year
(1970-71) two workshops were held. Before the end of the school year this year
every faculty member will have attended a one-week workshop in human relations.
I feel very strongly that the YWCA is indirectly responsible (available ESAP
funds are directly responsible) for this intensive effort in communications
being made. Our total community is being affected by this project.

"Finally, the YWCA is the first voluntary organization in Wilmington that
is courageously attempting to launch a project on a totally integrated basis...

"....I feel that Wilmington will see that a strong positive stand is being
taken by a dedicated and courageous group in spite of a four-year history of
racial turmoil, in a city where its citizens are just beginning to become fully
aware of the true worth of all its inhabitants."

-16-

YWCA grant documentation

Following is a portion of the information submitted for the grant.

Bobbie Jo Lineberger, who would later become executive director of the YWCA, compiled the special grant, adding the narrative I had rewritten. Our efforts were successful and we secured the grant.

New Hanover County Human Relations Commission

I spent a decade on the New Hanover County Human Relations Commission, serving as its chairman for one year. Other years I worked on numerous subcommittees, co-chairing Human Relations Month activities, mediating employee/employer relations, and presenting workshops for the New Hanover Sheriff's Office, the Wilmington Police Department, and schools and organizations in New Hanover and surrounding counties.

I attended a number of workshops or sensitivity sessions sponsored by the City of Wilmington in an effort to provide New Hanover County with some emotional and racial stability during those trying times.

During one such session in the late 1970s, Seymour Alper and the late William "Bill" Kingoff looked to be smiling as I was making some heated comments to the group. This was a little disconcerting given the serious nature of my remarks. In a later conversation, Bill Kingoff brought up my comments and said, "Bertha, I know that you saw Seymour and me looking at each other in somewhat of an amused manner. It might help you to know that many years ago we made those same comments to some citizens too." I thanked Bill for the feedback, comforted

that the two prominent Jewish merchants shared my sentiments.

Alpha Kappa Alpha Sorority, Incorporated

Founded on the campus of Howard University in Washington, DC in 1908, Alpha Kappa Alpha Sorority is the oldest Greek-letter organization established by African American, college-trained women.

For a period of three years, I served as president of Alpha Psi Omega Chapter of Alpha Kappa Alpha Sorority, Inc. I also chaired the debutante committee for many years, was the first chair of the local chapter's Ebony Fashion Fair in 1969. This program continued to be sponsored by

EBONY FASHION FAIR
INTERMISSION PROGRAM

October 22, 1969

SPONSORED BY

Alpha Psi Omega Chapter
Alpha Kappa Alpha Sorority
Wilmington, North Carolina

.... Soror Thelma W. Williams

soring Chapter

Fashion Fair .... Soror Bertha Todd

.... Mrs. Inez Childs Scoggins

Court ..... Soror Mary Moore, Basile s

Copy of program when I chaired the 1st Ebony Fashion Fair sponsored by Alpha Psi Omega Chapter of Alpha Kappa Alpha Sorority, Incorporated. This sorority facilitated the presentation of the Ebony Fashion Fair for a period of 40 years. Betty Cameron and Anne Rowe were invited by me to attend this event held at Brogden Hall.

the local sorority chapter until 2008 – a period of 39 years. Serving at the national level of the Alpha Kappa Alpha Sorority, Incorporated as one of its NAACP Representatives was an honor.

Wilmington Chapter of The Links, Incorporated

I became a member of the Wilmington Chapter of the Links, Inc. in 1955. The international organization was established in 1946 and is comprised of 12,000 professional women of color in 270 chapters in 42 states, the District of Columbia and the Commonwealth of the Bahamas. The local chapter was chartered by Celeste Burnett

Eaton, wife of Dr. Hubert A. Eaton, Sr. When I was elected chapter president, we hosted the Southern Area Conference, which included chapters in seven states. The conference was held in March of 1967 at the Blockade Runner Hotel and Resort in Wrightsville Beach. The Link program "Links Salute Young Americans" was initiated by me and the program continued for approximately seven years.

Serving as coordinator of the documentary project in 1989-90 was truly a challenge. This documentary entitled "The Talented Tenth: Heritage Rediscovered"

Serving as mistress of ceremonies and president at the The Links' Incorporated Southern Area Conference held at the Blockade Runner Hotel in March of 1967. Dr. Heyward Bellamy (far right end) and Mayor OO Allsbrook (my immediate left) were seated on the dais. Link Alma Lennon is seated to my immediate right.

Talented Tenth Video Program

paid homage to five southeastern North Carolina families that left an indelible mark in the southeastern region. This film has also been shown on The History Channel. Highlighted were the Jervay, Sadgwar, Scott, Spaulding, and Taylor families. As a result of this video, the Wilmington City Council voted to

establish an African-American Heritage Commission. Dick Snyder, former city councilman, presented the idea.

The local chapter holds the distinction of presenting the first intercultural programs in southeastern North Carolina from 1970-1976. Several were held at the Hannah Block Community Arts Center and others in conjunction with the University of North Carolina at Wilmington.

Wilmington, NC Chapter of Jack & Jill of America, Incorporated

Jack and Jill of America was founded in 1938 in Philadelphia, Pennsylvania by a group of 20 mothers who wanted to bring children together in a social and cultural environment. Today, Jack and Jill of America is a national organization with over 225 chapters in seven regions encompassing thirty-five states and the District of Columbia. Membership has grown to over 9,500 mothers and associates, and more than 30,000 family members.

Having served as president of the local chapter, I later assumed the role of co-advisor the teenage group. During this period, the first parent appreciation banquet was organized. I also traveled once a month to the Hillcrest public housing complex with my daughter, Rita, to teach African-American history to youth. This project lasted for a period of one year.

Bellamy Mansion

While serving on the board of directors of the Bellamy Mansion, I gained a greater appreciation for the superior workmanship of free and enslaved blacks who built the mansion. The Bellamy Mansion has meticulously preserved one of the remaining examples of urban slave quarters.

A Few "Rosa Parks" Moments
Azalea Festival Float

One of Wilmington's biggest events is the Azalea Festival Parade which draws thousands of people annually. In the early 1970's, a well-established department store, which shall go nameless, entered a beautiful float. As I watched the parade, I realized that only white children rode on the store's float. When I thought about all of the money I owed to this particular department store, I became incensed! Not only did I owe lots of money to the store, my friends also had large balances on their accounts.

At the time I was president of the local chapter of Alpha Kappa Alpha sorority and hastily sent a notice to the store's management expressing displeasure that they didn't include children of all ethnicities on the float. I also contacted my friends who were serving as presidents of their organizations and they followed suit. That was the last year the Belk department store ever sponsored a float in the Azalea Festival Parade.

Waiting Rooms

Another pet peeve was the segregated waiting rooms of a certain set of doctors. When their new building was erected near New Hanover Regional Medical Center during the early 1970's, the waiting rooms were desegregated. However, courtesy titles were still reserved for white patients only. I continued to address this condescending practice until every person was afforded the same courtesy.

One day, at the end of a long work day in 1971, I visited the office of an eye, ear, nose and throat specialist. I knew that the waiting rooms of this doctor were still segregated, but I decided to sit in the area designated for whites only. I picked up a magazine and began reading it – just waiting to see how the receptionist was going to handle this one. She surprised me when she approached me immediately and asked me to see the doctor first. Though I was early for my appointment, I've always believed that was the receptionist's way of handling my act of defiance.

Floral Deliveries

During the early 1960's, some well known florists also made racial distinctions between black and white clientele. If a patient at Community Hospital (which served the black community) received flowers, no courtesy titles were used. When a patient from the all-white James Walker Hospital received flowers, courtesy titles were used. Since the florist did not know if the recipient was black or white, all flowers delivered to Community Hospital had names without titles. The entire group of flowers delivered to James Walker Hospital included courtesy titles.

Having been a patient in both hospitals, I saw this firsthand after receiving flowers from the same florists. Twice I wrote the owner of one of the floral shops about this practice, which a black deliveryman confirmed was the case.

"The Wilmington 10"

When New Hanover County Schools desegregated in September, 1968, black students in the two high schools (New Hanover and Hoggard) either boycotted schools or attempted sit-ins to bring attention to their grievances.

In January of 1971, approximately 100 black students from both high schools gathered at Gregory Congregational Church at 609 Nun Street to bring attention to the concerns they felt had not been addressed. Fearing that the Rights of White People and the Ku Klux Klan would make good on repeated threats on his life, the Rev. Eugene Templeton, white pastor of the black congregation, asked for assistance from the Commission for Racial Justice of the United Church of Christ. The young Benjamin Chavis was sent to Wilmington on Feb. 1, 1971 to assist students with organizing a boycott.

No stranger to struggle, the Oxford, NC native had integrated the all-white libraries in his hometown by the age of 13. After graduating from high school, he attended St. Augustine"s College in Raleigh where he became a youth coordinator for the Southern Christian Leadership Conference and also served on the advance team for the Rev. Dr. Martin Luther King, Jr. Shortly after graduating from the University of North Carolina at Charlotte, he was appointed as Southern Regional Program Director for the United Church of Christ Commission for Racial Justice.

Over the course of a week, violence flared up around the city and several buildings were burned, including Mike's Grocery on Sixth & Ann streets. Firefighters responding to the blaze were fired upon, allegedly by snipers from the roof of Gregory Congregational. The National Guard was called in and 10 boycotters said to have been barricaded at Gregory Congregational were arrested and charged with firebombing the store and conspiracy to fire upon firefighters and law enforcement officers. The Wilmington 10, as they became known, were the Rev. Ben Chavis, then 24; Jerry Jacobs, 19; Wayne Moore, 19; Marvin Patrick, 19; Willie Vereen, 18; Reginald Epps, 18; James McKoy, 19; Connie Tindall, 21; and Joe Wright, 19. The only female was Ann Shepard, 35, a white social worker.

They were tried, found guilty, and handed prison sentences ranging from 15-34 years, a total of 282 years in all. Their convictions were based on the testimony of two black witnesses who claimed to have been in the church the night of the store bombing. As history would record, the church was empty when the National Guard stormed it and testimony by the two black witnesses was later recanted.

For these reasons, I appealed to the governor for a commutation of their sentences

Service to the Governor

During Governor James B. Hunt's first term, I was nominated to a seat on the North Carolina Human Relations Council by the late architect Herb McKim. I told Herb that I did not feel that there were enough hours in the day for me to serve in yet another capacity. Herb, who was also very active in the

STATE OF NORTH CAROLINA

OFFICE OF THE GOVERNOR

RALEIGH 27611

JAMES B. HUNT, JR.
GOVERNOR

June 22, 1977

Dear Bertha:

Pursuant to G.S. 143B-392, I hereby appoint you to serve on the North Carolina Human Relations Council. Your appointment is effective immediately and as a member of this Council you serve at the pleasure of the governor.

It is with great pleasure that I enclose your commission. I have every confidence you will make an outstanding contribution to the progress of this Council.

I am also enclosing the oath of office. Please have the oath properly executed before a judge, clerk of court, deputy clerk of court, register of deeds, notary public, magistrate or mayor, and return the original and two copies to my office.

My warmest personal regards.

Sincerely,

Mrs. Bertha B. Todd
114 Mercer Avenue
Wilmington, North Carolina 28401

Enclosures

Appointment by then Governor James B. Hunt to the North Carolina Human Relations Council. My service lasted for a period of eight years.

Serving as mistress of ceremonies
for a North Carolina Human Relations Council Program in Raleigh, NC.

community, felt I could offer a sorely needed perspective from southeastern North Carolina. The Council, comprised of members from across the state, met once a month, usually in Raleigh.

My most memorable experience during the eight years I served was meeting with the governor regarding the "Wilmington 10". At one of the council's meetings, the members voted to schedule a conference to discuss the lengthy sentences handed down to the ten. The council then voted to send a committee of three to meet with the governor. I was selected since I knew seven of the 10 who had attended Hoggard or whom I had met in the community. I was tapped to serve as spokesperson at our meeting with Governor Hunt, who did not pardon the 10 but substantially reduced their sentences.

The case garnered international attention and the U.S. Department of Justice asked for the sentences to be overturned. In December, 1980, the 4th Circuit U.S. Court of Appeals overturned the charges, a year after the last member of the Wilmington 10, Ben Chavis, had been paroled.

Healing and Hope: A Speech on the 25th Anniversary

Below are excerpts from a speech I was invited to deliver on the 25th anniversary of the Wilmington 10 arrests. The commemoration was held on the campus of the University of North Carolina at Wilmington.

Healing and Hope: Where We've Been and Where We're Going

"Ladies and gentlemen, good evening to all of you. Having been an educator who was employed by the New Hanover County School System during the period of desegregation of the school system, I have been asked to share an educator's perspective with you. I realize that the program this evening is to focus primarily on where you're going or where we need to be going. I would like for you to indulge a retired educator to share a bit of information with you that you may or may not know.

Where we have been – yes, I was very much involved in the school system and the community during the desegregation of this school system. You see, at the time, I knew seven of the members of the "Wilmington 10" quite well. Their dreams, however, may be compared to the words of the poem entitled, "Dream Deferred" by Langston Hughes. Quote:

What happens to a dream deferred?
Does it dry up like a raisin in the sun?
Or fester like a sore-- And then run?
Does it stink like rotten meat?
Or crust and sugar over-- like a syrupy sweet?
Maybe it just sags like a heavy load.
Or does it explode?

There are some bits of information that – as I reflect – that I feel that you need to know. I feel very strongly that most of you do not know. After twenty-five years – you need to know.

1. I visited and remained all day at Gregory Church on the very first day of the boycott. I also returned for one or two visits during the early days of the boycott. I wanted to learn more about the deep concerns and grievances of the African-American students who were attending New Hanover High and Hoggard High Schools at the time. I wanted to learn about the concerns that motivated them to boycott school. As a very

concerned educator, I wanted to know and needed to know. These concerns were expressed orally and also placed in writing. I took a copy with me.

2. When members of the 'Wilmington 10' were incarcerated, I corresponded with several of the ones whom I knew and even sent some of them a few dollars. I was concerned about all of the ten – I knew seven of them quite well, because I had worked closely with them while serving as an assistant principal at Hoggard High School.

Finally, and now – Where do we go from here? From one who is quite aware of the fact that our soul or spirit has no color – I have accepted this reading by Helen Steiner Rice as one of my favorites. Please allow me to share it with you.

"Teach Us To Live"

God of love, forgive, forgive

Teach us how to truly live

And someday may men realize that all the earth, seas, the skies

Belong to God who made us all

The rich, the poor, the great, the small

And in the Father's holy sight

No man is yellow, black or white

And peace on earth cannot be found

Until we meet on common ground

And every man become a brother

Who worships God and loves each other!!!

May we all strive to understand that this is God's world. Let us plan programs and activities that will enable us all to live in peace with one another.

Speechmaking/Conducting Workshops - A Way of Life

Because I maintained such a visible presence in the community and within the organizations to which I belonged, I was often called on to make presentations. According to my records, I have had more than 300 speaking engagements in the state of North Carolina and throughout the United States.

Presenting to a group

Politically Speaking

Though I have often been approached about running for public office on the local and state levels, I have never been so inclined. The closest I ever came was in 1971 when I began assisting others who had political aspirations. In December of 1971, Wendy Block, Katherine McKim and I became officers of the first chapter of Democratic Women of New Hanover County.

Throughout my adult life, I have felt driven to demand respect for all human beings. I have tried to align myself with individuals and organizations that share that passion. My sole purpose in sharing my involvement is to illustrate that each of us is uniquely positioned to effect positive change in our communities.

Bertha, an activist? No!   Bertha, a strategist? Maybe.

Additional Organizations

National Association for the Advancement of Colored People – Life Member

Women in Action for the Prevention of Violence and Its Causes – Member

The Wilmington Excellence Committee – Charter Member

The Cape Fear Community Foundation – Charter Member

New Hanover County Cancer – Board of Directors

Day Care Centers, Inc. – Secretary

Cape Fear Area Red Cross Board of Directors – Member

Chamber of Commerce Education Committee – Member

Partner for Economic Inclusion Relationship Committee – Member

UNC-Wilmington Foundation Board of Directors – Member

New Hanover County Department of Social Services – Member

"A True Warrior"
Chapter 11

*"Reading maketh a full man, conference a ready man,
and writing an exact man."*
-Francis Bacon

The Late Thomas C. Jervay, Sr. - Owner and Editor of The Wilmington Journal

My mother always subscribed to a daily newspaper, usually the *News & Observer* of Raleigh, which I continued reading until I completed my master's degree at North Carolina College. One year my mother subscribed to Wilmington's daily newspaper, so I was familiar with the *Wilmington Morning Star* when I arrived in 1952.

My landlady subscribed to the paper and I became a daily reader. While some of the coverage of the black community was positive, most of the articles were negative. Glaringly obvious to me was the absence of courtesy titles for blacks. This infuriated me, and several of us signed a petition and forwarded it to the paper, prompting a call from the *Morning Star*. We were prepared to boycott the paper if they did not change the practice.

My landlady was also the one who introduced me to the *Wilmington Journal*. I remember being so proud to read about black *achievement* for a change. The paper's publisher, Thomas C. Jervay or "TC" was a fearless journalist who challenged the social dictates of the day. In an August 1953 edition of the *Journal*, he called on the city of Wilmington to employ black firemen and policemen, and asked voters to elect blacks to Wilmington City Council, the New Hanover County Board of Commissioners, the New Hanover County Board of Education and the Wilmington Housing Authority. He also spoke out for more affordable housing for blacks, paved streets in black neighborhoods, and a black-owned drug store and supermarket.

His popular weekly column, "Uncle Tom" Sez", challenged whites and blacks on the issues of the day. Some of the unrest created by desegregation persisted well into the 1970's. As a result, I suggested that, in addition to the current queens and courts at Hoggard, another be added -- hoping that eventually a black female would

Uncle Tom Sez

It is good news that Hoggard High School has named one of our young women as "Miss Hoggard." The photo and story are on the front page. This is a first, though it took about five years, but it is an indication of progress. Also, it should serve as an inspiration for other blacks not to hold back from participation in school activities and to achieve in scholarship. This is one of the main aims of the Williston Alumni Association: to help motivate our students. There would not have been the racial trouble here that we had had city problems not spilled over into the schools. Young people, usually, can find common interests. It's only when negative thoughts are drilled into their heads by their parents that the problem is compounded. We can credit Mrs. Bertha Todd and others, who have worked hard and long for this day and other accomplishments, for their patient but insistent work towards our young people taking their rightful places in the sun. And, the parents should teach their children that color is skin deep and that it is ability that counts and to say in there and hang on until your aims are accomplished.

Young people, get involved in your student affairs and activities. Don't let ridicule by some hold you back and because they don't want to fight to make the system work, you keep on trying! We shall continue to emphasize that all of us make up the system. And, the system is what all of us demand of it. If you don't fight, you deserve what you get!

The following editorial from the desk of the publisher of the Atlanta Voice is appropriate at this point:

EDUCATION: A TWO WAY STREET

As most parents can testify our children here in Atlanta started to school on August 30. To many of our parents it was a great relief gone, at least temporarily, are those obstreperous brats who played their noon naps and kept interrupting their favorite soap opera. Children ought to go to school. It is essential to their maturation and growth but too often during this period it is "out of sight out of mind." Many parents still look upon school days as mini holidays it frees them for their own selfish diversions. This should not be. School days are crucial to the childs development at home and at school.

stand a chance of being elected. The idea worked and had a noticeable effect on the level of pride among the black students.It was during this time that I had the first of many conversations with Tom Jervay.

One day when I delivered an article for publication, he told me he hadn't seen much of me lately and asked if I was all right. I expressed to him how dejected I was feeling and questioned whether my efforts were in vain.

To which he replied, "Mrs. Todd, you continue to do all that you can to serve and fight injustice. Please do not permit the apathy or negative thinking to rub off on you."

Later, when I was appointed to serve on the North Carolina Human Relations Commission, I was one of three members to meet with then Governor James B. Hunt to discuss the lengthy sentences given to the "Wilmington 10".

When I returned from Raleigh, Mr. Jervay called me and said, "Mrs. Todd, I hear that you and two ministers were talking with Governor Hunt."

I have always been guarded about my strategy, believing that premature disclosure invites too many suggestions from too many people, thereby jeopardizing the desired outcome. So I was quite surprised by his knowledge of my activities and asked, "Mr. Jervay, how did you learn of this? Who told you about this conference?" He then replied, "Oh well, I have my ways." I should have known that the Dean of the Black Press would get the scoop.

The *Wilmington Journal* has been a beacon in southeastern North Carolina and for natives around the country. Though the "True Warrior" died on December 28, 1993 at the age of 79, his legacy lives on. In 1999, he was posthumously enshrined into the National Newspaper Publishers

Association Black Press Archives at Howard University in Washington, DC. The same year, he was inducted into the North Carolina Journalism Hall of Fame at the University of Chapel Hill.

The newspaper passed on to his heirs. Ms. Willie Jervay, TC's widow, is now the publisher emeritus. His daughter, Katherine, is retired after 29 years of service in the family business, where she served as co-publisher and business manager.

His daughter, Mary Alice Jervay Thatch, is presently editor and publisher. Grandchildren Shawn Thatch, Robin Allen, and Johanna Thatch Briggs and great-grandson Jonathan Allen work in various capacities.

"A Couple with Courage"
Chapter 12

"When true friends meet in adverse hour;
'Tis like a sunbeam through a shower."
- Sir Walter Scott

The palpable tensions between blacks and whites in Wilmington during the era of school desegregation resulted in violent episodes in schools and in the community at large. Several people took on the daunting task of trying to quell the unrest in the early 1970's, including Dan and Betty Cameron.

I first met Dan during a meeting at the Dale K. Spencer Building, which then served as the central office for the New Hanover County School system. We were both in attendance at a meeting to examine how to diffuse lingering racial tensions. Weeks later I learned that the man who had offered such thoughtful insights was Dan Cameron.

Despite his many business interests, as general partner in the MacMillan & Cameron Company, president of Atlantic Telecasting Corporation, WECT, and chairman of Atlantic Pepsi Cola Building Corporation, Dan was equally committed to bridging the growing divide caused by desegregation.

A graduate of New Hanover High School and Virginia Military Institute, Dan had been engaged in five European campaigns during World War II, for which he was awarded the Bronze Star. An Army captain at the age of 21 and a major at age 24, the decorated soldier's valor did not end on foreign soils.

Dan and I would work together on many projects over the years, including an advisory panel to address programming issues at WECT.

WECT NBC Television channel **6**

THE TALLEST TV TOWER IN THE EAST

August 18, 1972

Mrs. Bertha Todd
114 Mercer Avenue
Wilmington, North Carolina 28401

Dear Mrs. Todd:

I would like to invite you to a dinner meeting to discuss
programming ideas relevant to the black community and the
formation of a committee to meet regularly with WECT
representatives in this regard.

The meeting will be held in the new banquet room at Whitey's
Elberta Restaurant, Wednesday, August 23, at 6:30 p.m.
Whitey's is located at the intersection of Kerr Avenue and
Market Street.

Please call my secretary or Wayne Jackson (791-8070) and let
us know if it will be possible for you to attend. We do need an
estimate of the number of persons who will attend.

We look forward to meeting with you Wednesday evening.

Sincerely,

Dan D. Cameron
President

DDC:jgw

Atlantic Telecasting Corporation

322 SHIPYARD BLVD.   P. O. BOX 1087
WILMINGTON, N. C. 28401   FAYETTEVILLE, N. C. 28302
PHONE 919 791-8070   PHONE 919 463-4146

Letter to me from Dan

December 13, 1972

Mr. Dan D. Cameron
404 W. Renovah Circle
Wilmington, N. C. 28401

Dear Mr. Cameron:

As the year of 1972 is drawing to a close, please permit me
to express my opinions to you concerning the worthwhile civic
contributions that you have made during this year.

You are to be commended for the forward strides that have been
made in public and human relations. I feel certain that you
were influential in initiating many positive efforts that have
been taken by various businesses in the City of Wilmington.

Best wishes for continued progress through humanistic civic
approaches.

Sincerely,

Bertha B. Todd
Director of Human Relations

hf

Letter to Dan from me

Dan Cameron also became the first white person to sit on the board of directors of the
Community Boys Club, raising more than a half million dollars toward its construction.
His devotion to the club is evidenced in an early letter to Tom Jervay, late publisher of the
Wilmington Journal.

DANIEL D. CAMERON
WILMINGTON, NORTH CAROLINA 28406

March 29, 1989

Mr. Tom Jervay
Wilmington Journal
P.O. Box 1618
Wilmington, NC 28402

Dear Tom:

Thanks for sending me the clipping from Encore. It was a good story but only touched on the many interests and accomplishments you have participated in over a long period of service to your community. With another twenty years to go just think what you will get done!

It was nice visiting with you last Friday over lunch, and as usual we didn't finish covering all the subjects that were raised. In particular the issue of the Boys Club's new emphasis got waylaid, so let me take a minute to outline some of the things I had on my mind.

First off, let me reiterate my belief in the quality of our new board of directors. A better group would be hard to find.

Secondly, the development of new programs to better serve the crying need of inner city boys is well under way and only requires far greater financial support than the United Way is able to give it to make a strong impact on this need.

This brings up the subject of the recent commitment from the Trustees of the D. D. & Elizabeth H. Cameron Foundation to partially fund this new effort with a one time $25,000.00 donation. It is hoped that this money will act as a springboard to encourage others to get behind our project to enable us to better serve the urban areas, get boys off the street, inspire them to pursue higher goals and help eradicate the dreadful drug epidemic that is overtaking our city.

In my mind, now is the time for action. Tomorrow will be too late! We earnestly solicit the good offices of you and your newspaper to help our dedicated board members accomplish their avowed purposes.

Sincerely,

Dan D. Cameron

DDC:p

Letter from Dan to Tom Jervay courtesy of the Wilmington Journal.

In 2010, the main building at 901 Nixon Street was fittingly renamed the Daniel D. Cameron Unit in his memory.

I have yet another reason to be thankful for my decades-long friendship with Dan. As a man of means, Dan owned a jet for personal and business trips. Our son, Brian Edward had earned a B.S. degree in aeronautical science from Embry Riddle Aeronautical University and returned home to accrue the flight hours required to pilot commercial airlines. He was able to log some hours as a pilot for Eastern Delivery Service, owned by Katherine Bell Moore, former educator and Wilmington City Councilwoman.

After learning of an opening in Wilmington for a pilot instructor at Aeronautics, Inc., Brian applied for the position and waited for a response, to no avail. Sensing his frustration at not being able to start the aviation career he had worked so hard for, I called Dan Cameron. Dan informed me he already had a pilot, but Brian would be welcome to ride along with them. That kind gesture, though, would not satisfy the flight time requirements. I then told Dan about the opening at Aeronautics (where Dan's plane was serviced). He had me tell Brian to bring his resume to him, which Brian did the very next morning. After several days Aeronautics granted Brian an interview and hired him to teach flight lessons. Brian remained with Aeronautics for two years and has now been a pilot with Delta Airlines for 25 years; a captain for 15. Dan Cameron, who died in July 2005, will be remembered by many, but few are as grateful as I am for this man of courage.

Elizabeth "Betty" Cameron

It's remarkable that I would first meet Betty through our mutual involvement with the YWCA the year the organization adopted the national mission "to eliminate racism". It also happened that the county's two high schools were grappling with the pangs of desegregation. At the time there were two YWCA chapters: the main branch and the Phyllis Wheatley branch. Louise MacRae and Bessie Faye Hunt served as executive directors of the Phyllis Wheatley and main branches, respectively.

Over the course of two years, the two directors convened a series of discussions aimed at eliminating racism. Among those participating in the series were Alice Von Oeson, Betty Cameron, and Betty's sister, Pickett Taylor, all from the main branch. From the Phyllis Wheatley branch were Louise MacRae, Caronell Chestnut, and me. Sometimes other African-American women would participate.

In the beginning we met twice a week. It was during those heated sessions that Betty and I began to learn more about each other. The spirited discussions focused on differences and commonalities and presented our first opportunity to be candid without feeling threatened or intimidated.

To encourage youth participation, I would

often transport Hoggard students, black and white, to the sessions. After another major disturbance at Hoggard in 1970, Betty sent me a note of encouragement.

Those early years formed the basis of our enduring friendship. In addition to our involvement with the Y, we worked closely on the political scene. Betty

Personal note from Betty

would ask me about African-American candidates being considered for various offices and would host fundraising receptions in her home.

Later a group of Wilmington women, concerned with mounting violence in the schools and community, formed the local chapter of Women in Action for the Prevention of Violence and Its Causes. The group's founder was Mrs. Asa Q. Spaulding, whose family founded North Carolina Mutual Insurance Company family in Durham.

Newspaper Article
Star News – December 7, 1971
"With words of caution and warning about the cause they were undertaking, the initiator of the Women-in-Action Movement in North Carolina, Mrs. Asa Q. Spaulding of Durham addressed a group of 75-100 New Hanover County women Sunday. The organizational meeting was held in answer to the challenge issued to the City of Wilmington by Mrs. Spaulding in mid-October to begin a corps of interested women in the community who would

Letters to the Editor
Women in Action

EDITOR'S NOTE: Letters submitted for publication must be signed and correct address given, and must not exceed 300 words. Letters considered libelous or in bad taste will not be published.

To the Editor:
Last Fall an organization was started here called WOMEN IN ACTION FOR THE PREVENTION OF VIOLENCE AND ITS CAUSES. This group is patterned after and affiliated with the Durham organization by the same name which has received many honors and awards for its success in mobilizing women in a common cause — "the challenge of creating a community climate which respects the dignity and worth of all human beings, which encourages every citizen to develop to her or his greatest potential, and which enriches the quality of life of the total community".

The Wilmington Chapter of WOMEN IN ACTION FOR THE PREVENTION OF VIOLENCE AND ITS CAUSES shares this same cause and has as its basic goal "the prevention of violence — overt acts of unlawful behavior or the more subtle violence found under conditions where persons are denied the rights to life, liberty and the pursuit of happiness. WOMEN IN ACTION believe that the best way to prevent violence is to eliminate the conditions that cause it."

For several years concerned women have been asking, "What can I do?" in regards to human relations problems in our community and there seemed to be no blueprint to supply directions or answers. It seems to me this organization offers these women an opportunity to work together in a calm rational way, looking for causes and solutions and broadening understanding of

racial tensions and community unrest.

Any interested women are welcome at the meeting to be held this Sunday, April 30th at St. Paul's Episcopal Church, 16th and Market Streets at 4 o'clock. Mr. Dudley Flood, Human Relations Director for the North Carolina Department of Public Instruction and Mr. Gene Causbey of the same department will be speakers on the program. Both these men are nationally known for being outstanding in their field.
MRS. DAN CAMERON
Wilmington, N. C.

Letter to the Editor from Mrs. Dan D. Cameron

listen to and help solve the problems of the community. A temporary group of officers were selected at this initial meeting.

Mrs. Spaulding also told the group, "This will be a new experience for many women. It's the first time black and white women will be sitting down together."

I admired Betty for assuming the presidency of this worthwhile organization. One time we met for a special event at Dame Catherine Carpenter's home at 16th & Princess Streets. As we were leaving, there were two police cars parked outside. The officers informed us that we would have to stop these kinds of meetings.

Fortunately we didn't stop meeting. For forty years, Betty and I have shared so many wonderful experiences – whether she accompanied me to an Ebony Fashion Fair Show or she invited me to speak with her Adult Sunday School class at First Presbyterian Church.

Born Elizabeth Henderson, Betty is a lifelong member of First Presbyterian and has been active in the choir. After graduating from New Hanover High School in 1939, she attended Agnes Scott College in Decatur, Georgia, returning to Wilmington after she had earned a degree in English.

With the country in the midst of World War II upon her return, Betty did office work in the Wilmington Shipyard before moving to New York City, where she lived until Dan wooed her back to their hometown.

On August 14, 2008, I was present for the ribbon cutting for the Betty Cameron Women's and Children's Hospital on the campus of New Hanover Regional Medical Center. I was proud to bear witness to this lasting legacy for a dear friend!

Betty also served as the first female chair of the board of trustees at Agnes Scott College, where the Elizabeth Henderson Cameron Reading Terrace has been established in McCain Library.

At a time when Dan and Betty Cameron could have hidden behind a wall of wealth or clung to close-minded claims, they were at the forefront of efforts to reconcile community relations. Our friendship may have been borne of a critical need during a critical era, but its longevity is a testament to our mutual love and admiration for each other.

"The Challenges of a Coup d'état"
Chapter 13

"Every moment wasted looking back keeps us from moving forward."
– Hillary Rodham Clinton, June 7, 2008

In 1996 I was sitting in on a planning session for a Wilmington 10 commemoration when Dr. Melton McLaurin, now history professor emeritus at UNC-Wilmington, said, "Bertha, you know that in 1998, one hundred years will have passed since the violence occurred in 1898 here in Wilmington." I glanced at him and replied, "Oh, yes!"

My "Oh, yes" meant that I had no ready reply and no further comment. I detected the intimation that I participate in something. But I was mourning the recent deaths of my husband and elder sister who died within six weeks of each other. I had also had my fill of community organizing while serving at Hoggard years before. I thought no more controversy for *me*!

Later in 1996 Dr. Bolton Anthony, who was managing a grant on race relations for UNCW, requested a conference with me in my home. I agreed and we talked for hours! After several other conversations over time, Bolton asked if I would call a meeting of black and white females. Questions were formulated and the meeting was held in a conference room at the main branch of the public library. I thought, "Now just what he is planning to do with this information?"

Months later Bolton informed me that a group had been organized and that he and attorney William "Bill" Fewell were serving as co-chairs. The group would come to be called the 1898 Centennial Foundation. Unbeknownst to each other, Bolton and Bill would call me to get my take on ideas and I'd often hear them repeated back to me from the other. But I willingly shared my views with both of them.

I decided to attend one of their meetings later that year and learned that Bill had returned to Pennsylvania – for good. The organization's structure mandated a white and black co-chair and now the group needed a black co-chair.

When I was asked, I replied that I was in the grieving process and not willing to become involved in any more controversial projects. I did, however, offer to make contact with six people who were recommended, to no avail. Two phone numbers couldn't be tracked down, two said they would give my request some thought, and two had relocated due to their jobs.

With much prayer and meditation, I agreed to serve as co-chair of The 1898 Centennial Foundation on an interim basis. As soon as the group recruited a black co-chair, I would gladly step down.

I began meeting regularly with Bolton Anthony in late 1996 or early 1997. He was concerned about not getting a response from New Hanover County Commissioners, Wilmington City Council, or the Greater Wilmington Chamber of Commerce. I asked Bolton if he had sent written requests to these groups. He replied that all contact had been by telephone.

The first order of business was getting printed stationery, composing a letter, and mailing a written request for representation from various business and governmental entities to assist in planning the commemoration. The letters were followed up by phone calls. The strategy was effective and we had our first speaking engagement with the Greater Wilmington Chamber of Commerce. I began to bone up on background information and prepared a short presentation for the Chamber's regular business meeting. I thought that Bolton would do the same.

We were both anxious as we prepared to address Chamber members. After the president officially convened the meeting, he said, "Now, we will hear from Mrs. Bertha Todd and Dr. Bolton Anthony who will talk about their project".

The room was quiet as I made my way to the front. The members were staid and, to me, some frowned a bit. In my opening remarks, I stated that this wasn't *our* project, but belonged to everyone – the state of North Carolina, New Hanover County and the City of Wilmington – all of us!

Then it was Bolton's turn. Since he had been involved in the project much longer than I had, I think he felt that no outline

was necessary. Bolton talked on and on, sharing his dreams and aspirations for this controversial effort and made some remarks that some members were definitely not ready to hear. After noting some of the members' facial expressions, I wondered if I should go to the front, get Bolton and walk out of the meeting or if I should walk out by myself. When he finally finished his remarks, we left immediately. Our first presentation received the coldest reception we ever experienced at our many speaking engagements.

When we were invited to speak to groups, my co-speakers were Dr. Bolton Anthony, Dr. James Megivern, or Dr. Melton McLaurin, each of whom would ask me to make opening remarks. I had honed my presentation by listening to the questions from previous audiences.

When a few members of the Chamber contacted me and requested an audience with me alone, I agreed and asked that those present be committed to speaking candidly about the issue. I met with a very small group and talked for about four hours. As a result of this lengthy discussion, three representatives from the Greater Wilmington Chamber of Commerce became three of the strongest supporters of the 1898 endeavor.

Word about the 1898 Centennial Foundation's plans began to spread and we were inundated with invitations to discuss our goals. A representative from one civic organization asked that I present without my co-chair, Bolton. I simply replied, "One black and one white. If my partner is not going to be invited, I shall not appear either." Both of us attended and each made a short presentation. Bolton delivered an excellent speech!

As the foundation worked toward the centennial commemoration to be held at Thalian Hall in November of 1998, many meetings were held in my home -- usually because we couldn't locate a meeting place.

Needless to say, the project was consuming most of my time. And despite the fact that we each had the same goal, there were mounting tensions among members of the foundation. Some suggested that the organization needed to get rid of certain committee co-chairs. Others threatened to start another group working toward the same effort. Still others suggested I replace my co-chair. Drawing on more than two decades in administration, I was accustomed to making decisions. I would simply pray, think things over and make the decisions – whether good or bad.

One thing was sure; the foundation needed seed money in order to accomplish its mission. When Bolton asked if I would appear before Wilmington City Council during their budget hearing, I had already make plans to assist my recently-retired sister in Greensboro with a personal project. I learned later that Dr. Earl Sheridan appeared before the council.

Upon my return from Greensboro two weeks later, Bolton called regarding a budget hearing with New Hanover County Commissioners, which I agreed to. As I prayed for the right words regarding this controversial project, the following thought came to me:

1898 Foundation Philosophy

"No one living in Wilmington today was a participant in the events of 1898. Consequently, none among us bears any personal responsibility for what happened. But all among us – no matter our race or history, whether we have arrived here only recently or come from families that have called Wilmington home for generations – all among us are responsible for 1998. On each of us falls the personal responsibility to make our community one where economic justice and racial harmony flourish. Surely this is a challenge we are willing to accept."

When I shared my thoughts with Bolton, he changed some of the words, but this became the official 1898 Philosophy from 1997 through 2008. Many times I informed the members that if this philosophy was not printed on programs, I would cease my role as co-chair. By this time, I realized that my interim position had become a permanent one.

1898 Foundation Mission Statement

To "tell the story" of 1898 and make the real history known;

To "heal the wounds" of the racial division which continue in the city;

To "honor the memory" of those who lost lives and property in 1898; and

To "restore the hope" through efforts to foster economic inclusion.

Videos

Local filmmaker Francine DeCoursey produced and directed "Remembering 1898...Moving Forward Together," a 23-minute documentary film with an historical overview and remarks about the importance of the commemoration by me and other community members.

A Drama Worth Remembering

Unforeseen circumstances forced the foundation to secure another playwright for a commissioned drama based on the events of 1898. With about two months before the production was to be staged, Dr. Anne Russell, noted professor and playwright, wrote "No More Sorrow to Arise." Her sensitive treatment told the story of the 1898 coup through actual letters written by Carrie Sadgwar Manly, the widow of black newspaperman Alex Manley. The full-length drama was presented November 5–7, 1998 on the main stage at Thalian Hall.

Hugh MacRae, II – A Supporter of 1898 Programs and Activities

As co-chair I began to develop programming strategies that would include all, including living descendants whose grandfathers were involved in the violence of 1898. I wanted to impress upon them that the foundation's goal was not to point fingers, but to shed light on the "secret" in order to move forward.

I called Hugh MacRae II who agreed to meet with me. When I walked into his Hanover Center office, I introduced myself to Hugh, a tall, stately man, and he motioned for me to be seated. I had prepared comments just in case the reception was a cold one, but it was not. After talking to him about the purpose of my visit, I asked if he would be willing to join us as the foundation implemented its planned programs, activities, and public commemoration to be held in 1998. He replied that he had heard of the 1898 violence and knew that his grandfather was involved, but was not fully aware of what had transpired in 1898. He ended by saying that he would participate as much as he could, given his busy schedule.

True to his word, he attended meetings and spoke at several events, including one held at Screen Gems Studios. Hugh and one of his daughters, Marguerite "Meg" MacRae, also served on committees and made generous financial contributions. Several of his family members attended events sponsored by the foundation.

It was during a picnic sponsored by the Wilmington Baha'i' faith and the 1898 Centennial Foundation in the summer of 1998 that Hugh addressed another controversial issue surrounding his family. His grandfather had reportedly stipulated in his will that Hugh MacRae Park was for whites only.

In a prepared statement, Hugh MacRae II affirmed that the park was open to all.

I wrote a letter to the editor of the *Star News* after a man from Roanoke, Virginia, the descendant of a Confederate mercenary, reprimanded individuals and groups other than whites for using Hugh MacRae Park.

Rather than go on the defensive about the actions of their forebears, Hugh MacRae II and several other descendants supported our efforts to commemorate the tragedy of 1898 in both word and deed.

ETTERS TO THE EDITOR

MacRae helps

EDITOR: ... The four goals of the 1898 Centennial Foundation were (and continue to be): 1. Tell the story; 2. Honor the memory; 3. Heal the wounds; and 4. Restore the hope.

Hugh MacRae II began working with the foundation members in the early planning stages.

(He) spoke publicly on numerous occasions, attended several programs, and financially contributed to the foundation's efforts.

MacRae, accompanied by several members of his family, attended a picnic sponsored by the 1898 Centennial Foundation and members of the Ba-ha'i community.

MacRae and his family members attended this event in order to made an announcement. MacRae, in a prepared speech, announced that Hugh MacRae Park welcomes individuals and groups from all ethnicities.

The 1898 Foundation informed the news media of all programs and activities. However, this event was not covered.

Hugh MacRae II has been and continues to be a strong supporter of the foundation. A memorial is scheduled to be erected in 2007.

A corresponding publication is also in progress.

The 1898 Foundation and the 1898 Race Riot Commission are two separate entities.

The late state Sen. Luther Jordan Jr. and Rep. Thomas Wright were former members of the 1898 Centennial Foundation.

Bertha Boykin Todd
Wilmington

EDITOR'S NOTE: The writer was a co-chairman of the 1898 Centennial Foundation.

WRITE US

We invite your opinions on issues mentioned recently in our news and opinion columns. Only one letter per month, please, of no more than 225 words. All letters are subject to editing and condensation.
Address: Editor, P. O. Box 840, Wilmington, N.C. 28402.
E-mail: letters@starnewsonline.com
Please include signature, address and telephone number. If you don't have a listed number, bring letters, along with identification, to our receptionist at 1003 South 17th St.

Public Kick-off of 1898 Centennial Year Observances

While Bolton Anthony and I were serving as co-chairs and planning for the opening ceremony, we discussed a theme for the observance. Three words sprang to my mind: Moving Forward Together. When I shared them with Bolton, he responded, "Bertha, you certainly are optimistic!" I replied, "We can at least give this a try. If we do not believe in the end results of this project, who will?"

Bolton had a banner made with those three words that set the perfect tone for the throngs of people who turned out for the opening ceremony in January 1998 at Brogden Hall. He was a master at implementing ideas and offered the perfect counterbalance to my restless energy.

1898 Commemoration at Thalian Hall

Trish Snyder chaired the committee charged with producing the centennial ceremony.

When she informed me that the main auditorium at Thalian Hall had been reserved for a film screening and our commemoration would have to be held in one of the smaller meeting rooms, I was upset.

Not knowing what to expect, given the fact that not everyone was in agreement with the foundation's goals, my primary concern was whether we would be able to contain a large group in a small area. A day before the commemoration was to be held, members of the program committee received word that the group planning to use the stage deferred to our event. Did I breathe a sigh of relief!

Hundreds of people representing a broad cross-section of Wilmington turned out on November 10, 1998 to remember the blacks and whites who had been run out of town and the unknown number of African-Americans who were killed November 9-10, 1898.

Passing the Torch as Co-Chair

Now that the big event was over, the members of the 1898 Centennial Foundation changed the name of the organization to the 1898 Foundation. Some goals still had not been realized. Jim Megivern and I decided to resign as co-chairs in 1999. Bolton, by this time, was serving as executive director of the foundation. Following are the individuals who committed to serve as co-chairs of the 1898 Foundation – always one white and one black.

Co-Chairs

Dr. Bolton Anthony & William "Bill" Fewell
Dr. Bolton Anthony & Bertha B. Todd
Bertha B. Todd & Dr. James Mcgivern
Barbara Sullivan &
Linda Upperman–Smith
Dr. Thomas Schmid & Herbert Harris
Dr. Melton A. McLaurin & Lethia Hankins
Robert Gerlach & Lethia Hankins
Lethia Hankins & Laura Padgett

Recruiting 1898 Foundation Co-chairs

Only a few members of the foundation chose to remain following the public program on November 10, 1998. When Bolton moved to Chapel Hill to pursue another project, I began feeling somewhat lost, but I was determined to continue. One final goal had not been accomplished — the memorial.

I begged Melton McLaurin to remain with us for two terms as co-chair, even though I was aware that he was in the process of writing another book, this one on the Montford Point Marines. Sensing the desperation in my voice, he acquiesced.

A black co-chair was now needed. I sought out my AKA sorority sister and friend, Lethia S. Hankins, and promised her that I would remain in the background and help familiarize her with the foundation's previous activities. She agreed.

When Melton finally stepped down, I contacted Rob Gerlach and told him that Lethia and I would do the work if he would serve as the white co-chair. Rob worked very hard for the foundation for several years before resigning for personal reasons.

By this time, we were nearing the final goal. It was too late to recruit a new person. Laura Padgett, who had served the organization in many capacities over the years, was serving on Wilmington City Council. I said, "Laura, please consent to serve as co-chair with Lethia. All you need to do is sit here and be white." Although Laura was extremely busy with her other duties, she looked at me, smiled, and agreed to serve as Lethia's co-chair until the memorial was completed. I said to myself, "Thank God!"

1898 Memorial Plan Almost Derailed

THE VISION BEHIND THE CREATION OF THE 1898 MEMORIAL PARK

The 1898 Memorial Park offers a rare opportunity to grasp again a vision once shared over a century ago by the citizens of Wilmington, North Carolina. The vision was of a city which, although knowing its share of economic hardship, offered a future of prosperity and progress to all who claimed the vision as their own and the city as their home.

As history has told us, the original vision for a growing, progressive Wilmington was dashed in the racial violence of November 1898. Diversity of race and class became a catalyst which ignited and, in one day, destroyed the tenuous race relations which then existed in the growing Port City. The incident fragmented race relations in Wilmington for decades to come.

The purpose behind the creation of the 1898 Memorial Park is to restore the promise of racial progress and to salute the forward-looking residents of Wilmington. In this way the city once again stands as a mecca for many races, colors and creeds who seek a new life in the South – a South aware of its past but more focused on the future – a South not of what was but of what will be.

Just as the foundation put out an international call for entries for design of the memorial park, state Representative Thomas Wright publicly stated at a Community Action Group meeting in March 2002 that a grocery store would be a better use of the site.

In the meantime, the foundation had tapped the Odeleye Group, whose proposed monument and park design was overwhelmingly endorsed through a public process.

Rep. Wright promised to exchange the original site of the park for a nearby lot. However, Leigh Lane, head of the state's Public Involvement and Community Studies Unit of the Department of Transportation, stated that the DOT was legally bound to build a park on the site. If a park was not developed on the site, the state would have to seek a new memorandum of agreement with various federal, state and local offices that were involved in the initial agreement. (Wilmington Morning Star, Saturday, March 2, 2002).

The unanticipated opposition posed a challenge for the foundation. Committee members were faced with three options if the 1898 Memorial Park was not developed.

1. Return the money to donors and say we can't build the memorial.

2. Go to court to force the issue at the 3rd and Davis Streets' site. This would be without the support of a majority of the current City Council and without a signed contract with Odeleye. Both realities begged the question of whether or not a court fight over a memorial dedicated to reconciliation was worth the struggle.

3. Make the best of the current situation by agreeing to another site and getting the memorial built. This option hinged on:

a. The 1898 Foundation obtaining a new, acceptable site, gratis
b. Odeleye agreeing to site modifications, i.e. landscaping revisions to his original plan for the memorial.

Representative Wright did not follow through on his commitment to provide us with another site, gratis. By this time, fundraising plans had stalled which left members wondering if we could recapture the momentum.

Below is one letter of support that helped us regain our motivation.

BONEY
Architecture
Design
Consulting
Development

WILMINGTON
RALEIGH
CHARLOTTE

BONEY, PLLC
2528 Independence Blvd.
Suite 200
Wilmington, NC 28412
T 910.790.9901
F 910.790.3111
info@boneyarchitects.com
www.boneyarchitects.com

11 October 2002

Beth Becca, Director of Development
Cape Fear Community Foundation
PO Box 119
Wilmington, NC 27606

RE: 1898 Memorial Fund

Dear Beth,

I am pleased to enclose our check for $3,333.33 in partial fulfillment of our pledge for the 1898 Memorial. We plan to continue this amount until our pledge is complete.

We are honored to be a part of this community effort, and look forward to its completion.

Sincerely,

BONEY, PLLC

Charles H. Boney, Jr., AIA
Director, Wilmington Operations

C: Mrs. Bertha Todd

Mrs. Todd —
Thanks for involving
us in this. Best
wishes —
Charles

A letter that helped us to regain our motivation from The Boney Architectural Firm

Senator Luther Henry Jordan, Jr.

State Senator Luther H. Jordan, Jr., who was a member of the 1898 Foundation, arranged for the group to meet with the North Carolina Legislative Black Caucus in Raleigh. The meeting motivated Luther to present a resolution calling for the formation of a legislative commission to study the 1898 violence and its impact.

My relationship with Luther began early in his political career. We both belonged to Chestnut Street Presbyterian Church (USA) where I watched him mature into a true statesman.

One day Luther came to me and said he wanted to run for Wilmington City Council and asked if I would assist him with composing a letter to voters. I ended up composing the letter, typing the letter, purchasing stamps and mailing the letters to a list of people he supplied to me.

Luther did not win this particular election, but continued to run as a candidate for city councilman until he won a seat, which he held for six years. He was then elected as a state senator representing the Seventh District, which included parts of New Hanover, Onslow, Pender, Jones and Lenoir counties. His decade in the senate included serving as majority whip.

Over the years, Luther had come to me for so much advice that I began to consider him one of my socially adopted sons. I was deeply saddened by his untimely death on April 23, 2002 at the age of 51.

Moving Forward Together

The idea for a book occurred to me after Bolton's departure. I realized that not everyone would have an opportunity to visit Wilmington and view the monument. I also wanted to ensure that there was a written legacy for the hundreds of black and white citizens who had given of their time and skills over the course of 13 years. The book would also serve as a tribute to those who had been run out of Wilmington or killed during the violence of 1898.

In keeping with the organization's goal of pairing blacks and whites, journalists Rhonda Bellamy and Si Cantwell served as the editorial team for "Moving Forward Together: A Community Remembers 1898." The publication has been distributed throughout the United States.

Outgrowths of The 1898 Centennial Foundation
Partners for Economic Inclusion

One of the more visible outgrowths was the formation of Partners for Economic Inclusion. Chaired by Rob Gerlach and Peter Grear, the group's mission was to facilitate dialogue and develop strategies for economic inclusion in the Lower Cape Fear Region. The Partners met annually for several years, later merging with the Greater Wilmington Chamber of Commerce.

Study Circles

Wilmington was designated as one of 55 host cities for the National Days of Dialogue on Race Relations. The foundation's Reconciliation Committee set a goal of recruiting and training 100 facilitators to produce 50 racially balanced teams, which would meet with small groups of 10-15 participants in five two-hour sessions. All told more than 500 black, white and Hispanic citizens participated in the dialogue sessions which continue through the YWCA.

Ministerial Roundtable

The Ministerial Roundtable was organized in 1998 to bring the city's clergy together to participate in the commemoration. Initially co-chaired by The Rev. Dr. June Highfill of Pearsall Memorial Presbyterian Church and Rev. Johnny Calhoun of St. Stephen AME Church, the Roundtable continues to be active in the community, organizing the annual Sunday Service in memory of the Rev. Dr. Martin Luther King, Jr.

At Last! 2008 Dedication of the 1898 Memorial Park

At long last, the foundation had raised enough funds for sculptor Ayokunle Odeleye and his team to complete the memorial according to the contract.

The Odeleye Group maquette, designed by Odeleye, Marianne Weinberg-Benson, and the landscape architects at jon Benson + associates, was the overwhelming favorite among a seven-member 1898 panel and among the general public ballots collected at the New Hanover County Public Library where the models were displayed. The design features six paddles are symbolic of water, an important element in the spiritual belief systems in Africa and their descendants who resided in Wilmington during the 1800's.

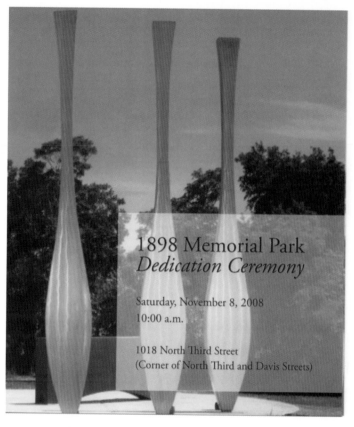

Cover of the Dedication Program

A prolific public sculptor, Odeleye trained at Virginia Commonwealth University and Howard University. He is a tenured professor of art at Kennesaw University, where he has taught since 1989.

Our capital campaign was so successful that we had funds to commission the book "Moving Forward Together," which chronicled the community's efforts at reconciliation. The book was edited by Rhonda Bellamy, assisted by Si Cantwell.

The park was finally dedicated on November 8, 2008. As I looked over the crowd assembled on that beautiful fall morning, I was filled with tears and pride. Silently I thanked God for the good-heartedness of those who stayed true to the cause so many years after we began.

Below is a copy of my remarks at the dedication of the 1898 Memorial Park.

The Present and the Future
November 8, 200

Ladies and gentlemen, good morning.

The Present
Today, the reality of this vision, this goal, was not achieved instantly. This 1898 monument and memorial park are standing solidly on the shoulders of those individuals who began pursuing a vision more than 12 years ago. A small group of people began to expect great things to happen! Great things did happen because of the courage and unwavering faith of many of you who are standing here with us today.

Today, the present is simply a realistic assessment of a vision pursued, the progress toward a goal fulfilled, accompanied with a sense of pride and awe. The journey has been a challenging one – without a doubt. Nevertheless we have come this far by faith in God, faith in humanity, faith in many of you here today and faith in many, many citizens living throughout these United States – especially those living in southeastern North Carolina.

The Future
Abraham Lincoln stated, and I quote, "The best thing about the future is that it comes one day at a time," end of quote. H.G. Wells stated, and I quote, "that the future is the shape of things to come," end quote. Senator Hillary Clinton stated only a few months ago, "Every moment wasted looking back keeps us from moving forward."

Our book published by the foundation is entitled "Moving Forward Together." Edited by Rhonda Bellamy and assistant editor Si Cantwell, this publication represents a testament to the work of the 1898 Centennial Foundation, currently called the 1898 Foundation. Let us ALL make a profound commitment to move forward together in unity to render services for the betterment of humanity.

Surely this is a challenge all of us are willing to accept!

The 1898 Foundation was officially dissolved in February 2009.

Recommended readings include "We Have Taken a City" by Leon Prather, "Democracy Betrayed" by David Cecelski and Timothy Tyson, and "Moving Forward Together" by Rhonda Bellamy and Si Cantwell.

1898 Centennial Foundation Involvement

Serving as co-chair of the 1898 Centennial Foundation was a challenging, but worthwhile experience. The following log of activities was compiled from my daily planning calendar beginning in 1996 and ending in 1999.

Each telephone call, each meeting, each event was important toward developing and maintaining a superior level of quality this commemoration warranted. All efforts, programs, and activities focused upon unifying all ethnic groups instead of further widening a chasm between the races that has existed since 1898.

1898 CENTENNIAL FOUNDATION INVOLVEMENT
BERTHA B. TODD

January 1996 – December 1996

DATE	EVENT	TIME
6/3	Met with NHC Women Leaders at Public Library	12:00 – 2:00 PM
7/96	No Activity	
8/96	Telephone conversations w/Bolton Anthony	
8/96	Telephone conversations w/Bill Fewell	
9/96	Telephone conversations w/Bolton Anthony	
9/96	Telephone conversations w/Bill Fewell	

Many telephone conversations were held with Bolton Anthony and Bill Fewell regarding the planning and organization process.

1898 CENTENNIAL FOUNDATION INVOLVEMENT
BERTHA B. TODD

January 1997 – December 1997

DATE	EVENT	TIME
1/7	Radio Station – WHOR	7:00 PM
1/16	NAACP Office	2:00 – 4:00 PM
1/21	NAACP Office (Interviews)	2:30 – 4:00 PM
2/4	NHC Public Library (Meeting)	7:00 – 9:00 PM
2/19	Chamber of Commerce (Meeting)	12:00 – 1:00 PM
3/14	Bolton Anthony (Meeting)	2:00 – 4:00 PM
4/97	No Activity	
5/6	NHC Public Library (Meeting)	7:00 – 9:00 PM
5/14	Town Hall (Meeting)	3:30 – 4:30 PM
5/29	Town Hall (Meeting)	5:30 – 7:30 PM
6/2	County Commissioners (Meeting)	6:30 – 9:30 PM
6/10	Sub-committee Meeting	2:00 – 3:00 PM
6/16	Town Hall (Meeting)	5:30 – 7:30 PM
7/1	Bolton Anthony & Gerry McCants (Meeting)	9:00 – 10:00 AM
7/3	Bolton Anthony (Meeting)	4:00 – 6:00 PM
7/9	Bolton Anthony (Meeting)	
7/11	Cape Fear Museum (Meeting)	3:00 – 5:00 PM
7/24	NHC Public Library (Meeting) (Ill – My daughter represented me.)	7:00 – 9:00 PM
8/12	Anthony Wade (Breakfast Meeting)	9:00 – 11:00 AM
8/14	Bolton Anthony (Video Meeting)	2:00 – 4:00 PM
8/15	Jim McGivern & Bolton Anthony (Lunch Meeting at Annabelle's)	1:00 – 3:00 PM
8/16	Terry Gandy (Meeting)	2 hours
8/18	Executive Committee Meeting	7:00 – 9:00 PM

1898 CENTENNIAL FOUNDATION INVOLVEMENT
BERTHA B. TODD

January 1997 – December 1997
(continued)

DATE	EVENT	TIME
8/20	Bolton Anthony & Doug Tanner (Lunch Meeting)	2:00 – 4:00 PM
8/22	Glen Barefoot (Meeting)	11:00 AM – 12:00 PM
8/22	Bolton Anthony (Meeting) (Scottish Rite Temple)	1:00 – 2:00 PM
8/26	Bill Caster (Meeting)	11:00 AM – 12:30 PM
8/26	Economic Development Committee (Meeting)	5:30 – 7:30 PM
8/27	Wilmington Excellence (Meeting at UNC-W)	7:45 – 9:45 AM
8/28	Chancellor James Leutze (Meeting at home)	1:00 – 3:00 PM
9/2	Chamber of Commerce (Meeting)	11:30 AM – 12:30 PM
9/4	1898 Centennial Council (Meeting)	4:00 – 6:00 PM
9/8	Special Workshops	
9/10	Z. Smith Reynolds (Interview)	1:30 – 2:30 PM
9/25	History in Black & White (Presentation w/John Godwin at UNC-W)	7:00 – 9:00 PM
9/30	Bolton Anthony (Meeting) (Azalea Inn)	1:00 – 3:00 PM
10/2	1898 Centennial Council (Meeting)	7:00 – 9:00 PM
10/5	Bellamy Mansion (Presentation)	5:00 – 7:00 PM
10/8	NHC Retired Teachers (Presentation)	
10/19	St. Mark Episcopal Church (Presentation Series)	3:00 – 5:00 PM
10/20	Chamber of Commerce (Conference)	2:00 – 4:00 PM
10/23	North Fourth Street (Presentation)	5:30 PM

2.

1898 CENTENNIAL FOUNDATION INVOLVEMENT
BERTHA B. TODD

January 1997 – December 1997
(continued)

DATE	EVENT	TIME
11/97	Church Women United (Presentation)	
11/9	1898 Waterfront Vigil	7:00 PM
11/10	First Union National Bank (Meeting)	
11/11	Wilmington Star News	11:00 – 11:30 AM
11/12	Presbyterian Ministers (Meeting)	11:00 AM
11/13	Wilmington Star News	2:00 – 3:00 PM
11/16	Cape Fear Museum	3:00 – 4:30 PM
11/18	NHC Public Library (Meeting)	6:00 – 7:30 PM
11/19	Leave for Raleigh	11:00 AM
	(Meeting w/Betty McCain)	2:00 PM
11/20	Chamber of Commerce (Meeting)	7:30 – 9:30 AM
11/20	Cynthia Henry (Meeting)	10:00 AM
11/20	NHC Retired Teachers (Presentation)	10:30 AM
11/20	1898 Centennial Foundation (Meeting)	7:00 – 9:00 PM
11/21	Facilitator Training	9:00 AM – 12:00 PM
11/22	Meeting	9:00 – 11:00 AM
11/25	St. Phillips (Meeting)	6:00 – 9:00 PM
12/4	North Fourth Street (Meeting)	3:00 PM
12/10	Doug Tanner & Angela Bryant (Meeting)	4 hours
12/22	Wilmington Policemen	
	(Presentation w/Bolton Anthony)	
12/31	Forester's Restaurant	12:00 – 1:00 PM
	(Lunch Meeting)	
12/31	Sgt. McKinney/WPD (Meeting)	10:00 AM – 12:00 PM

1898 CENTENNIAL FOUNDATION INVOLVEMENT
BERTHA B. TODD

January 1998 – December 1998

DATE	EVENT	TIME
1/8	Coast 97.3/Rhonda Bellamy's Radio Show (Presentation)	7:00 AM
1/13	Hubert Eaton Memorial Committee (Meeting) (Distributed materials & answered questions)	11:30 AM
1/14	Martin Luther King, III Program/UNC-W (Distributed materials)	8:00 PM
1/15	Group conducting survey from Durham (Met & distributed materials)	6:00 PM
1/16	WAAV/Don Ansell's Radio Show (Presentation)	8:30 AM
1/17	1898 Centennial Foundation/Brogden Hall (Opening Ceremony)	4:00 PM
1/20	1898 Ad Hoc Committee/St. Stephen Church (Meeting)	4:00 - 6:00 PM
1/20	1898 Centennial Foundation Executive Council (Call Meeting)	7:00 PM
1/21	St. James Episcopal Church (Presentation preparation meeting)	6:30 PM
1/22	UNC-W Foundation (Meeting) (Distributed materials)	12:00 PM
1/25	St. James Episcopal Church (Panel Discussion) (Other panel members - Barbara Sullivan, Thomas Wright, Rev. Jack Ormond, & Kenneth Davis)	10:00 AM
1/27	North Fourth Street Partnership (Board Meeting)	6:30 PM
1/28	Phil Harvey (Meeting)	2:00 PM
1/29	Drama Committee (Meeting)	10:00 AM
1/30	Presbyterian Dialogue Group	10:00 AM
2/4	Civitans Group (Presentation)	12:50 PM
2/4	Wilmington Black & White Session	7:30 PM
2/12	Wilmington Black & White Session	7:30 PM
2/13	Mary Alice Jervay Thatch (Meeting)	10:00 AM

1898 CENTENNIAL FOUNDATION INVOLVEMENT
BERTHA B. TODD

January 1998 – December 1998
(continued)

DATE	EVENT	TIME
2/15	St. John's Episcopal Church	11:00 AM
2/16	"The Talented Tenth" Panel Discussion	3:00 - 5:00 PM
2/16	"The Young at Heart Club" & Nayo Watkins (Meeting)	11:00 AM
2/16	"The Harvard Jennings" Radio Talk Show	2:00 PM
2/19	Wilmington Black & White Session	7:30 PM
2/20	Hugh MacRae (Meeting)	11:00 AM
2/20	1898 Executive Committee (Meeting)	9:45 AM
2/26	Wilmington Black & White Session	7:30 PM
3/10	1898 Executive Committee (Meeting)	
3/13	Economic Development Committee (Meeting)	8:00 AM
3/15	Booksigning at Books-A-Million	2:00 PM
3/16	Doug Tanner & Angela Bryant (Meeting)	8:30 AM
3/20	Cape Fear Rotary Club (Presentation)	7:30 AM
3/20	"Let My People Go" (Presentation) Community Arts Center	8:00 PM
3/24	1898 Centennial Foundation (Annual Meeting)	6:30 PM
3/27	Murial Rose (Interview)	3:00 PM
3/31	YWCA (Dialogue Session)	6:30 PM
4/2	Hugh Morton into The Walk of Fame (Induction)	6:45 PM
4/2	Wilmington Black & White Session	7:30 PM
4/14	YWCA (Dialogue Session)	6:30 PM
4/20	1898 Executive Committee (Meeting)	7:00 PM
4/21	YWCA (Dialogue Session)	6:30 PM
4/23	Caletha Powell (Breakfast Meeting)	7:00 AM
4/24	Mayor Hamilton Hicks (Meeting)	9:00 AM

1898 CENTENNIAL FOUNDATION INVOLVEMENT
BERTHA B. TODD

January 1998 – December 1998
(continued)

DATE	EVENT	TIME
4/25	Ministers & Community Leaders (Meeting)	8:00 AM
4/27	Christian Science Monitor Journalist (Meeting)	2:00 PM
4/27	Hugh MacRae (Meeting)	3:15 PM
4/29	Caletha Powell & Others (Meeting)	5:30 PM
4/30	Economic Development Committee (Meeting)	7:30 PM
5/2	Caletha Powell & Others – Town Hall (Meeting)	7:20 AM
5/12	Plantation Village (Presentation)	4:00 PM
5/20	Chancellor James Leutze (UNC-W)	10:00 AM
5/20	1898 Centennial Foundation (Meeting)	10:00 AM
5/21	CEO Corning Representative (Meeting)	8:30 AM
5/21	1898 Executive Committee (Meeting)	7:00 PM
5/22	1898 Committee (Meeting)	1:00 PM
5/26	Lifewise- 5th Anniversary (1898 Exhibit)	10:00 AM
5/27	ARCH Meeting	1:00 PM
5/27	1898 Executive Committee (Meeting)	7:30 PM
6/1	Fund Raising Committee (Meeting)	4:30 PM
6/2	1898 Executive Board Meeting	6:00 PM
6/4	1898 Executive Board Meeting	7:00 PM
6/6	Meeting	7:00 AM
6/11	Chamber of Commerce (Meeting)	8:00 AM
6/13	Bahai' Picnic at Greenville Park	10:00 AM
6/16	1898 Executive Committee (Meeting)	7:00 PM
6/17	Rob Gerlach (Meeting)	3:00 PM
6/18	Hugh MacRae (Meeting)	11:00 AM
6/25	Committee Meeting	6:00 PM
6/22 - 7/5	Boston, MA - The Links, Incorporated/National Meeting	

(Made an effort to distribute 1898 Newsletters to Link Members).

1898 CENTENNIAL FOUNDATION INVOLVEMENT
BERTHA B. TODD

January 1998 – December 1998
(continued)

DATE	EVENT	TIME
7/5 – 7/10	Chicago, IL – Alpha Kappa Alpha Sorority, Incorporated National Meeting	
	(Made an effort to distribute 1898 Newsletters to Sorority Members).	
7/13	Hugh MacRae & Hugh Morton (Telephone calls)	
7/14	YWCA (Dialogue Session)	7:30 PM
7/15	Screen Gems Studio (Presentation)	6:00 PM
7/15	Economic Development Committee	7:00 PM
7/18	North Fourth Street (Street Fair)	3:00 PM
7/20	Fund Raising Committee (Meeting)	4:00 PM
7/20	Church of the Good Shepherd (Dialogue Session)	7:30 PM
7/23	UNC-W Foundation (Meeting)	12:00 PM
7/25	Church of the Good Shepherd (Dialogue Session)	7:30 PM
7/29	1898 Centennial Foundation (Meeting)	5:00 PM
7/30	Dr. John Morris – NHCS Superintendent	4:00 PM
8/4	Fund Raising Committee (Meeting)	2:00 PM
8/5	Chamber of Commerce (Meeting)	8:00 AM
8/5	Minority Businesses (Meeting)	6:30 PM
8/6	1898 Centennial Foundation (Meeting)	6:00 PM
8/6	Dr. Wooley/Cape Fear Museum	7:30 PM
8/6	Alex Manley/Cape Fear Museum	7:30 PM
8/12	Bolton Anthony (Meeting)	11:30 AM
8/12	Bolton Anthony & Don Ansell (Meeting)	12:00 PM
8/13	Chamber of Commerce (Meeting)	8:00 AM
8/13	Economic Development Committee (Meeting)	7:00 PM
8/15	Henry Weyerhauser (Meeting)	7:00 PM
8/16	Reconciliation Committee Picnic	2:00 PM
8/17	Fund Raising Committee (Meeting)	2:00 PM

1898 CENTENNIAL FOUNDATION INVOLVEMENT
BERTHA B. TODD

January 1998 – December 1998
(continued)

DATE	EVENT	TIME
8/18	Drama Committee (Meeting)	10:00 AM
8/18	1898 Centennial Foundation (Meeting)	2:30 PM
8/18	Nations Bank (Meeting)	3:30 PM
8/18	Economic Development Committee (Meeting)	6:30 PM
8/21	Fund Raising Committee (Meeting)	7:30 AM
8/22	Black Leadership (Meeting)	8:00 AM
8/25	Education Committee (Meeting)	4:00 PM
9/1	Chancellor James Leutze (Meeting)	11:30 AM
9/1	Drama Committee (Meeting)	2:00 PM
9/1	1898 Executive Committee	7:00 PM
9/2	Economic Development (Conference)	7:30 AM
9/9	NC Legislature/Black Caucus (Presentation)	4:00 PM
9/22	Lawrence Epps (Meeting)	10:00 AM
9/24	Anita Haynes (Book Review Series)	7:00 PM
9/25	Bolton Anthony & Francine DeCoursey	3:00 PM
9/27	St. Matthew Lutheran Church (Presentation)	10:0 AM
9/27	"Friends of David Walker" Celebration	3:00 PM
9/29	Pearsall Memorial Church (Distributed materials)	6:00 PM
10/1	Wes Beckner & Bolton Anthony	8:00 AM
10/1	Hannah Gage (Meeting)	10:00 AM
10/2	Church Women United (Presentation)	9:30 AM
10/6	Fund Raising Committee (Meeting)	4:00 PM
10/8	Chamber of Commerce (Meeting)	8:00 AM
10/8	Hugh MacRae (Meeting)	9:30 AM

1898 CENTENNIAL FOUNDATION INVOLVEMENT
BERTHA B. TODD

January 1998 – December 1998
(continued)

DATE	EVENT	TIME
10/15	Laura Padget (Presentation preparation)	
10/17	Barnes & Noble (Booksigning)	7:00 PM
	(Dr. Leon Prather)	
10/20	WWAY Television Studio (Talk Show)	1:00 PM
10/21	Associated Press (Meeting)	
10/21	Al Corbett (Meeting)	
10/23	UNC-W 1898 Symposium	9:00 – 3:00 PM
10/24	UNC-W 1898 Symposium	9:00 – 3:00 PM
10/27	Hargrove (Interview)	4:00 PM
11/2	Katherine Moore (Meeting)	4:00 PM
11/4	Emergency Meeting	3:00 PM
11/5	Drama – "No More Tears"	
11/6	Bellamy Mansion	
11/9	Rehearsal for November 10th	7:30 PM
11/10	Commemoration Day	7:00 PM
11/17	Charles Anderson, Wilmington Star News	3:00 PM
11/18	Emergency Meeting	
	(compilation of news magazine)	
12/3	Wachovia (Luncheon Meeting)	10:00 AM
12/3	First Baptist Church (Meeting)	7:30 PM
12/18	Peace Prize Presentation	12:00 PM

1898 CENTENNIAL FOUNDATION INVOLVEMENT
BERTHA B. TODD

January 1999 – June 1999

DATE	EVENT	TIME
1/7	1898 Executive Committee	
1/14	1898 Executive Council	7:30 PM
2/2	Cape Fear Museum (Lunch) (distributed materials)	12:00 PM
2/11	Tourism (Meeting)	10:00 AM
2/12	Cape Fear Museum	
2/16	Retired School Personnel (presented and distributed news magazine)	10:00 AM
2/23	1898 Nominating Committee (Meeting)	7:15 PM
2/25	Cape Fear Community College (presentation)	6:00 PM
3/3	Memorial Committee (Luncheon Meeting)	
3/15	Z. Smith Reynolds Foundation	11:30 AM
3/18	New York Graduate Student	2:30 PM
3/24	Dr. James Leutze (Conference Meeting)	3:30 PM
3/29	Honorary Co-chairs (Luncheon Meeting)	11:30 AM
3/31	Executive Committee (Meeting)	
4/3	Delores Williams (Meeting)	10:30 AM
4/8,9,10	Charlotte Conference (Distributed materials)	
4/13	United Methodist Church (Presentation)	10:00 AM
4/22	St. Andrews Covenant Presbyterian Church (Presentation)	6:15 PM
4/28	1898 Executive Committee	12:30 PM
4/29	1898 Executive Council	7:00 PM
5/7	Mary Gorto, City Manager (Meeting)	3:00 PM
5/18	Partners for Economic Inclusion (Seminar - Coastline Convention Center)	8:00 AM

1898 CENTENNIAL FOUNDATION INVOLVEMENT
BERTHA B. TODD

January 1999 – June 1999
(continued)

DATE	EVENT	TIME
5/24	Bolton Anthony & Windell Daniels (Luncheon Meeting)	12:00 PM
5/27	Committee Meeting	2:00 PM
6/4	Partners for Economic Inclusion (Wachovia)	8:00 AM

"The WHAT Mentality"
Chapter 14

*"But I believe we have a higher level of mentality within us,
but we have to use the power in the right way."*
-Tina Turner

In 1997 I attended a lecture at St. Mark's Episcopal Church where Dr. David Celceski, a noted historian and professor, was discussing blacks who lived in Wilmington and other parts of southeastern North Carolina in 1898. A question and answer period followed.

A native Wilmingtonian who was sitting directly in front of me said, "Now, I know just what happened during this period of violence. Some of us were run out of town, some of us were killed and those of us who remained found our places and stayed there."

His remarks succinctly conveyed the reason it had been so difficult in finding blacks to assist me during the turbulent desegregation era. His words stuck with me and, shortly thereafter, I coined the phrase "The 1898 Mentality" to describe people I encountered who continued to limit their interactions with others based on the prescribed customs of yesteryear.

All of us, no doubt, have met people with the "WHAT" Mentality.
- Those who have no regard for other ethnic groups living in the area,

- Those who are content to reminisce about the good ole' days rather than face current realities and **actively** pursue remedies,

- Those who constantly complain about how things are, but choose not to participate in helping to improve conditions.

- Those who seek to remain in contact with "people like me" instead of reaching out to those who are not like them, and

- Those who are afraid of "upsetting the apple cart" when efforts are made to balance the playing field.

This mentality was peculiar to some Wilmington natives and readily apparent to those of who moved here from other places. Our interactions were not burdened by the profound effect the 1898 coup d'état had on the native families that remained.

Fortunately, between 1952 and 2010, I have also met from many natives who refused to succumb to this mindset or have worked to shed these inhibitions. And it is to them that I would like to pay special tribute for giving of themselves for the betterment of all in the greater Wilmington region.

The word "WHAT" is in no way related to the acronym for Wilmington Health Access for Teens, founded by Connie Parker, whom I have long respected for her impassioned work in the healthcare field. In addition to WHAT, she was instrumental in the establishment of New Hanover Regional Medical Center's Hospitality House, and she presently serves as executive director of the NC School Community Health Alliance, where she advocates for school health centers across the state. Ms. Parker is a recipient of the *Star News'* 2010 Lifetime Achievement Award.

A Tribute to Deceased Participants

Baskervill, Lillian Gladys Whiteman

New Hanover County Schools (Educator); Tapestry, Inc. Board of Directors; Ministers' Wives, The Alumnae Chapter of Delta Sigma Theta Sorority, Chestnut Street Presbyterian

Berry, Jr., Lisbon

Civil Rights Attorney; New Hanover County Airport Commissioner; Thalian Hall Center for the Performing Arts; Board of Community Penalties; NAACP Life Member; Board of Directors' Community Boys & Girls Club (Chairman)

*Spouse (Shirley Berry (living))** has contributed greatly to Southeastern North Carolina. Ms. Berry was not born in any of the counties used in the established criteria.

Boone, Martha Blanks

New Hanover County Schools (Educator); The Links, Incorporated (Southern Area Director); Alpha Psi Omega Chapter of Alpha Kappa Alpha Sorority, Incorporated; Chestnut Street Presbyterian

Boykin, Hartford Edwin

New Hanover County Schools (Employee); World War II Veteran; North Carolina Magistrate Judge; Licensed Pilot; St. Mark Episcopal

Bryant, Thelma Brewington

New Hanover County Schools (Educator); Cape Fear Chapter of The American Red Cross; The Wilmington Alumnae Chapter of Delta Sigma Theta Sorority, Incorporated; Chestnut Street Presbyterian

Bryant, William (Bill) Dean

New Hanover County Schools (Educator); New Hanover County Retired Teachers (President); National Cash Register (Director of Personnel); Greensboro City Schools Vocational Education (Director); Omega Psi Phi Fraternity, Incorporated; Chestnut Street Presbyterian

Burnett, E. William

RR Taylor Homes (Manager); US Postal Service (Postman); St. Mark's Episcopal; Civic & Community Volunteer; Omega Psi Phi Fraternity; Chestnut Street Presbyterian

*Spouse (Anna Gardner Burnett). She contributed much to New Hanover County.

Mrs. Burnett was not born in any of the counties used in the established criteria.

Chestnut, Caronell Carter

New Hanover County Schools (Educator); New Hanover Regional Medical Center (Board of Trustees); Cape Fear Area United Way (Board of Directors); Family Service Traveler's Aid (Board of Directors); Women in Action for the Prevention of Violence and Its Causes (Treasurer); The Wilmington Alumnae Chapter of Delta Sigma Theta Sorority, Incorporated

Childs, William (Bill) Thomas

City of Wilmington Juvenile Court (Probation Officer); New Hanover County Schools (School Attendance Officer); NC Self Improvement Center (Chief Court Counselor); Greater Wilmington Chamber of Commerce; Omega Psi Phi Fraternity; Cape Fear Rotary Club; New Hanover County Department of Aging (Advisory Board); 1898 Centennial Foundation, Inc.

Crosby, Charles

Crosby Taxi Cab Company (Owner); One of the 1st Black Businesses in Southeastern North Carolina since 1898.

Davis, Derrick

UNC-Wilmington (Professor Emeritus); City of Wilmington Parks & Recreation (Director); NC Recreation & Parks Society (President/1st Black Elected); Cape Fear Memorial Hospital (Board of Trustees); Arts Council of the Lower Cape Fear (Board of Directors); Wilmington Housing Authority (Board of Directors); New Hanover County Senior Citizens (Board of Directors)

Davis, Bennye Newell

Davis Funeral Home (Co-owner & Director); Wilmington Alumnae Chapter Delta Sigma Theta Sorority, Incorporated; The Wilmington Chapter of The Links, Incorporated; Community & Civic Volunteer

Davis, French I.

Davis Funeral Home (Owner & Director); Kappa Alpha Psi Fraternity; Community & Civic Volunteer

Evans, Bredell
Federal Express Airlines (Captain)

Finley, James Daniel
Finley's Driver Training School (Owner); The only driver training school in North Carolina for a number of years.

Forden, Harry
North 4th Street Partnership (Organizer); Community Activist & Civic Volunteer

Freeman, Mae Rachel
New Hanover County Schools' Board of Education; Civic Volunteer

Hall, Rebecca
New Hanover County Schools (Educator); New Hanover County Home Extension Agency (Agent)

Hatcher, William (Buddy)
New Hanover County Schools (Teacher, Principal); Community & Civic Volunteer

Howie, Jr., Samuel Joseph
New Hanover County Schools (Teacher, Assistant Principal, Principal, Assistant Superintendent); NC Secondary Committee for the Southern Association of Colleges and Schools (Consultant); Community Boys' Club (Board of Directors); Board of Family Services Travelers' Aid; Cape Fear Area United Way (Board of Directors); Phi Delta Kappa Education Fraternity; St. Luke AME Zion

*Spouse (**Lydia Howie, living**). She has contributed much to New Hanover County. Ms. Howie was not born in any of the counties used in the established criteria.

Jervay, Thomas C.
The Wilmington Journal (Owner/Editor)

Jervay, Jr. Thomas C.
The Wilmington Journal (Advertising Manager/Photographer); Co-authored a publication with Hugh Morton on the life of Meadowlark Lemon as a fundraiser for the Community Boys' and Girls' Club.

Johnson, Dorothy Jackson
New Hanover County Schools (Educator); New Hanover County Board of Education (Member)

Jordan, Jr. Luther Henry

Jordan Funeral Home (Owner & president); Wilmington City Councilman (Mayor Pro-Tem); North Carolina Senator/7ᵗʰ District; NC Legislative Black Caucus (Chairman); Omega Psi Phi Fraternity, Incorporated; Chestnut Street Presbyterian

Keith, Eddie Joel

Keith's Dry Cleaners (Owner); Realtor - One of the first of two blacks in the real estate business in Southeastern North Carolina since 1898.; Kappa Alpha Psi Fraternity, Incorporated; Chestnut Street Presbyterian

*Spouse (Jeanne Barksdale Keith Harris (living). She has contributed much to New Hanover County. Ms. Harris was not born in any of the counties used in the established criteria.

King, Addie Whiteman

New Hanover Regional Medical Center (Volunteer); New Hanover County Department of Social Services (Volunteer); Pine Forest Cemetery (Board of Directors); Educator; Tapestry, Incorporated (Board of Directors); Cape Fear Chapter of The American Red Cross (Volunteer); Chestnut Street Presbyterian

Lowe, Sr., William Grady

New Hanover County Schools (Educator); Community & Civic Volunteer

Mallette, Henry

Mallette's Window Cleaning and Janitorial Service – The 1ˢᵗ in Southeastern North Carolina

Merrick, Winslow

Continued to manage his Uncle's (also named "Winslow Merrick") barbershop at 315 North Front Street until it was destroyed by fire in the 1970s. The Merrick Males were businessmen who opened several barbershops in 1909. Their clientele were white businessmen who had offices in the area of Front Street. Taken from *Strength Through Struggle* by William M. Reaves

Moore, Delores Foy

New Hanover County Schools (Employee); New Hanover County Branch of NAACP (President); Community activist

Moore, Mary Quick

New Hanover County Schools (Educator); Community Boys' & Girls' Club (Board of Directors); Las Amigas, Incorporated (Co-Founder of National Organization); Community volunteer

Murphy, William E.

City of Wilmington Department of Parks and Recreation (Athletic Director); Mentored and coached many young males and females in football and softball in New Hanover County

McDuffie, William

Organized tenants in Wilmington Housing Projects; Organized the 1st NAACP Youth Chapter; Historic Preservation Society (Chairman); Worked closely with Martin Luther King, Jr. Parade and Activities

McGowan, Isabel Boney

New Hanover County Schools (Educator); Macedonia Missionary Baptist; Eastern Stars; Grand Orders of Salem; Williston Alumni Association; Wilmington Community Association; New Hanover County Senior Citizen Fellowship (President)

Norman, George Norwood

North Carolina Security Commission (Representative); UNC-Wilmington Seahawks' Club (Lifetime Member); Retired Governmental Employees' Association

Shaw, Jr. Willie

John H. Shaw's Funeral Home (Owner); Musician; Omega Psi Phi Fraternity, Incorporated

Shoeber, Lillian

New Hanover County Public Library (Librarian); *Began in 1942; retired from the Red Cross Street Branch in 1958; Public libraries were integrated in 1962; Father (Dr. James Francis Shoeber; 1st black physician to practice in the state of North Carolina; Chestnut Street Presbyterian

*Taken from *Strength through Struggle* by William Reaves

Swain, Ernest A.

New Hanover County Schools (Principal/Three Elementary Schools); World War II Veteran

Upperman, Callie Smith

New Hanover County Schools(Better Schools Committee); The Wilmington Chapter of The Links, Incorporated; Fannie Norwood Home Board of Directors; The Wilmington Chapter of Jack & Jill of America, Inc.; Chestnut Street Presbyterian

*Spouse (Dr. Leroy W. Upperman) contributed greatly to Southeastern North Carolina. Dr. Upperman was not born in any of the counties used in the established criteria.

Wheeler, Dr. William J.

1st African American Ophthalmologist in Southeastern North Carolina.

NOTE: Drs. Eaton, Gray, Roane and Upperman were not born in Southeastern North Carolina. They relocated to New Hanover County as adults.

White, Kenneth C.

New Hanover County Schools (Principal/Several elementary & middle schools); Community & Civic Volunteer; Refree – basketball

Whitted, Laverne Davis

New Hanover County Schools (Educator); UNC-Wilmington Department of Education (Employee); Bellamy Mansion (Board of Directors)

Wright, Carrie Taylor

New Hanover County Schools (Educator); YWCA (Board of Directors); Tapestry Theatre, Incorporated (Board of Directors); Chestnut Street Presbyterian (Grandfather, Henry Taylor, was one of the founders of Chestnut Street Presbyterian. He was also one of the builders of the Bellamy Mansion.)

A Tribute to Living Participants

Barfield, Janice Grainger

PRESENT – Mary Kay Cosmetics (Senior Sales Director)

PAST – New Hanover Regional Medical Center Hospitality House; Thalian Hall Performing Arts (Board of Directors); Elderhaus (Board of Directors); YWCA (Board of Directors)

Barfield, Joe

PRESENT – Real Estate Developer

PAST – New Hanover County Commissioner

Barfield, Jonathan

PRESENT – New Hanover County Commissioners (Vice Chairman); Barfield & Associates Reality, LLC (Owner); Cape Fear Council of Government; Cape Fear Museum (Advisory Board); Cape Fear Public Transportation Authority; Lower Cape Fear River (Advisory Board); New Hanover County Board of Health; New Hanover County "Smart Start" Program (Board of Directors); Southeastern Center Area (Board of Directors)

PAST – New Hanover County Human Relations Commission; Cape Fear Habitat for Humanity (Board of Directors); Affordable Housing Coalition of Southeastern North Carolina (Chairman); New Hanover County Children's Museum (Board of Directors)

Beatty, Harold

PRESENT – New Hanover County Branch of NAACP (President); American Heritage Tours, Incorporated (Co-owner)

PAST – Pfizer, Incorporated (Foreman); US Navy (Chief Petty Officer)

Beatty, Karen Clay

PRESENT – "Focus on Leadership" Initiative; New Hanover County NAACP (Executive Board)

PAST – New Hanover County Human Relations Commission

Bellamy, John

PRESENT – New Hanover County NAACP (2nd Vice President); New Hanover County Democratic Party (Executive Committee); New Hanover County Precinct #15 (1st Vice Chair); New Hanover County Black Caucus; Willis Richardson Players (Board of Directors); Macedonia Missionary Baptist

PAST – US Navy; Corning (Machine Operator)

Bellamy, Rhonda

PRESENT – Cumulus Broadcasting's Wilmington Market (News Director/WGNI, WMNX, WAAV, WWQQ, WKXB); The Black Arts Alliance(Co-founder); North Carolina Black Film Festival (Director); Cape Fear Habitat for Humanity(Board of Directors), Cameron Art Museum (Member); Wilmington Downtown, Inc. (Member); Eastern Area Radio Reading Service (EARRS/Member); New Hanover County Library Foundation (Member); North Carolina Arts Council's Wilmington (Steering Committee)

PAST – The Dreams Center for Arts Education (Founding Instructor); Domestic Violence Shelter and Services (Board of Directors); The Wilmington Children's Museum (Board of Directors); The City of Wilmington's African-American Heritage Commission (Charter Member), the Azalea Festival Multicultural Committee; The Mayor's Convention Center Task Force (Mayor Hamilton Hicks); The Mayor's Task Force on Arts and Cultural Affairs (Harper Peterson/Co-chair); *Moving Forward Together: A Community Remembers 1898* (Editor)

Bennetone, Sonya J.

PRESENT – Democratic Women of New Hanover County (President); City of Wilmington Commission on African-American History; New Hanover County NAACP; Rev. Isaiah J. Jackson Foundation, Inc. (Founder); Community Organizer for OFA

PAST – Democratic Party Precinct Chair CFO5; Martin Luther King, Jr. Celebration (2006-2008)

Bibbs, Julia

PRESENT – Retired Teachers of the Cape Fear Area; Macedonia Missionary Baptist; Civic Volunteer

PAST - New Hanover County Schools (Educator); New Hanover County Democratic Women (Chairman); Cape Fear Museum (Volunteer); YWCA (Board of Directors; Retired Teachers of the Cape Fear Area (President)

Boykin, Patrick

PRESENT – First Citizens (Business Banker/ Vice-President); Greater Wilmington Sports Hall of Fame (Executive Committee); Cape Fear Council Boy Scouts of America (Executive Board); New Beginnings Christian; Kappa Alpha Psi Fraternity; Giblem Lodge #2 PHA/ Masonic Lodge; YMCA (Board of Directors)

PAST – Cape Fear Council Boy Scouts of America (Field Director); Pursuit of a degree

Boykin, William

PRESENT – John H. Shaw's Funeral Home (Manager)

PAST – Jordan Funeral Home (Manager); Ordained Minister

Bragg, Sarah

PRESENT – Bragg Catering Business (Owner)

PAST – Sarah's Kitchen and Restaurant

Braye, Lydia Davis

PRESENT – Retired; Alpha Psi Omega Chapter of Alpha Kappa Alpha Sorority, Incorporated; The Wilmington Chapter of The Links, Incorporated

PAST – The Saint Mary Catholic Pre-School (Principal); Smart Start Partnership for Children (Board of Directors); Returned to New Hanover County

*Spouse (Lt. Colonel James Braye)** has contributed greatly to Southeastern North Carolina. Lt. Colonel Braye was not born in any of the counties used in the established criteria.

Brewington Code, Carmen

PRESENT – North Carolina Retired School Personnel (Chairman/Constitution & By-Laws Committee); The Wilmington Alumnae Chapter of Delta Sigma Theta Sorority, Incorporated; Chestnut Street Presbyterian

PAST – New Hanover County Schools (Educator) Wilmington Alumnae Chapter of Delta Sigma Theta Sorority, Incorporated (President); New Hanover County Chapter of NC Retired School Personnel (President); New Hanover Association of Educators (President, Vice-President); New Hanover County Association of Classroom Teachers (President, Vice-President)

Briggs, Hollis

PRESENT – Figure Island Yacht Restaurant (Chef); The Family and Neighborhoods Institute of North Carolina, Incorporated (President); Martin Luther King, Jr. Celebration (President); St. Philip AME Zion

PAST – Returned to New Hanover County; Wilmington Tree Commission; Campaign Manager (several political candidates)

Brown, Brenda

PRESENT – Verizon (Human Resource Consultant); Community & Civic Volunteer

PAST – New Hanover Regional Medical Center (Employee); Alpha Psi Omega Chapter of Alpha Kappa Alpha Sorority, Incorporated

Brown, Carl

PRESENT – Cape Fear Community College (Vice-President, Institutional Services); New Hanover Regional Medical Center (Board of Trustees)

PAST – US Air Force School of Aviation Medicine (Laboratory Technician); US Atomic Energy Commission (Radio Chemist); New Hanover County Commissioners (Former Candidate); Returned to New Hanover County

Brown, Cynthia

PRESENT – New Hanover County Community Action, Incorporated (CEO/Executive Director); UNC-W School of Nursing (Advisory Board); UNC-W Cameron School of Business/Executive Network; Historic Wilmington Foundation (Board of Trustees); Pine Forest Cemetery (Board of Trustees); Alpha Psi Omega Chapter of Alpha Kappa Alpha Sorority, Incorporated; The Wilmington Chapter of The Links, Incorporated; "People to People" Ambassador Program; St. Stephen AME

PAST – Returned to New Hanover County; Downtown Wilmington Rotary Club; New Hanover County "Smart Start"; The Wilmington Chapter of The Links, Incorporated (President)

Brown, Henry

PRESENT – State Farm Insurance (Agent); Mt. Olive AME

PAST – New Hanover County Insurance Advisory Commission; Civic & Community Volunteer

Bunting, Simuel and Delores

PRESENT – Sim's Quick Release Bonding Company (Owners)

PAST – Civic Volunteers

Byrd, Carl

PRESENT – New Hanover County (Community Affairs Specialist)

PAST – New Hanover County Human Relations Commission (CEO/Director)

Byrd, Grace Mosley

PRESENT – Alpha Psi Omega Chapter of Alpha Kappa Alpha, Sorority Incorporated; St. Mark's Episcopal; National Alliance of Black School Educators; North side Resource Center (Advisory Board)

PAST – New Hanover County Schools (Educator); Educational Advisory Commission (Governor James Martin); Cape Fear Museum (Board of Trustees)

Campbell-Dereef, Pamela

PRESENT – Constituents Service Assistant Community Outreach Liaison for Congressman Mike McIntyre/7th Congressional District; Social Security Housing Urban and Development – United States Department of Labor (Special Case Worker); African American Episcopal AME Church of the Southern District

PAST – Representative (Retired Congressman Charlie Rose/7th Congressional District; Internal Revenue Veterans Administration; United States Military, Immigration, Federal Communication Commission (Social Security); United States Passport; Farmers Home Administration; United States Postal; Department of Education; Corp of Engineers

Cliette, Richard

PRESENT – Retired; Civic Volunteer

PAST – Friends of David Walker (President); City of Wilmington Code Enforcement (Officer)

*Spouse (Patricia Cliette) has contributed greatly to Southeastern North Carolina. Mrs. Cliette was not born in any of the counties used in the established criteria.

Clinton, Lottie Drye

PRESENT – North Carolina State Employees' Association; North Carolina Association for Retired Government Employees'

PAST – UNC-Wilmington Accounting Department; NC State of Ports Authority (Administrative Supervisor); Intermodal Systems (Administrative Supervisor, developed this system, the 1st of its kind in the United States); New Hanover County Board of Elections (Election Assistant); American Business Women/Liberty Light Azalea Chapter (President); New Hanover County Community Health Center (Board of Directors); City of Wilmington Service to Disabled Persons; Cape Fear Community College (Curriculum Advisory Board); Cape Fear Museum (Advisory Board); North Carolina 1898 Race Riot Commission

Cooper-Freeman, Cheryl

PRESENT – BB & T (Banking Officer/Small Business Services); Mt. Pilgrim Baptist; Price Cathedral AME Zion; Civic Volunteer

PAST – Greater Wilmington Chamber of Commerce; Black Expo Committee

Cooper, Freddie

PRESENT – New Hanover County Schools (Apprenticeship Coordinator); Price Cathedral AME Zion; Mt. Pilgrim Baptist

PAST – ROCAME (Coordinator & Board Member)

Daniels, Euran S.

PRESENT – Relocated; Regional Transportation Consultant; Project Management and Event Planning; Daniels Tours, LLC (Manager)

PAST - Pursuing a degree

Daniels, Wilma

PRESENT – Daniels Development Corporation, LLC (President); Daniels Tours, LLC (President);

William Hooper Apartments (Owner); Smart Shop Dress Shop (Manager); YWCA (Board of Directors); New Hanover County Health Center (Advisory Board); Habitat for Humanity (Advisory Board); UNC-Wilmington Athletics Teal Club; Cape Fear Community College (Foundation Board Member); New Hanover County Chapter of the NAACP; Macedonia Missionary Baptist

PAST – Greater Wilmington Area Chamber of Commerce (Executive Board)

Davis, Delores
PRESENT – UNC-Wilmington (Administrative Associate/Office of Admissions); Macedonia Baptist; Alpha Psi Omega Chapter of Alpha Kappa Alpha Sorority, Incorporate

PAST – Girls' Incorporated (Board of Directors); Alpha Psi Omega Chapter of Alpha Kappa Alpha Sorority, Incorporated (President);

Davis, EB
PRESENT – North side Resource Center/6th Sense Community Skills Center (Director/Founder); Wilmington Precinct #26 (Chairman); ILA Local 1426 International Longshoremen AFL/CIO (Executive Board Member); First Baptist

PAST – Wilmington Precinct #6 (Chairman); New Hanover County Democratic Party (Vice-President)

Davis, Harry
PRESENT – Professional Artist

PAST – US Office of Equal Opportunity and Civil Rights; US Armed Forces

Davis, John
PRESENT-Professional Photographer; St. Stephen AME Zion

PAST – Girls', Incorporated (Board of Directors); Human Relations Commission; 1898 Centennial Foundation; 1898 Foundation

*Spouse (**Barbara Ennett Davis**) has contributed a great deal to Southeastern North Carolina.

Davis, Joselia Mapson
PRESENT – Retired; Civic Volunteer; New Hanover County Precinct #10 (Chair); Saint Andrew AME Zion

PAST – New Hanover County Schools (Educator); Relocated; New Hanover County Black Caucus; New Hanover County NAACP

Davis, Karen Y.
PRESENT – Davis Funeral Home/Jordan Chapel (Owner); Greater Wilmington

Area Chamber of Commerce; Wilmington Alumnae Chapter of Delta Sigma Theta Sorority, Incorporated; The Wilmington Chapter of The Links, Incorporated; New Hanover County of the NAACP; The Cape Fear 50

PAST – YWCA (Board of Directors); Historic District Commission; North side Resource Center

Davis, Kenneth

PRESENT - New Hanover County Parks & Recreation (Advisory Commission); New Hanover County Community Action; Friends of Maides Park

PAST – 1898 Centennial Foundation; 1898 Foundation; Commission of African-American History (Member & Chairman); North Carolina 1898 Race Riot Commission

Davis, Jr., Russell

PRESENT – New Hanover County Public Defenders' Office (Assistant Public Defender); First Citizens' Bank (Board of Directors); Cape Fear Community College; (Advisory Board/ Paralegal Program); St. Luke AME Zion

PAST – Civic Volunteer; Represented indigent defendants; Davis & Davis Attorneys at Law; Shaw University CAPE Program (Criminal Justice Instructor); North Carolina Public Television (Board of Directors); North Carolina Child Advocacy Commission (State and Local Boards); Cape Fear Museum (Board of Directors)

*Spouse (Regina Davis) has contributed greatly to Southeastern North Carolina. Mrs. Davis was not born in any of the counties used in the established criteria.

Davis Graham, Sadie

PRESENT – Davis Funeral Home/Jordan Memorial Chapel (Vice-President, CEO); American Cancer Society; Bellamy Mansion (Board of Directors); Elderhaus (Board of Directors); Greater Wilmington Chamber of Commerce; The Wilmington Chapter of The Links, Incorporated; The Wilmington Alumnae Chapter of Delta Sigma Theta Sorority, Incorporated

PAST – Returned to Southeastern North Carolina

DeShields, Dorothy

PRESENT – New Hanover County Schools' Board of Education; The Lower Cape Fear Chapter of League of Women Voters; New Hanover County Democratic Party; Cape Fear Area of United Way (Planning & Investment Committee); YWCA (Women of Achievement Committee); Mt. Nebo Baptist ; The Wilmington Chapter of The Links, Incorporated

PAST – UNC-Wilmington Watson School of Education (Instructor); Community Boys' and Girls' Club (Board of Directors); New Hanover County Schools (Administrator)

DeShields, Francine

PRESENT – Returned to New Hanover County; The Wilmington Chapter of The Links, Incorporated; Ebenezer Missionary Baptist

PAST - US Postal Service (Customer Service Supervisor/Acting Manager); Girls', Incorporated (Board of Directors); National Association of Postal Supervision (Treasurer for 10 years)

Drain, Samuel Cecil

PRESENT – Adkins-Drain Funeral Home (Owner)

PAST – US Postal Service (Postman)

Spouse (Allene Drain) has contributed greatly to Southeastern North Carolina. Mrs. Drain was not born in any of the counties used in the established criteria.

Drain Greene, Constance

PRESENT – Adkins Drain Funeral Service (Director/Manager); The Wilmington Chapter of The Links, Incorporated; St. Stephen AME

PAST – Returned to New Hanover County

Emerson, Dr. Diane E.

PRESENT – New Hanover County Schools Pre-K Education (Director); Dorothy B. Johnson Pre-K Center (Principal)

PAST – Returned to New Hanover County; NC General Assembly/Office of the Speaker (Education Director); NC Department of Public Instruction (Education Consultant); 1898 Foundation Committee; United Way (Vision Council); New Hanover County School System (Educator)

Ennett, Kathryn B.

PRESENT - Retired

PAST – New Hanover Regional Medical Center (Word Clerk); New Hanover County Senior Center (RSVP); St. Mary Catholic School (Library Assistant); Knights of Columbus Auxiliary (Secretary); Catholic Daughters (Regent); League of Women Voters; New Hanover County Democratic Party; Elderhaus; Cape Fear Museum (Receptionist & Docent)

Epps, Lawrence

PRESENT - Larry's Florist (Owner/Operator)

PAST – New Hanover County Schools (Educator)

Faison, Jr., James H.

PRESENT – Retired Teachers of the Cape Fear Area; Relocated

PAST – New Hanover County Schools (Teacher); New Hanover County Schools (Director of Vocational Education); Cape Fear Community College (Instructor); Omega Psi Phi Fraternity

Faison, III, James H.

PRESENT – District Court Judge – 5th Judicial District (Serving New Hanover and Pender Counties); YMCA (Board of Directors); Ordained Minister; Community Boys' and Girls' Club (Board of Directors); Charter Day School (Board of Directors); NOTT Foundation (Advisory Board); The Family and Neighborhoods Institute of North Carolina, Inc. (Board of Directors)

PAST – Yahweh Center (Board of Directors); Alternative Dispute Resolution Center (Board of Directors)

Faison, Jimmy

PRESENT – Retired Teachers of the Cape Fear Area (President); New Hanover County Schools (Hearing Panel Board Member); Ordained Minister

PAST – New Hanover County Schools (Educator); Bellamy Mansion (Jon Konu Planning Board); Wilmington Historic Commission Researcher; Relocated to New Hanover County

Fennell, Alice Boykin

PRESENT – Sickle Cell Association (Board Chair/Member); NAACP (Life Member); US Navy (Retired Civil Service)

PAST – Returned to New Hanover County

Fennell, Jr., Homer W.

PRESENT – Civic Volunteer

PAST – Fennell's Florist (Owner); Fennell's Barbershop (Owner); OSHA (State Law Enforcement Safety Officer); City of Wilmington (Fireman); Longshoreman; New Hanover County Soil and Water Agency (Elected official)

Fennell, Janice Bryant

PRESENT – First Citizens' Bank (Bank Teller); The Wilmington NC Chapter of The Links, Incorporated; St. Luke AME Zion

PAST – Wilmington Housing Authority (Board of Directors); Wachovia/Wells Fargo (Employee); The Wilmington Chapter of The Links, Incorporated (President)

Fennell, Jerome

PRESENT – Property Management (Director); Kappa Alpha Psi Fraternity; St. Luke AME Zion

PAST – Community Boys' and Girls' Club (Board of Directors)

Fields, Jacqueline Delores

PRESENT – Retired; Chestnut Street Presbyterian Church

PAST – Cashier/Bookkeeper; Wilmington Housing Authority (Counselor)

Flowers, Gwendolyn Richardson

PRESENT – Realtor; Fair Housing Committee/Board of Realtors (Chairman); Historic Preservation Society Committee

PAST – Civic Volunteer

Franklin, Margaret

PRESENT – Wilmington Preparatory Academy (Principal/Dean); Mt. Olive AME; Community In Schools; Ordained Minister

PAST – Headstart (Teacher/Supervisor); New Hanover County Schools (Educator); Elderhaus, Inc. (Volunteer); Jack & Jill of America, Incorporated; The Wilmington Chapter of The Links, Incorporated

Fredlaw, Sr., Clarence

PRESENT – Fannie Norwood Home (Board of Directors); St. Stephen AME

PAST – City of Wilmington Police Department (Sgt./Professional Standards Division)

Fredlaw, Margaret Bailey

PRESENT – Fannie Norwood Home (CEO); Alpha Psi Omega Chapter of Alpha Kappa Alpha Sorority, Incorporated; The Wilmington Chapter of The Links, Incorporated; St. Stephen AME

PAST – Fannie Norwood Home (Chair/Board of Directors); Girls, Incorporated (Board of Directors); Community Arts Council

Freeman, William E.

PRESENT – International Longshoremen Association (Supervisor Team IL)

PAST – International Longshoremen Association #1426 (Executive Board); Seabreeze Heritage Committee; Freeman Park Advisory Committee

Fullwood, Ernest B.

PRESENT – Relocated

PAST – Senior Resident 5th District Superior Court Judge; New Hanover County Human Relations Commissions (Director); Fullwood & Morgan Attorneys at Law; North Carolina Central University (Professor of Law)

Fullwood, James (Woody)

PRESENT - Developer

PAST – 2nd Judicial Division Court (Chief Officer); New Hanover County (Intensive Probation & Parole Officer); US Army (Pay & Disbursement Specialist); Southeastern Mental Health/Mental Retardation/Substance Area (Board of Directors); New Hanover County Family Services (Board of Directors); Offender Aid Restorative, Incorporated (Board of Directors); Cape Fear Area United Way (Board of Directors); New Hanover County District Court Farm Committee (Founder/Chairman/Board of Directors)

Gailes-Crumdy, Marion

PRESENT – Relocated

PAST – New Hanover Regional Medical Center (Registered Nurse); *The Wilmington Journal* (Advertisement Sales); St. Luke AME Zion

Gailes-Mallette, Marlyn

PRESENT – Relocated

PAST – New Hanover County Schools (Educator); Council of Governments (Advisory Board); The Wilmington Alumnae Chapter of Delta Sigma Theta Sorority, Incorporated (President); Community Activist; St. Luke AME Zion

Garrison, Robert (Bob) Fuller

PRESENT – Retired; Civic Volunteer

PAST – City of Wilmington (Recreation Manager); New Hanover County Schools (Eliminating the Achievement GAP); Wilmington Access for Teens (WHAT); New Hanover County (Juvenile Justice Committee); US Army National Guard; NAACP (Life Member)

Gerald, Ethel Thomas

PRESENT – YMCA (Volunteer); New Hanover County Schools (Snipes' School Grandparent Volunteer); Mt. Zion AME Zion

PAST – UNC-Wilmington (Employee)

Grear, Cathy Davis

PRESENT – Greater Diversity News (President/Co-Owner & Publisher); The Spirit of Truth Ministry (Elder); The Next Realm in Glory Apostolic International Higher Praise Apostolic Center (Marketing Director); For Your Glory Ministries (Board Member); Alpha Kappa Alpha Sorority, Incorporated

PAST – In God's Name Mission Choir (Founder)

Grear, Joyce Theodora

PRESENT – Professional storyteller; The Family and Neighborhoods Institute of North Carolina, Inc. (Program Director); Macedonia Missionary Baptist

PAST – City of Wilmington (Parks and Recreation); Friends of Maides Park

Grear, Peter

PRESENT – Attorney at Law; Greater Diversity News (Co-Owner & Publisher); Community Activist

PAST – NC Black Leadership Caucus; 1898 Centennial Foundation; Partners for Economic Inclusion (Co-Founder)

Grear Brown, Gwendolyn

PRESENT – Retired; Civic Volunteer; New Hanover County Schools' Smart Start (Board of Directors)

PAST – Returned to New Hanover County; US Department of Defense; Office of the Inspector General; Director/Supervisor of Criminal Investigations

Greene, Sonja Bull

PRESENT – United Order of Tents/Royal Degree Circle (Financial Secretary); Warner Temple AME Zion; Precinct #29 (Secretary)

PAST – New Hanover County Schools (Secretary/Personnel/Secretary/Staff Development/Accountability/Chapter 1)

Gurganious, Lavern

PRESENT – Educational Programs and Projects (Volunteer)

PAST – New Hanover County Schools (Teacher/Assistant Principal/Principal); Educational Consultant; Baker and Daniels Consulting (Instructional Leadership Partner); The Family and Neighborhoods Institute of North Carolina, Inc. (Board of Directors); Volunteer (Educational Programs and Projects)

Hamilton, Gwendolyn Vernice

PRESENT – Wilmington Housing Authority (Director of Resources/Resident Services/Youth Build); Domestic Violence Shelter (Volunteer); Cape Fear Gospel Rescue Mission; A Better Community, Incorporated (Project Task Force); Williston Alumni Association (President); Mt. Nebo Missionary Baptist

PAST – Wilmington Housing Authority (Interim Executive Director); Wilmington Housing Authority (Tenant Selection Supervisor); *The Wilmington Journal* (Office Manager); New Hanover County Democratic Party (Office Manager); Bedford Fair (Credit Department); Shaw

University (Adjunct Professor); New Hanover County (Friends of the Library); New Hanover County Schools (Board Redistricting Committee); Community Boys' Club (Board of Directors); Girls' Incorporated (Board of Directors); Fannie Norwood Home (Board of Directors); YWCA (Board of Directors)

Hankins, James

PRESENT – J. Hankins Realty (Owner); J. Hankins Construction (Licensed General Contractor); Youth Build (Construction Manager) This is a program designed to teach construction skills to youth ages 16 – 24 who have dropped out of schools. Students also work toward completing their GEDs; The Family and Neighborhoods Institute of North Carolina, Inc. (President/Board of Directors); NAACP (Life Member)

PAST – New Hanover County Chapter of NAACP (President); Friends of *The Wilmington Journal* (Co-chair)

Hankins, Lethia S.

PRESENT – YWCA (Member & Volunteer); Cape Fear Community College (Board of Trustees); Alpha Psi Omega Chapter of Alpha Kappa Alpha Sorority, Incorporated; First Baptist

PAST – New Hanover County Public Library (Advisory Board); City of Wilmington (City Council); Voting Precinct #13 (Chairperson); Willis Richardson Players (Director); Wilmington Housing Authority (Chairperson); United Way of Lower Cape Fear; Retired Teachers of the Cape Fear Area; Cape Fear Museum Associates, Incorporated (Docent & Member); New Hanover County Democratic Women; NAACP (Education Committee); Human Relations Commission; 1898 Foundation (Co-chair); YWCA (Board of Directors); Creekwood Learning Center; Thalian Hall Center for Performing Arts (Board of Trustees); Cancer Community Outreach Board; Alpha Psi Omega Chapter of Alpha Kappa Alpha, Incorporated (President); New Hanover County Schools (Teacher)

Harris, Jr. Herbert

PRESENT – Consultant; Author; Public Speaker

PAST – Attorney at Law; 1898 Foundation (Co-chair); Community Action (Board of Directors)

Hayes, Ivey

PRESENT – Professional Artist

PAST – Community Volunteer

Hewett, Russell

PRESENT – New Hanover County Schools (Educator); "100 Black Men"; Williston Middle School (Volunteer Tutor); Good Shepard (Volunteer)

PAST – Returned to Southeastern North Carolina

Hill, Willie Rae Corbett
PRESENT – Cosmetologist; Sisters of Giblem Lodge #646; Ebenezer Baptist

PAST – Cape Fear Community College (Board of Directors); Returned to New Hanover County

Hines, Lewis
PRESENT – ILA Local #1426 International Longshoremen AFL/CIO; NAACP (Silver Life Member/Business Agent)

PAST – A. Philip Randolph Institute (President); Charlie O's Fashions (Owner); Slicks "n" Chicks, Incorporated (Owner)

Jackson, Russell
PRESENT – Adkins/Drain Funeral Home (Employee); St. Mark Episcopal

PAST – City of Wilmington (1st African American Fireman since 1898); DuPont (Operator)

*Spouse (Emma H. Jackson). Educator and administrator has contributed much to New Hanover County. She was not born in any of the counties used in the established criteria.

Jervay Tate, Katherine
PRESENT – Relocated

PAST – *The Wilmington Journal* (Editor/Publisher)

Jervay, Willie
PRESENT - Retired

PAST – *The Wilmington Journal* (Editor and Publisher)

Johnson, Carolyn
PRESENT – City of Wilmington (Attorney); St. Luke AME Zion

PAST – Returned to New Hanover County

Johnson, Flora Sampson
PRESENT – Civic Volunteer; Chestnut Street Presbyterian

PAST – New Hanover County Schools (Educator); Gregory School of Science, Math and Technology (Tutor); "Meals on Wheels"; China Plate Club (for Youth in Community); Jack and Jill of America, Inc.; Alpha Psi Omega Chapter of Alpha Kappa Alpha Sorority, Inc.; The Wilmington Chapter of The Links, Inc.; Daughters of Isis

*Spouse (Theodore Johnson, Sr.) has contributed greatly to Southeastern North Carolina. Mr. Johnson was not born in any of the counties used in the established criteria.

Johnson, Joyce Jackson

PRESENT – UNC-Wilmington Randall Library (Supervisor/Library Circulation)

PAST – Civic Volunteer

Kaazim, Ali

PRESENT – Nation of Islam (Minister Consultant); Ministerial Roundtable; YWCA (Race Relations Program); 100 Black Men; Wilmington Improvement Association

PAST – Million Man March (to Washington, DC)

Kane, Barbara Chestnut

PRESENT – New Hanover County Retired School Personnel (Vice-President); St. Mark Episcopal; The Wilmington Chapter of The Links, Incorporated; Alpha Psi Omega Chapter of Alpha Kappa Alpha Sorority, Incorporated

PAST – New Hanover County Schools (Educator); New Hanover County Human Relations Commission (Secretary, Co-chair, Chair); WAVE Transit Authority; Jack & Jill of America, Incorporated (Wilmington Chapter); Alpha Psi Omega Chapter of Alpha Kappa Alpha Sorority, Incorporated (Treasurer); The Wilmington Chapter of The Links, Incorporated (President, Vice-President, Treasurer)

*Spouse (Paul N. Kane) has contributed greatly to Southeastern North Carolina. Mr. Kane was not born in any of the counties used in the established criteria.

Lee, Carolyn Sumlin

PRESENT – "Elegant Accents" Catering Company (Owner/Operator); The Family and Neighborhoods Institute of North Carolina, Inc.: New Beginnings Christian

PAST – Civic Volunteer

Lee, Helena J.

PRESENT – Chestnut Street Presbyterian; Civic Volunteer

PAST – UNC-Wilmington – Upperman African American Cultural Center (1st Director); Cape Fear Community College (Director of Learning Lab); Alpha Psi Omega Chapter of Alpha Kappa Alpha Sorority, Incorporated; 1898 Centennial Foundation; City of Wilmington (Sister City Committee); African American Heritage Commission (Member); Presbytery of Coastal Carolina (1st African American female to serve as Associate Executive Presbyter)

Lennon, Rena

PRESENT – Davis Funeral Home/Jordan Memorial Chapel (Employee); Community Volunteer

PAST – New Hanover County Schools/Dale K. Spencer Building (Personnel Department/Receptionist)

Lewis, Barbara Shannon

PRESENT – Elderhaus (Board of Directors); Williston Alumni Association (Treasurer)

PAST – Wachovia/Wells Fargo (Banker); Children's Museum (Board of Directors); Cape Fear Museum (Board of Directors); Domestic Violence & Shelter (Board of Directors); Veterans of Foreign Wars (Board of Directors); Community Boys and Girls Club, Incorporated (Board of Directors)

Little, Lula

PRESENT - Las Amigas, Incorporated (President/Mentoring Programs at Bellamy and Gregory Elementary Schools); New Hanover County Schools' Retired School Personnel (Secretary); Retired Teachers of the Cape Fear Area; Alpha Psi Omega Chapter of the Alpha Kappa Alpha Sorority, Incorporated; Ebenezer Baptist

PAST – New Hanover County Department of Health Volunteers; Bellamy Mansion Program Committee; New Hanover County Schools (Teacher)

Lofton, Wayne

PRESENT – Community Boys' and Girls' Club (Executive Director/CEO); Ordained Minister

PAST – Returned to New Hanover County

Lomax, Diane Elizabeth

PRESENT – Domestic Violence Shelter and Services (Director of Operations); Cape Fear Association of Fundraising Professionals (Treasurer); Macedonia Missionary Baptist

PAST – Relocated to New Hanover County

Mallette, Andre

PRESENT – New Hanover County (Assistant County Manager)

PAST – Civic Volunteer

Mallette Sparrow, Angela

PRESENT – New Hanover County Regional Medical Center (Volunteer); Williston Alumni Choral Ensemble

PAST – WECT TV 6 (Community Relations/Black Advisory Board); The Jim Burns Show (Co-host); WWAY TV 3 (Reporter/Field Anchor/Interview Host); Wilmington Children's Museum (Board of Directors); Community Boys' and Girls' Club (Board of Directors); Jack & Jill of America, Incorporated; Challenge Academy (Coordinator/Afterschool Middle School Student Program)

MacCrae-Stevens, Louise Moore

PRESENT - Relocated

PAST – YWCA Phyllis Wheatley Branch (Director); Newly built YWCA (Director of Special Activities from 1974 until retirement)

MacRae, Linda

PRESENT – Retired; Civic Volunteer

PAST - UNC-Wilmington (Associate Director of Admissions); Domestic Violence Shelter (Board of Directors/Chair); Village at Greenfield (Workshop on Study Skills)

Melvin, Patricia

PRESENT - Senior Ambassador - International Embassy of Holiness, Incorporated

PAST – New Hanover County (Assistant County Manager); New Hanover County Crime Prevention Council; New Hanover County Criminal Justice Partnership (Advisory Board); New Hanover County Transportation Advisory Board (Director); Wilmington Health Access for Teens (WHAT); UNC-Wilmington's Historically Underutilized Business Advisory Board; Cape Fear Regional Community Development Corporation; North Carolina Azalea Festival (Co-Chairman, Multicultural Committee); Partners for Economic Inclusion; Good Friends of Wilmington (Executive Board); North Carolina Commission for Domestic Violence

Merrick, Velma H.

PRESENT – "Meals on Wheels" (Volunteer); New Hanover County Retired School Personnel; Retired Teacher of The Cape Fear; St. Stanislaus Catholic

PAST – Food Bank (Volunteer); Girls' Incorporated (Volunteer Tutor); New Hanover County Schools (Educator)

Metts, Owen

PRESENT – The Benefit Connection (Owner); Licensed Realtor/Broker/Certified Housing Counselor; Ordained Minister

PAST – Civic Volunteer; Developer

Monroe, Dr. Lee Everett

PRESENT – Shaw University (Director of Development)

PAST – Florida Memorial College (President); Paul Quincy College (President); Vorhees College (President); Shaw University/CAPE Program (Creator); Gregory Elementary School (Provided funding for literacy program); Community Boys' and Girls' Club (Chairman/ Board of Directors); Community Development Corporation (Assisted Wilmington Southside in obtaining 1.2 million dollars for weatherization purposes for residents.)

Moore, James

PRESENT – City of Wilmington (Deputy Police Chief); New Hanover County Smart Start Program (Board of Directors); North Carolina Police Executive Association; Coastal Carolina Chapter/100 Black Men of America

PAST – New Hanover County Human Relations Commission; New Hanover County Community Health Center; New Hanover County Community Action (Board of Directors); Community Boys' and Girls' Club (Board of Directors)

Moore, Katherine Bell

PRESENT - Relocated

PAST – Wilmington City Council/14 years (Mayor Pro Tem/Member); New Hanover County Schools (Educator); Eastern Delivery Service (Owner/Operator); UNC-Wilmington (Board of Trustees); Cape Fear Community College (Instructor); Women in Action for the Prevention of Violence and its Causes; Alpha Psi Omega Chapter of Alpha Kappa Alpha Sorority, Incorporated; The Wilmington Chapter of The Links, Incorporated

Moseley, Rosalind Moore

PRESENT – African American Heritage Foundation (Board of Directors); Alpha Kappa Alpha Sorority, Incorporated; 1898 Foundation (Secretary of Executive Committee)

PAST – Returned to New Hanover County

Moseley, Mary

PRESENT – The Family and Neighborhoods Institute of North Carolina, Incorporated (Founder); New Hanover County Schools Lakeside High School renamed The Mary S. Mosley Performance Learning Center; Alpha Kappa Alpha Sorority, Incorporated

PAST – Returned to New Hanover County

McCrimmon, Marvis

PRESENT – The Family and Neighborhoods Institute of North Carolina, Inc. (Volunteer); Zeta Phi Beta Sorority, Inc.; Ebenezer Baptist; Retired Teacher of the Cape Fear

PAST – New Hanover County Schools (Educator); Women in Action for the Prevention of Violence and Its Causes

McDonald, Alfredia

PRESENT – Wilmington Housing Authority (Board of Commissioners); Back to School Project (Coordinator)

PAST – 1898 Centennial Foundation; 1898 Foundation; Creekwood Development Association (President)

McGlone-Webb, Deidre

PRESENT – Suntrust Bank (Vice-President/Branch Manager); USS North Carolina Battleship Commission (Board Member); YWCA (Ex-Officio Board Member); North Carolina Azalea Festival (Chair/Sponsor Relations)

PAST – New Hanover County Friends of Human Relations (President); North Carolina Azalea Festival (Chair, Azalea Pride/Co-chair, Official Party/Assistant, to the 59th Festival President); SunTrust Triangle Diversity Site Council (Member and Corporate Diversity Facilitator); Alpha Psi Omega Chapter of Alpha Kappa Alpha Sorority, Inc.

McIntyre, Harris

PRESENT – New Hanover County Schools (Director/Safety & Hearing Officer); St. Paul AME; Omega Psi Phi Fraternity

PAST – US Army (Military Police); New Hanover County Schools (Teacher, Assistant Principal, Director of Custodial Services, Director of Facilities, Director of Support Services, Education & Training; Girls' Incorporated (Board of Directors); Cape Fear Area United Way (Appropriations Committee); Omega Psi Phi Fraternity, Incorporated (President, Vice-President, Secretary)

McLaurin, Kenneth

PRESENT – Relocated

PAST – New Hanover County Schools (Teacher, Assistant Principal, Principal); City of Wilmington (1st African American City Councilman elected since 1898)

McQueen, Jr., Joseph

PRESENT – Retired; Civic volunteer

PAST – New Hanover County (Sheriff) – Five successful elections for sheriff. Approximately three decades with the New Hanover County Sheriff's Department; New Hanover County Sheriff's Department (Chief of Detectives, Commander of Support Services Division); Governor James B. Hunt, Jr.'s Crime Commission; North Carolina Sheriff Trainers and Standards Council; SAFE Summer Project; DARE Project

Newsome, Mercedes Jones

PRESENT – Alpha Psi Omega Chapter of Alpha Kappa Alpha Sorority, Incorporated; The Wilmington Chapter of The Links, Incorporated; St. Mark Episcopal

PAST – New Hanover County Schools (Educator); League of Women Voters (President); Cape Fear Community Foundation; Retired Teachers of the Cape Fear Area (President); New Hanover County School Personnel (Program Chair); YWCA (Board of Directors); New Hanover County Democratic Party (1st Black Vice-Chair); New Hanover County

Human Relations Commission; Community Boys' and Girls' Club (Board of Directors); New Hanover Regional Medical Center Foundation (Board of Directors); United Negro College Fund (Co-chair); Girl Scout of America (Troop #52 Leader); Jack & Jill of America, Incorporated (Local President/National Foundation Board/National Editor/National Treasurer/National Program Co-Chair);   Girls, Incorporated (Board of Directors);   The Wilmington Chapter of The Links, Incorporated (President)

*Spouse (Carter Newsome) has contributed greatly to Southeastern North Carolina. Mr. Newsome was not born in any of the counties used in the established criteria.

Nixon, Charles
PRESENT - Recycling Business (Owner & Operator)

PAST - NC State Ports (Foreman & Shift Supervisor)

Nixon, Hannah
PRESENT - Retired

PAST – Cape Fear Museum (Volunteer/Receptionist); League of Women Voters; New Hanover County Mental Health Center (Volunteer)

Nixon, Julius Augusta
PRESENT - NC State Ports (Foreman & Shift Supervisor)

PAST – Civic Volunteer

Nixon, Wesley O.
PRESENT – Retired; Civic Volunteer

PAST – New Hanover County Planning Board; New Hanover County (Sub-division & Site Plan Review Commission); Federal Point Democratic Precinct #1 (#4); Retired US serviceman

Nixon Dunlap, Addie
PRESENT – Alpha Kappa Alpha Sorority, Inc.; Chestnut Street Presbyterian; Civic Volunteer

PAST – New Hanover County Schools (Counselor); Old New Hanover County Genealogical Society (Secretary); Alpha Psi Omega Chapter of Alpha Kappa Alpha Sorority, Incorporated (President)

Owens, Marguerite MacRae
PRESENT - Retired

PAST – City of Wilmington Recreation (Director); Wilmington Housing Authority

(Coordinator of Recreation); Wilmington Food Bank/Cheese and Butter Distribution; New Hanover Regional Medical Center (Women's Auxiliary); City of Wilmington Parks and Recreation Department (Special Olympics)

Pearce, Linda A.

PRESENT – Elderhaus, Incorporated (CEO); New Hanover Community Health Center (Board of Directors); Davis Health Care Center (Board of Directors); New Hanover Regional Medical Center (Investigative Review Board for Clinical Students); UNC-Wilmington (Board of Trustees); USS Gravely Commissioning Commission; Wilmington Rotary Club

PAST – New Hanover County Regional Medical Center (Board of Trustees); PPD (Clinical Investigation Review Board); New Hanover County Regional Medical Center (Foundation); New Hanover County Regional Medical Center (Pastoral Care Commission); Greater Wilmington Area Chamber of Commerce (Board of Directors)

Pridgen, Columbus

PRESENT – Powell Bail Bonding (Agent)

PAST – New Hanover County Schools (Educator & Civic Volunteer)

Rhodes, Delores Hassell

PRESENT – UNC-Wilmington/School of Education (Host Coordinator for NC Teach Program); Bellamy Mansion Museum (Board of Directors/Chair of Education Committee); Cape Fear Literacy Council (Advisory Committee); Relocated to New Hanover County

PAST – Children's Museum (Board of Directors); Landfall Grants (Scholarship Committee)

Rhodes, Keith

PRESENT – Catch Restaurants located on Princess Street and Market Street (Owner and Chef);

PAST – Deluxe Restaurant (Chef)

Rhodes, Jr., Nick

PRESENT – New Hanover County Partnership for Children; African-American Heritage Foundation; UNC-Wilmington/Cameron School of Business (Cameron Executive Network); Cape Fear Area Resource Center (Advisory Board); New Hanover County Schools' (Board of Education)

PAST – Relocated to New Hanover County; US Air Force (Lt. Col.); Price Waterhouse Corporation (Senior Manager); WHQR (Board of Directors)

Richardson, Inez

PRESENT – Elderhaus (Board of Directors); NC Retired School Personnel

PAST – New Hanover County Schools (Educator); YWCA (Board of Directors); New Hanover

County Mental Health (Board of Directors); Williston College (Branch of UNC-Wilmington before the merger between Wilmington College and the Williston Branch of Fayetteville State University; American Association of University Women; Alpha Psi Omega Chapter of Alpha Kappa Alpha Sorority, Incorporated (Life Member)

Richardson, Terry L.

PRESENT – Attorney at Law; Price Cathedral AME Zion

PAST - New Hanover County (Assistant District Attorney); Pender County (Assistant District Attorney); New Hanover County Human Relations Commission; Cape Fear Chapter of the American Red Cross (Board of Directors); New Hanover County Democratic Party (2nd Vice Chairman); Wilmington Chapter of the Salvation Army (Board of Directors); Town Hall Community Education Cultural Center (Owner and President)

*Spouse (**Charlene Bell Richardson**) has contributed greatly to Southeastern North Carolina. Mrs. Richardson was not born in any of the counties used in the established criteria.

Roberts, Frankie

PRESENT – LINC (Executive Director)

PAST – New Hanover County Department of Social Services (Chairman/Board of Directors)

Robinson Evans, Constance

PRESENT – UNC – Wilmington (Perkins Specialist)

PAST – Civic Volunteer

Robinson, Marva Mapson

PRESENT – Wilmington Symphony (Board of Directors); Dreams of Wilmington (Teacher); Performing Artist (Lyric Soprano); Wilmington Alumnae Chapter of Delta Sigma Theta; Wilmington NC Chapter of The Links, Incorporated

PAST – Brunswick County Schools (Educator); St. Luke AME Zion (Minister of Music); Dreams of Wilmington (Board of Directors); Wilmington NC Chapter of The Links, Incorporated (Chairman/Southern Area Ritual Chair); The Wilmington Alumnae Chapter of Delta Sigma Theta (President)

Rogers, Margaret Sampson

PRESENT – Local Historian; National Association of Physically Handicapped, Incorporated (Cape Fear Chapter)

PAST – 1898 Centennial Foundation (Historian); The 1898 Foundation; 1898 Lecturer; Carolina Broadcasting Company; Pocomoke Public Radio; Duke University (Preservation of Black History Project); UNC-Wilmington (Assisted graduate student with historical information for research projects.) ; Alpha Kappa Alpha Sorority, Incorporated

Rowell, Helenda Simpson

PRESENT – Civic Volunteer; Retired; St. Luke AME Zion

PAST – New Hanover County Schools (Records Clerk); Community Citizens' Participation Group (Assistant Director); Alpha Psi Omega Chapter of Alpha Kappa Alpha Sorority, Inc

Rowell, Wilbur

PRESENT – International Longshoremen's Association (Assistant Secretary/Treasurer – One of the top four executive officers of the national union)

PAST – International Longshoremen's Union/Local #1426 AFL-CIO (President); NC Ports (Employee)

Scavella, Betty

PRESENT - Retired

PAST – "Smart Shop" (Owner); Community Involvement; Mt. Olive AME

Shaw, Marie

PRESENT – John H. Shaw Funeral Home (Owner)

PAST – Civic Volunteer

Shepard, Leo

PRESENT – NC Ports Authority (Employee); Ebenezer Baptist; Chestnut Street Presbyterian

PAST – A. Phillip Randolph Institute (Director); New Hanover County Department of Social Services (Chairman/Board of Directors); Civil Rights Activist

*Spouse (Jennie Price Shepard) has contributed greatly to Southeastern North Carolina. Mrs. Shepard was not born in any of the counties used in the established criteria.

Sheridan, Dr. Earl

PRESENT – UNC-Wilmington (Professor/Political Science); City of Wilmington (Councilman); Cape Fear Region Community Development Center (Board of Directors); Thalian Hall (Board of Directors); Mt. Olive AME

PAST – New Hanover County Branch NAACP (President); Domestic Violence Shelter and Services (Board of Directors); Bellamy Mansion (Board of Directors); 1898 Centennial Foundation; 1898 Foundation; UNC-Wilmington (Political Science Department Chair); *Wilmington Star News* (Guest Columnist)

Sheridan, Dr. Sandra J.

PRESENT – Chamber of Commerce (Educational Foundation Board); Cape Fear Museum (Advisory Board/Secretary); New Hanover County Partnership for Children (President);

State Employees' Credit Union (Advisory Board); The Wilmington Alumnae Chapter of Delta Sigma Theta Sorority, Incorporated (Journalist); St. Mark Episcopal

PAST – New Hanover County Schools (Educator/Principal/Director of Personnel/Assistant Superintendent); New Hanover County Democratic Party (First Vice-Chairman); Wilmington Railroad Museum (Board of Directors)

Simpson, Helen

PRESENT – Housing Rehabilitation Loans (Chairperson/Loan Review Committee); Chestnut Street Presbyterian

PAST – New Hanover County Schools (Educator); The Wilmington Alumnae Chapter of Delta Sigma Theta Sorority, Incorporated

Simpson, Vonnie Michelle Goodson

PRESENT – BRIDGES (Building Rapport with Individuals Divided by Gaps, Economic, and Social Structures) (Co-Founder); New Hanover County Health Department (Social Worker)

PAST – Coastal Horizons Substance Abuse Center; Alpha Psi Omega Chapter of Alpha Kappa Alpha Sorority, Incorporated

Smalls, Beverly Elese

PRESENT – Cape Fear Community College (Coordinator, Teacher Certification/Self Support Program Assistant); African-American Historical Society of the Lower Cape Fear (Gullah-Geechee Caucus); New Hanover County School System (Core Professional Development Team);

PAST – Cape Fear Museum (Educational Coordinator); Child Development Center of Wilmington; Thalian Hall Center for the Performing Arts (Board of Trustees)

Smith, Evelyn B.

PRESENT – New Hanover County Public Library (Advisory Board); New Hanover County School System/Sunset Elementary School (Director/After School Program); Mt. Olive AME

PAST – International Union AFL-CIO TCU-ASD (Industrial Trades Section) (Vice-president); AFL-CIO (Legislative Committee); Political Activist (under Dr. Hubert Eaton, Sr. Kenneth McLaurin, LM Newsome, Dorothy DeShields, and Dr. Earl Sheridan); Community Action Program (under the leadership of McCluey Hewett)

Smith, Shirley

PRESENT – The Wilmington Alumnae Chapter of Delta Sigma Theta Sorority, Incorporated; Mt. Zion AME; Civic Volunteer

PAST – Retired Teachers of the Cape Fear Area (President); Returned to New Hanover County

Sneed, Lavinia E.

PRESENT – Retired Teacher of the Cape Fear; St. Luke AME Zion

PAST – New Hanover County Schools (Principal); Shuffler Building (Transportation Volunteer)

Sneed, Virginia P.

PRESENT – New Hanover County Department of Aging (Volunteer/Coach Computer Training

PAST – US Customs Federal Women's Program (EEOC); NC Agricultural (Advisory Board); Human Relations Commission (Fair Housing Committee Chairperson); YWCA (Board of Directors); Cape Fear Council of Government (Care Givers Board Member); Returned to New Hanover County

Sparks, Ronald

PRESENT – Spark's Engineering, PLLC (Owner); City of Wilmington (Councilman); Seven Day Adventist

PAST – New Hanover County (Project Manager/Several Projects); Project Engineer (New Hanover County and other states); Author (several publications)

Spaulding-Hughes, Sandra

PRESENT – NC House of Representatives (District 18); Co-author

PAST – Family and Consumer Science Educator (NHC Cooperative Extension Service); City of Wilmington (Council member); New Hanover County Arts Council; Screen Gems Film Commission; DARE (Commission); YWCA (Board of Directors); Community Action Group (Co-Founder); North 4th Street Partnership (Board); New Hanover County Prison (Board of Directors)

Speller, Islah

PRESENT – Burnett Eaton Museum (Founder & Owner)

PAST – Civic Volunteer

Spicer-Sidbury, Penelope

PRESENT – City of Wilmington (City Clerk); YWCA (Board of Directors/Treasurer); NC League of Municipalities (Board of Directors)

PAST – Wilmington City Council (Administrative Assistant to the Mayor and Council); Wilmington Industrial Development, Incorporated (Administrative Assistant); North Carolina Azalea Festival (President); North Carolina Association of Municipal Clerks (President); Gregory School of Science, Math and Technology (PTA President)

Thatch, Mary Alice Jervay
PRESENT – *The Wilmington Journal* (Editor/Publisher); The Wilmington Chapter of The Links, Incorporated; Alpha Kappa Alpha Sorority, Incorporated

PAST – Returned to New Hanover County

Thatch, Shawn Jervay
PRESENT – *The Wilmington Journal* (Chief Executive Officer); Alpha Psi Omega Chapter of Alpha Kappa Alpha Sorority, Incorporated

PAST – Relocated to New Hanover County

Thatch Briggs, Johanna
PRESENT – *The Wilmington Journal* (Assistant Editor); Alpha Kappa Alpha Sorority, Incorporated

PAST – Relocated

Thomas, Loretta Evans
PRESENT – Spring Arbor Retirement and Nursing Home (Executive Director); Shiloh Missionary Baptist

PAST – New Hanover County Department of Social Services (Hardship Hearing Committee)

Thomas, Alfred
PRESENT – New Hanover Community Health Center, Incorporated (CEO)

PAST – Returned to New Hanover County

Thompson, Lela
PRESENT – Willis Richardson Players (President/Board of Directors); Play Performances; St. Stephen AME

PAST – Center for the Performing Arts, Incorporated (Thalian Association); Community Arts Committee/Downtown Plan/Vision 20/20; Arts Council of the Lower Cape Fear; Piney Woods Cultural Heritage Festival; Lower Cape Fear Historical Society Tour by Candlelight

Thompson, Melvin
PRESENT – Willis Richardson Players; St. Stephen AME

PAST – New Hanover County Schools (Social Worker); Piney Woods Cultural Heritage Festival; Lower Cape Fear Historical Society "Tour by Candlelight"; Accord Theatre Group; Free Masonry Participation in North Carolina

Thompson, Paul

PRESENT – Thompson House Rentals, LLC (President); Phoenix Employment Ministry (Job Developer); Chemical Process Elementis Chromium (Supervisor); Chestnut Street Presbyterian

PAST – New Hanover County Juvenile Services Center (Program Counselor)

Upperman Smith, Linda

PRESENT – UNC-Wilmington "Stompin' at the Savoy (UNC-W Scholarship Fundraiser Organizer); NAACP

PAST – Returned to New Hanover County; UNC-Wilmington (Foundation Board); UNC-Wilmington (Board of Trustees); Great Expectations; UNC-Wilmington HUB Advisory Committee; 1898 Foundation (Co-chair); 1898 Foundation (Leadership Team); Good Friends (Board of Directors); Thalian Hall Center for Performing Arts (Board); Cape Fear Museum (Board of Directors); The Wilmington NC Chapter of The Links, Inc.

*Spouse (Dr. Howard Rasheed) has contributed greatly to Southeastern North Carolina. Dr. Rasheed was not born in any of the counties used in the established criteria.

Utley, James

PRESENT – Civic Volunteer; Ordained Minister; Activist

PAST – Wilmington Ministerial Alliance (Chairman); NC Legislative Representative (Candidate)

Waddell, Ruchadina L.

PRESENT – Chestnut Street Presbyterian; Delta Sigma Theta Sorority, Incorporated; Relocated

PAST – New Hanover County Assistant County Attorney; Habitat for Humanity; Family Services of the Lower Cape Fear; After School Enrichment Program (President); Business and Professional Women (Vice President & President-Elect); New Hanover County Bar (Board of Directors); Juvenile Crime Prevention Council; Ocean House Mental Health Advisory Board; 1898 Executive Committee; Heritage Tourism

Wade, Dr. Anthony E.

PRESENT - Relocated

PAST – New Hanover County Human Relations Commission (Director)

Warren, Florence Johnson

PRESENT – New Hanover County Schools (Educator); St. Stephen AME

PAST – New Hanover County Board of Education (Candidate); Civic worker and community organizer

Washington, Gregory

PRESENT – International Longshoremen's Union/Local #1426 AFL-CIO (President); Spectrum Photography (Owner); Hanover Lodge #14; Habib Temple #159; New Hanover County Community Action; City of Wilmington Loan Review Committee; EASY Program (Board Chairman); *The Wilmington Journal* (Freelance Photographer); Wilmington Consistory #63

PAST – Hanover Lodge #14 (Worshful Master Past Master)

Weller, Frances

PRESENT – WECT TV6 (News Anchor for 25+ years); Community Boys' and Girls' Club (Board of Directors); Willie Stargell Foundation; Pink Pack (Breast Cancer Self-Awareness); Fran's Fans (Fan collection for distribution to the needy.); Fran's Wheels (Bicycle collection for children at Christmas)

PAST – Pursuit of degree

Weller, Katherine

PRESENT - Retired

PAST – John T. Hoggard High School/New Hanover County Schools (Administrative Secretary); Historic Wilmington Foundation, Incorporated; Women in Action for the Prevention of Violence and Its Causes

Weller-Stargell, Margaret

PRESENT – Coastal Horizons Center (President and CEO); Willie Stargell Foundation (Established in honor of her late husband, Willie Stargell (former major league baseball player for the Pittsburg Pirates), for the purpose of furthering kidney disease research and treatment.

PAST – Pursuit of degree

Williams, Antoinette R.

PRESENT – A. Williams Tax Express, Incorporated (Owner)

PAST – Pursuit of degree

Williams, Arthalia Bordeaux

PRESENT – Returned to New Hanover County; New Hanover Regional Medical Center (Ethics Committee); Meals on Wheels (Volunteer); New Hanover County Board of Elections (Democratic Judge CF06); Topsail Island Fishing Club (Chair/Board of Directors); Moore's Creek Missionary Baptist (Health Fair Organizer); UNC-Chapel Hill (Interviewer/Evaluator – School of Public Health/Department of Maternal & Child Health)

PAST – New Hanover County Schools (Teacher/Assistant Principal/Principal); UNC-Chapel Hill (Instructor); Alpha Kappa Alpha Sorority, Incorporated

Williams, Eva
PRESENT – A. Williams Tax Express (Office Manager); Central Missionary Baptist

PAST – Zeta Phi Beta Sorority, Incorporated; Civic Volunteer; New Hanover County Schools (Educator)

Williams, Harry
PRESENT – New Hanover County Board of Elections; Precinct #6(Secretary); Mary C. Williams Elementary School (Volunteer); Northside Resource Center; St. Luke AME Zion

PAST – New Hanover County Schools (Teacher, Assistant Principal, Principal, Assistant Director, Central Office)

Wilson, Madafo Lloyd
PRESENT – Storyteller; Relocated

PAST – Brothers Reaching Out (Mentoring Program); Kwanzaa Coordinating Committee; Children's Theatre (Director); Racial Healing Discussions (Moderator)

Worthy, Helen Shaw
PRESENT – New Hanover County Black Caucus (Chair); Civic Volunteer

PAST – New Hanover County Democratic Party (Chair)

Wright, Thomas Edward
PRESENT - Relocated

PAST – NC Representative – NC House 18; Wilmington City Council (Councilman); City of Wilmington (Fire Department); Emergency Medical Technician

"My Journey Continues"
Chapter 15

"Too often we are so preoccupied with the destination, we forget the journey."
-Anonymous

Do I feel as restless as I did years ago? **NO**! I'm still just as driven -- just on a more selective basis.

My late husband, Mack would often say, as I'd scurry off to yet another community meeting, "Well, there you go again, trying to save the world."

But I have always believed that each of us has a calling to advance the cause of humanity, and sometimes it requires that we move out of our comfort zone. We need only pray and examine our hearts and minds to determine why we are in this place at this time.

Shakespeare wrote in "As You Like It",

All the world's a stage
All the men and women merely players
They have their exits and their entrances
And one man (woman) in his (her) time
plays many parts.

The part that I played was miniscule when one considers the totality of the human experience. Many others, in this state, this country, and all over the world, for that matter, have worked tirelessly to demand that the rights afforded one of us is afforded all of us. My life's work was not so much about changing *the* world as it was changing *my* world. I could not sit idly by while the schools in which I worked, the community I lived in, and the state I called home tried to wing their ways through one of the most turbulent times in our country's history.

My journey toward goal fulfillment has, for the most part, kept me from journeying geographically. Recently, however, I was fortunate to take some time to tour parts of Europe and the Middle East with a special group from Macedonia Missionary Baptist Church under the coordination of the Rev. Dr. Terry L. Henry.

Establishing an Endowment

As my journey continues, new goals are being pursued -- all in an effort to serve humanity in some way. In 2009, Myrtle and I began to reminisce about our early years in Sampson County. Myrtle suggested that to truly honor the Boykin educational legacy that we establish a Boykin endowment at Sampson Community College. Descendants of the four Boykin brothers were contacted and funds were solicited. We are pleased to announce that the endowment is approaching a quarter million dollars. It is our hope that many deserving students will be served by these annual scholarships. My cousin, Mary Boykin Brown, an instructor at Sampson Community College and member of the Sampson County Board of Education, is serving as the endowment coordinator.

This endowment was established in honor of my father, Thomas, and his three brothers. My father and his two sisters were the educators, but each of his siblings believed in a strong work ethic and encouraged their children to pursue an education.

In Memoriam

Junious A. Boykin (my stepfather)

James C. Boykin

Thomas J.L. Boykin (my father)

Benjamin J. Boykin

Group picture taken at the luncheon establishing the Boykin Endowment for Sampson Community College, Clinton, NC. Back row: Dr. Stephen McCary Henderson, Thomas Barksdale, Franita Brown Barksdale, Dr. Robert R. Sampson, Rita Denise Todd, Derrick Edison Boykin Front row: Mary Boykin Brown, Dr. Bertha Boykin Todd, Dr. Myrtle Boykin Sampson, Ernest Lamarr Boykin

JUNIOUS A. BOYKIN DESCENDANTS

Annie Boykin Carlton

Clarence Randolph Boykin

Mary Boykin Brown

David Junious Boykin

Joseph V. Boykin, Jr., M.D.

JAMES C. BOYKIN DESCENDANTS

Selena Boykin Reid

Cynthia L. Reid

THOMAS J.L. BOYKIN DESCENDANTS

Bertha Boykin Todd

Clarence C. Cooper

Derrick Edison Boykin

"Ricky" Ricardo Sampson

Myrtle Boykin Sampson

Rita Denise Todd

Brian Edward Todd

BENJAMIN J. BOYKIN DESCENDANTS

Jefferine Boykin Baskett

Ernest L. Boykin

Benjamin Boykin, II

In closing, I'm reminded of the great vision penned by poet Langston Hughes.

"I Dream"

A world where men

No other man will scorn

When love will bless the earth

And peace its paths adorn.

I dream a world where all

Will know sweet freedom's way,

Where greed no longer saps the soul

Nor avarice blights our day.

A world I dream where black, white, red, yellow and brown

Whatever ethnic group you be

Will share the bounties of the earth

And every man is free,

Where wretchedness will hang its head

And joy, like (man or woman)

Attends the needs of all mankind –

Of such I dream, my world!

Appendix A

The letters included here in chronological order may further exhibit my sense of restlessness through the years. Although many awards have been received as a result of my intense involvement, this book was not penned for the purpose of highlighting those accolades. I am profoundly humbled for being a recipient of these awards.

THE WINSTON-SALEM PLAN

TURNKEY III Home Ownership Counseling Program

1410 PLEASANT STREET / P. O. BOX 4807 / WINSTON-SALEM, N. C. 27107

DIVISION OF UNIVERSITY EXTENSION
Agricultural Extension Service Cooperating

September 24, 1971

Mrs. Bertha B. Todd
Administrative Assistant
Human Relations
114 Mercer Avenue
Wilmington, North Carolina 28401

Dear Mrs. Todd:

Thank you for your excellent program on Human Relations. It was a great asset to our Turnkey III staff conference at Wrightsville Beach. The need for better understanding is especially important in our work with people of such varied backgrounds. We appreciate your willingness to talk with us and share with us your experiences. You have a standing invitation to visit us in Winston-Salem. Thank you again for the fine program.

Very truly yours,

Robert W. Watts
Training Director

Letter of appreciation from Mr. Robert W. Watts

OFFICE OF THE
MAYOR

City of Wilmington, North Carolina

November 22, 1971

Mrs. Bertha B. Todd
114 Mercer Ave.
Wilmington, N. C.

Dear Mrs. Todd:

Thank you for accepting appointment to
the Human Relations Commission. I have high hopes
and great confidence in this Human Relations Commission under the able leadership of Mr. Bill Cullom.

You will be officially notified of the
time and place of the first meeting.

Again thank you for accepting this
appointment and your willingness to serve this
community.

Sincerely yours,

B. D. Schwartz
Mayor

Letter from the late Mayor BD Swartz

BROOKS HAYS, CHAIRMAN
THEODORE SPEIGNER, VICE CHAIRMAN

FRED L. COOPER, DIRECTOR

North Carolina
Human Relations Commission

ROBERT W. SCOTT, GOVERNOR

P. O. BOX 12525
RALEIGH, NORTH CAROLINA 27605
(919) 829-7996
829-3354

January 6, 1972

Mrs. Bertha Todd
114 Mercer Avenue
Wilmington, North Carolina   28401

Dear Mrs. Todd:

The North Carolina Human Relations Commission is very
impressed with the manner in which the citizens of Wilmington have
responded to the problems that became apparent during the civil
turmoil of last February.

We want to commend the citizens in general and give special
recognition to a few of the leaders for their outstanding
contributions and leadership in helping set up the machinery
that will hopefully lead to a better understanding and unity of all
people in Wilmington in the future.

You have been chosen as one of those to receive this special
recognition. We wish to extend to you a cordial invitation to
be in Raleigh, North Carolina on January 12, 1972, at 11:00 a.m.
for a ceremony honoring you for your efforts. The ceremony will
be held in the Methodist Building at 1307 Glenwood Avenue.

Please contact Mayor Schwartz, he is making arrangements for
transportation.

We are looking forward to seeing you on the 12th.

Sincerely,

Fred L. Cooper
Director

FLC:cw

Letter of invitation from Mr. Fred L. Cooper, Director,
North Carolina Human Relations Commission

North Carolina General Assembly
House of Representatives
State Legislative Building
Raleigh 27611

May 25, 1977

B. D. SCHWARTZ
12TH DISTRICT
HOME ADDRESS: 205 FOREST HILLS DRIVE
WILMINGTON, N. C.   28401
LEGISLATIVE COMMISSION ON CHILDREN WITH
SPECIAL NEEDS, CHAIRMAN

COMMITTEES:

ALCOHOLIC BEVERAGE CONTROL
CHAIRMAN
BANKS AND BANKING
VICE CHAIRMAN
APPROPRIATIONS COMMITTEE ON
HUMAN RESOURCES AND
CORRECTIONS
COMMERCIAL FISHERIES AND
OYSTER INDUSTRY
ECONOMY
HIGHER EDUCATION
STATE GOVERNMENT

Mrs. Bertha B. Todd
114 Mercer Avenue
Wilmington, North Carolina   28401

Dear Bertha:

The Governor has just informed me that you are being named
to the North Carolina Human Relations Council.

I pleasantly recall the input that you gave our Human
Relations Council which I helped organize in the City of
Wilmington.

With kindest personal regards and best wishes,

Sincerely,

B. D. Schwartz

BDS/gwc

Again Congratulations

Letter from the late Representative BD Swartz, NC House of Representatives

**AGRICULTURAL EXTENSION SERVICE
AGRICULTURAL AND TECHNICAL STATE UNIVERSITY**
GREENSBORO, NORTH CAROLINA

September 22, 1971

Mrs. Bertha B. Todd
Administrative Assistant, Human Relations
114 Mercer Avenue
Wilmington, North Carolina   28401

Dear Mrs. Todd:

I do appreciate the very practical approach you took
in presenting human relations information to our Turnkey III
counseling staffs. It was just what we needed. I hope we
can build on what we learned as we continue to work together
as a staff and to work with the disadvantaged families.

You are rendering a wonderful service to human beings
in your daily work and I feel the sincerity you have for
people.

Best wishes for a successful and happy year.

Yours very truly,

Helen W. Branford

(Mrs.) Helen W. Branford
District Home Economics Agent
Turnkey III Training Program

HWB/cc

COOPERATIVE EXTENSION WORK IN AGRICULTURE AND HOME ECONOMICS. NORTH CAROLINA STATE
UNIVERSITY AT RALEIGH, 100 COUNTIES AND U. S. DEPARTMENT OF AGRICULTURE COOPERATING

STATE OF NORTH CAROLINA
GOVERNOR'S OFFICE
RALEIGH 27611

ROBERT W. SCOTT
GOVERNOR

December 10, 1971

Mrs. Bertha Todd
Assistant Principal
Hoggard High School
Wilmington, North Carolina

Dear Mrs. Todd:

In order to alleviate the tensions and unrest within many of the public schools of our State, I am forming a citizens task force to look into this troublesome problem and to come up with recommendations.

I would like for you to serve as a member of this task force, which will hold its initial meeting on December 17 in the Conference Room of the State Administration Building here in Raleigh. Registration will begin at 10:15 a.m. at the conference site, with the meeting to start at 11:00 a.m.

I plan to open the meeting by speaking to the problem and to the work of the task force. After this, we plan to have brief preliminary remarks among members of the task force and then to recess for lunch. No provisions for lunch have been made, so you will be on your own. After the lunch break, we plan to reassemble and to divide into a number of workshop or seminar groupings, concluding later in the afternoon with a brief summary session.

I feel that you can provide input into this effort to maintain a proper climate of learning within our schools and to assure continuing public support for them.

I would appreciate a reply from you at your earliest convenience.

Cordially,

Robert W. Scott

THE WINSTON-SALEM PLAN

TURNKEY III   Home Ownership Counseling Program

1410 PLEASANT STREET / P. O. BOX 4807 / WINSTON-SALEM, N. C. 27107

DIVISION OF UNIVERSITY EXTENSION
Agricultural Extension Service Cooperating

September 24, 1971

Mrs. Bertha B. Todd
Administrative Assistant
Human Relations
114 Mercer Avenue
Wilmington, North Carolina 28401

Dear Mrs. Todd:

    Thank you for your excellent program on Human Relations.
It was a great asset to our Turnkey III staff conference at
Wrightsville Beach. The need for better understanding is
especially important in our work with people of such varied
backgrounds. We appreciate your willingness to talk with us
and share with us your experiences. You have a standing
invitation to visit us in Winston-Salem. Thank you again
for the fine program.

                      Very truly yours,

                    Robert W Watts

                    Robert W. Watts
                    Training Director

* Sponsored a human relations workshop
RWW/jbs for a group of approximately 30
Professionals from various divisions
within N.C.. Three persons were
from N.C. State in Raleigh. Faculty members.

New Hanover County Schools
Wilmington, North Carolina

Mrs. Bertha B. Todd
114 Mercer Avenue
Wilmington, N. C.

Dear Mrs. Todd:

You are invited and requested to serve as a MEMBER OF THE ADULT ADVISORY COMMITTEE ON SCHOOL AND COMMUNITY RELATIONS. YOU WERE RECOMMENDED AND SELECTED AS A CITIZEN WHO IS INTERESTED IN SCHOOL AND CIVIC MATTERS AND IT IS HOPED YOU WILL ACCEPT THIS INVITATION AND ACTIVELY SERVE.

As indicated by its name, this committee will act in an advisory capacity to the New Hanover County Board of Education and will serve as a liaison link between the Board and the adult population of our area. We all know there are many problems to be solved in the immediate future and hopefully this committee will aid tremendously in solving these problems by keeping abreast of the actions of the Board, by disseminating correct information, by helping eliminate half-truths and false rumors that so often cause a great deal of trouble among both students and parents, and by doing everything possible to promote the orderly operations of our schools over the entire County.

This committee will be composed of approximately 25 fine citizens, including yourself, and we should like to have you meet in the immediate future in preparation for the opening of school on September 1, 1970.

Will you please indicate your acceptance of committee membership by writing me in care of New Hanover County Board of Education, P.O. Box 390, Hemenway Hall, Wilmington, North Carolina, or calling the office of Dr. Heyward C. Bellamy, Superintendent of Schools, Telephone number 763-5431.

Sincerely,

E. A. Laney, Chairman
New Hanover County
Board of Education

EAL:DWP

1971

OFFICE OF THE
MAYOR

City of Wilmington, North Carolina

November 22, 1971

Mrs. Bertha B. Todd
114 Mercer Ave.
Wilmington, N. C.

Dear Mrs. Todd:

Thank you for accepting appointment to
the Human Relations Commission. I have high hopes
and great confidence in this Human Relations Commission under the able leadership of Mr. Bill Cullom.

You will be officially notified of the
time and place of the first meeting.

Again thank you for accepting this
appointment and your willingness to serve this
community.

Sincerely yours,

B. D. Schwartz

B. D. Schwartz
Mayor

BROOKS HAYS, CHAIRMAN
THEODORE SPEIGNER, VICE CHAIRMAN

FRED L. COOPER, DIRECTOR

North Carolina
Human Relations Commission

ROBERT W. SCOTT, GOVERNOR

P. O. BOX 12525
RALEIGH, NORTH CAROLINA 27605
(919) 829-7996
829-3354

January 6, 1972

Mrs. Bertha Todd
114 Mercer Avenue
Wilmington, North Carolina   28401

Dear Mrs. Todd:

The North Carolina Human Relations Commission is very
impressed with the manner in which the citizens of Wilmington have
responded to the problems that became apparent during the civil
turmoil of last February.

We want to commend the citizens in general and give special
recognition to a few of the leaders for their outstanding
contributions and leadership in helping set up the machinery
that will hopefully lead to a better understanding and unity of all
people in Wilmington in the future.

You have been chosen as one of those to receive this special
recognition. We wish to extend to you a cordial invitation to
be in Raleigh, North Carolina on January 12, 1972, at 11:00 a.m.
for a ceremony honoring you for your efforts. The ceremony will
be held in the Methodist Building at 1307 Glenwood Avenue.

Please contact Mayor Schwartz, he is making arrangements for
transportation.

We are looking forward to seeing you on the 12th.

Sincerely,

Fred L. Cooper
Director

FLC:cw

Seven Wilmingtonians honored by state Human Relations group

By WILEY McKELLAR
Staff Writer

RALEIGH — Seven Wilmingtonians were honored by the North Carolina Human Relations Commission here Wednesday for their efforts in building better race relations in a city which has been torn by civil strife several times over the past three years.

Certificates for outstanding leadership were presented to Mayor B. D. Schwartz, William Cullom, chairman of the Wilmington-New Hanover Human Relations Commission; Tom Jervay, editor and publisher of the Wilmington Journal; Mrs. Bertha Todd, assistant principal of John T. Hoggard High School in charge of human relations; Herb McKim, chairman of the Chamber of Commerce Human Relations Committee; and Miss Elaine Fields and Miss Angelia Wright, students active in human relations.

Fred Morrison, legal assistant to Gov. Bob Scott, presented the awards to the Wilmingtonians on behalf of the Governor, and conveyed to them a message from Gov. Scott, who was unable to attend the ceremonies.

"We are committed to equality for all citizens," said Gov. Scott in his message. "To deny this to any one citizen is wrong. I, as Governor, again call upon all citizens from every walk of life to help us work through our social problems in the spirit of justics, fairness and openness. Then and only then will we 'be rather than to seem.'

"It is very gratifying for me to join the North Carolina Human Relations Commission in paying tribute to seven Wilmingtonians who embody the kind of spirit, attitude, compassion and sense of fair play that will help us work through our human relations problems."

Aaron Johnson, public information officer of the Human Relations Commission, said that after more than its share of racial strife, Wilmington and its community leadership are emerging as a "very courageous and compassionate" force for human relations.

He said the leaders of Wilmington realized there were citizens with just grievances, and brought together people young and old, rich and poor, black and white for the purpose of discussing their mutual problems.

Perhaps the most important result of the Wilmington work was the formation of a new Human Relations Commission on a local level, said Johnson. He said the new commission involves representatives from just about every segment of the community from the black militants to Ku Klux Klan.

He said that the sooner the people of North Carolina and the rest of the country take heed from the Wilmington story, then the closer the world will come to harmony.

He said people must realize and "learn to live here with justice, equality and liberty, or we are going to die as fools."

Johnson introduced the seven Wilmingtonians to the meeting.

Mayor B. D. Schwartz — "the new breed of political leader," who during one period of racial crisis watched as his brother's furniture store went up in flames caused by arson.

Mrs. Bertha Todd — "the new breed of school administrator" who had worked into a job requiring the utmost skill — human relations in school.

William Cullom — "he's been in the middle and thick of things and he's done a tremendous job."

Tom Jervay — "courageous leadership" within the black community, "a man with a cool head and a heart full of compassion."

Herb McKim — the "new breed of businessman" with the capacity to bring the involvement of business in human relations.

Miss Elaine Fields and Miss Angelia Wright — "an outstanding job in human relations in the school."

Mayor Schwartz told the Human Relations Commission that he was proud to accept his award on behalf of the City of Wilmington, and added that there was still much work ahead for Wilmington's citizens.

"We haven't solved all our problems yet," said the Mayor. "But we are aware of them, and the people of Wilmington are moving ahead. They are getting involved. Each person that you see here today is heavily involved."

Mayor Schwartz said he had high hopes for the Human Relations Commission in Wilmington, and added that the formation of the group in November had opened up a whole new line of communication among people in every social stratum and every walk of life in Wilmington.

He said the involvement of people — not only the community leaders, but all citizens — will work into a more harmonious relationship between the races in the city.

Rogers   Jones   Asbury   Milnor   Todd   Lewis   Staff Photos Graham

These county citizens honored by bicentennial association Friday

Weitz

Heroes of peace honored in city

1975-76

Local "heroes of peace" were honored Friday in a special Memorial Day observance by a luncheon program at the Wilmington Hilton.

The program was sponsored by the Wilmington-New Hanover County American Revolution Bicentennial Association.

A panel of speakers, Fire Chief Robert Shipp, Chief of Police D. L. Bruestle, Sheriff H. G. Grohman, Highway Patrol 1st Sgt. J. B. Stewart, Cmdr. Robert Janecek of the Coast Guard, and Dr. Robert Fales of the medical profession, told of local heroes of peace within their profession.

The list included Highway Patrolman H. Griffin, killed last year near Burgaw, as a man who gave his life in his service, and Leon George, a Wilmington police officer, who died of disease contacted while helping others in an epidemic at the turn of the century.

Other speakers told of the dedication of Major Joe Johnson, the New Hanover County jailer who ably served those with whom he came in contact with, and fireman Martin Schnibbens, killed while racing to put out a fire.

Those attending the luncheon heard of the Midgett family, Coast Guardsmen on the Outer Banks, who dedicated their lives in the rescue and help of men lost at sea.

They heard of Doctor Dickson, a martyr in the 1862 yellow fever epidemic in Wilmington.

Other awards were made to those who have helped make the Bicentennial projects in New Hanover County a reality during the past year.

The award certificates were presented by Col. Robert S. Milner.

The Williston Concert Band provided music for the program. The band was under the direction of Betsy Talley.

May 29, 1976

Scott names 2 local people to task force

Mayor B. D. Schwartz and Mrs. Bertha Todd, Assistant Principal in charge of Human Relations at J. T. Hoggard High School, have been appointed by Governor Bob Scott to an 80 member Citizens' Task Force to study the unrest and tension in North Carolina's public schools.

The Task Force is being formed to look into the tension and unrest that has plagued many of the state's public schools, and to come up with recommendations to faD maintain a proper climate of learning in the schools.

An initial meeting of the Task Force will be held in all-day session Friday at the State Administration Building in Raleigh.

Governor Scott will preside over the session, at which seminar and workshop groupings will be formed.

1970'

UNCW *Shr News 9-16*

Five named to foundation board

Five new members have been elected to UNCW's foundation board of directors, which presides over the university's fund-raising arm. The new members will serve until July 1996.

The members are Michael Creed, president of McKim & Creed Engineers; Tom Dodson, NationsBank senior vice president; Jack Henriksen, president of Takeda Chemical Products; Betty Ann Sanders, owner of Sanders & Associates; and Bertha Boykin Todd, retired administrator of New Hanover County schools.

The board has 18 members who meet every three months. *1990'*

Meetings

Following is a list of meetings of organizations which are open only to members and their guests. The deadline for insertion of items in the Wednesday meetings list is 5 p.m. Monday. Information may be mailed to Meetings, Star, Box 840, Wilmington 28402. Information is not accepted by telephone.

Today

Kiwanis Club of Wilmington — Bertha Todd, a member of the N.C. Human Relations Council, will speak at a luncheon in the Boucan Room of the Heart of Wilmington Motel. *1980's*

North Carolina General Assembly

House of Representatives

State Legislative Building

Raleigh 27611

May 25, 1977

B. D. SCHWARTZ
12TH DISTRICT
HOME ADDRESS: 205 FOREST HILLS DRIVE
     WILMINGTON, N. C.   28401
LEGISLATIVE COMMISSION ON CHILDREN WITH
     SPECIAL NEEDS, CHAIRMAN

COMMITTEES:
ALCOHOLIC BEVERAGE CONTROL
     CHAIRMAN
BANKS AND BANKING
     VICE CHAIRMAN
APPROPRIATIONS COMMITTEE ON
     HUMAN RESOURCES AND
     CORRECTIONS
COMMERCIAL FISHERIES AND
     OYSTER INDUSTRY
ECONOMY
HIGHER EDUCATION
STATE GOVERNMENT

Mrs. Bertha B. Todd
114 Mercer Avenue
Wilmington, North Carolina   28401

Dear Bertha:

The Governor has just informed me that you are being named
to the North Carolina Human Relations Council.

I pleasantly recall the input that you gave our Human
Relations Council which I helped organize in the City of
Wilmington.

With kindest personal regards and best wishes,

                                    Sincerely,

                                    B. D. Schwartz

BDS/gwc

Again Congratulations

STATE OF NORTH CAROLINA

OFFICE OF THE GOVERNOR

RALEIGH 27611

JAMES B. HUNT, JR.
GOVERNOR

June 22, 1977

Dear Bertha:

Pursuant to G.S. 143B-392, I hereby appoint you to serve
on the North Carolina Human Relations Council. Your
appointment is effective immediately and as a member of
this Council you serve at the pleasure of the governor.

It is with great pleasure that I enclose your commission.
I have every confidence you will make an outstanding
contribution to the progress of this Council.

I am also enclosing the oath of office. Please have the
oath properly executed before a judge, clerk of court,
deputy clerk of court, register of deeds, notary public,
magistrate or mayor, and return the original and two
copies to my office.

My warmest personal regards.

Sincerely,

Mrs. Bertha B. Todd
114 Mercer Avenue
Wilmington, North Carolina 28401

Enclosures

FAMILY SERVICE ASSOCIATION OF AMERICA **STRENGTH TO FAMILIES**

Washington DC Field Office
Middle Atlantic & Southeastern Regions
1819 H Street N.W.
Washington D.C. 20006
(202) 659-8732

May 3, 1978

Mrs. Bertha B. Todd
114 Mercer Avenue
Wilmington, N. C. 28401

Dear Mrs. Todd:

Please accept thanks from the Family Service Association, from the South-eastern Region and from me, personally, for your generous contributions during the six years you served as a member-at-large to the Southeastern Regional Council. It is because of committed members like you that the family movement has maintained its position of strength and leadership in the community.

Again, thank you and hopefully, you will again be involved at some future time.

Sincerely,

Richmond G. Bernhardt Jr.
Vice President
Southeastern Region

North Carolina
Department of Administration

Howard Building   112 West Lane Street   Raleigh 27603

James B. Hunt, Jr., Governor
Joseph W. Grimsley, Secretary

Human Relations Council
Henry E. McKoy, Executive Director
(919) 733-7996

December 11, 1978

Ms. Bertha Todd
114 Mercer Avenue
Wilmington, N.C. 28401

Dear Ms. Todd:

The North Carolina Human Relations Council is preparing for its Annual Workshops and Banquet scheduled for February 16-17, 1979, at the Jane S. McKimmon Center, North Carolina State University, Raleigh.

We are pleased you have agreed to serve as a moderator at the workshop, "Competency Testing" on Friday, February 17, 1979 from 2:45 - 5:30 p.m. Your remarks should be limited to 10 minutes. The workshop will consist of two primary speakers, two reactors, a moderator and a recorder.

Thank you for your time and interest.

If you have any questions, please advise.

Sincerely,

Henry

Henry E. McKoy
Director

HEMcK/dd

North Carolina
House of
Representatives

 Carl J. Stewart, Jr., Speaker

Raleigh 27611
(919) 733-3451

July 15, 1980

Ms. Bertha B. Todd
114 Mercer Avenue
Wilmington, North Carolina 28401

Dear Bertha:

Congratulations on being appointed by Governor Hunt to
serve on the New Horizons Housing Task Force. I am sure
that you will do an outstanding job on this Task Force. I
wish you the very best.

With warmest personal regards, I remain

Very truly yours,

Carl J. Stewart, Jr.
Speaker of the House

CJSjr:crw

Southeastern Community College   P.O. Box 151, Whiteville, N.C. 28472

August 16, 1984

Mrs. Bertha Todd
Assistant Principal
Hoggard High School
4305 Shipyard Blvd.
Wilmington, N.C. 28403

Dear Mrs. Todd:

I would like to take this opportunity to thank you for your
excellent presentation in the Substitute Teacher Workshop
for the Columbus County School System personnel.

Your presentation received an overall rating of excellent
in the evaluation completed by the participants.

Thank you again for sharing your expertise with us.

Sincerely,

Harry W. Foley
Supervisor, Adult Education

HWF

cc: Dr. Richard Flynn
     Mr. Michael J. Saus

ATLANTIC TELECASTING CORP. / P.O. Box 4029 / Wilmington, N.C. 28406 / (919) 791-8070

KAREN FOX
Director of Community Relations

March 6, 1985

Mrs. Bertha Todd
Hoggard High School
4305 Shipyard Boulevard
Wilmington, N.C. 28403

Dear Mrs. Todd:

Thank you for agreeing to be a member of WECT's Minority Advisory Council. We at WECT hope the council will be a viable forum for the exchange of ideas to strengthen the relationship between the minority community and the station.

Our first meeting has been set for Friday, March 22 at 12noon at the Western Steer Family Steak House on the Carolina Beach road. We invite you to join us for lunch in their meeting room in the rear of the restaurant. The facility should give us the privacy we need to get acquainted and to find out what each other has on his mind.

I will call you prior to March 22 to confirm your attendance. I look forward to seeing you then.

Sincerely,

Karen Fox

522 Decatur Drive
Wilmington, N. C. 28403

June 05, 1985

Mrs. Bertha Todd
114 Mercer Avenue
Wilmington, N.C. 28401

Dear Mrs. Todd,

It made my heart glad to hear such enthusiam in your voice on the morning I spoke with you in the matter of being our Special Guest and Speaker at our 30th Anniversary Dinner-Dance and Social Hour.

I have taken the matter before our class and they, along with me eagerly await your brief message and fellowship.

The Dinner-Dance will be held at the I.L.A. Labor Temple, 1305 South Fifth Avenue, Friday, July 05, 1985 at 7:00 P.M. The attire for the evening will be semi-formal.

Please feel free to partake in all scheduled functions as this will be our wages to you. (smile)

Thank you very, very much for your acceptance.

We Love You Always,

THE CLASS OF "55"

Walter McAllister,
President

WMcA:ejcg

North Carolina Department of Administration

121 West Jones Street • Raleigh, North Carolina 27603-1334 • Telephone 919-733-7996

James B. Hunt, Jr., Governor
Jane Smith Patterson, Secretary

Human Relations Council
James W. Bowden, Executive Director

October 2, 1984

Mrs. Bertha B. Todd
114 Mercer Avenue
Wilmington, North Carolina 28401

Dear Mrs. Todd:

On behalf of the Council and staff, I would like to thank you for your dedicated service as a member of the North Carolina Human Relations Council.

Through your efforts, the Council was able to accomplish many of its objectives, such as passage of the Dangerous Weapons Law, Fair Housing Law, Jury Selection Law and the Staggered Terms Law and the many other studies and positions of the Council. In fact, I don't think that I would be overstating the facts if I said that you served on one of the most progressive and far-sighted Councils since its existence. So, when I suggest that your service was invaluable, I really do mean it and deeply regret that you will no longer be serving with us. However, we know that you will continue to make significant contributions to our society, for that's the kind of person you are. Should you find that we could be of assistance to you in your future endeavors, please know that we stand ready to do what we can to help you accomplish your objectives.

The Council would like to have you as our guest during our next meeting and properly express our appreciation for your many contributions. The staff will be in touch with you to let you know when in January we will be meeting.

Again, the Council and I really do appreciate your past service and we wish for you God's Speed as you turn your efforts to other areas of interest.

Thanks from all of us to you!

Sincerely,

Dr. Jerry Drayton, Chairman
N. C. Human Relations Council

/tbn

An Equal Opportunity / Affirmative Action Employer

Center
for Documentary
Studies
at Duke University

Snow Building
Suite 511
331 West Main Street
Durham, North Carolina
27701

(919) 687-0486

April 22, 1993

Mrs. Bertha Todd
114 Mercer Avenue
Wilmington, NC 28403

Dear Mrs. Todd:

Thank you so much for taking the time to meet with us last week to discuss the "Behind the Veil: Documenting African American Life in the Jim Crow South" project. We enjoyed meeting you and appreciate your assistance.

We felt that our two days in Wilmington were quite productive. With your help, we compiled a list of almost 75 people to contact! With your consent, we would like to use your name as one of our local "consultants" when we begin to contact people for interviews.

For your information, we are enclosing an article about the project which was recently published. We will keep you informed of our progress. We look forward to working with you.

Best,

Leslie Brown and Annie Valk
Research Coordinators

THE OLEANDER COMPANY, INC.
P. O. BOX 3145
WILMINGTON, NORTH CAROLINA 28406
TEL: 910-392-3300
FAX: 910-392-5123

November 18, 1998

Mrs. E. M. Todd
114 Mercer Avenue
Wilmington, NC 28403

Dear Bertha,

Congratulations to you and all of your colleagues who worked so hard to achieve the highly successful 1898 Commemoration events. The entire Commemoration and all of the fine events turned out very successfully and touched many people in the right way.

Particularly, I appreciate your thoughtfulness to me and your giving me the opportunity to be included. I learned and benefited much during the process, and I was very pleased to be able to support the Commemoration and to be a part of it.

I also feel that several new and meaningful programs have been set in motion. These will work for improvements in the future. I look forward to taking part in other occasions as I am able to do so. I will enjoy working with you on the Monument Commission, as all of this unfolds further.

Again, congratulations on the wonderful work which you and your colleagues have accomplished. I look forward to seeing you often as we work along together on the Bellamy Mansion restoration program and the Monument Commission for 1898.

With my best regards,

Hugh MacRae II

Hugh MacRae II

cc: Dr. Bolton Anthony

CAPE FEAR COMMUNITY COLLEGE

411 NORTH FRONT STREET • WILMINGTON, NORTH CAROLINA 28401-3993
PHONE (910) 251-5100 • FAX (910) 763-2279

January 28, 1999

Mrs. Bertha Todd
114 Mercer Avenue
Wilmington, North Carolina 28403

Dear Mrs. Todd:

Thank you for agreeing to be a member of the panel *Wilmington in the 1890s*. The panel is scheduled for Thursday evening February 25, 1999 from 6:00 - 7:30 p.m. in the auditorium of the McLeod Building. (Please refer to the enclosed map.) When you enter McLeod from the parking area, the auditorium is on the right. A parking space near the entrance will be reserved for you for the evening.

As I mentioned during our telephone conversation, this panel was originally planned for the students currently enrolled in my Introduction to Sociology classes. For their class project, I am requiring each student to conduct three to five interviews with people in the Wilmington area who are at least 70 and who know the area well. These interviews will be used to write a summary of the changes that Wilmington has undergone over the past one hundred years. In order to better understand what the area was like in the 1890's each student is required to read three to five sources on Wilmington during this time period. The panel may be used as one of these sources but more importantly, will provide students the opportunity to ask questions of people who are experts on the subject. The more I thought about the panel and spoke with people on campus, the more it became obvious that this panel would be of interest to the entire college community as well as the community at large. Thus the panel discussion will be open to the general public and be a part of Cape Fear Community College's celebration of *Black History Month*.

To assist you with your preparations for the panel, I have enclosed a copy of the instructions given to my students. Please do not view this as an exhaustive list of topics rather it is provided as reference. Comments from panel members should last approximately an hour leaving the final thirty minutes for questions from the audience. Light refreshments will be served at the conclusion of the program.

Again, thank you for your assistance in making this program a success. If you need additional information, please feel free to contact me at (910) 251-5692.

Sincerely,

Deborah L. Basket
Sociology Instructor

State of North Carolina
Office of the Lieutenant Governor

BEVERLY EAVES PERDUE
LIEUTENANT GOVERNOR

310 NORTH BLOUNT STREET
20401 MAIL SERVICE CENTER
RALEIGH, NC 27699-0401

July 3, 2001

TELEPHONE: (919) 733-7350
FAX: (919) 733-6595
e-mail: bperdue@ncmail.net

Bertha Boykin Todd
114 Mercer Avenue
Wilmington, NC 28403

Dear Bertha:

Congratulations on receiving the **Community Leadership Award** at the North Carolina Legislative Black Caucus Foundation's Sixteenth Annual Legislative Education and Scholarship Conference.

I commend your unselfish involvement in promoting positive race relations within New Hanover County. These efforts are vital as we move towards a more diverse North Carolina. Your civic and social involvement exemplifies the spirit of community service. Your accomplishments continue to inspire other citizens.

You are extremely worthy of the honor bestowed upon you by the North Carolina Legislative Black Caucus. Let me offer my greatest and most sincere appreciation for your hard work and persistence.

With warmest regards, I am

Sincerely,

Beverly Eaves Perdue

You are an outstanding North Carolinian.

BEP:dh

An Agency of New Hanover County

814 Market Street • Wilmington, NC 28401-4731
910.341.4350 • Fax: 910.341.4037
e-mail: cfm1@wilmington.net
www.co.new-hanover.nc.us/cfm/cfmmain.htm

September 13, 2001

Ms. Bertha Todd
114 Mercer Ave.
Wilmington, NC 28403

Dear Bertha:

I appreciate your contribution to our first *Bit of History*, Williston Memories. Your stories and memories provided audience members with a good idea of the struggles and celebrations that occurred at the high school. And as I listen to reports of Tuesday's horrific event, I am thankful there are people with your spirit in our community working for peace.

From our perspective, the program was a success. There were forty audience members, UNC Wilmington filmed the presentation for possible broadcast and media representatives from three different radio/television stations attended. The program was of interest to a wide audience and we appreciate your help in making it a memorable event.

Sincerely,

Jennie Ashlock
Education Coordinator

Where the Past has Presence

711 Iredell Street
Suite A
Durham, NC 27705
(919) 286-7186
Fax. (919) 286-7216.
E-mail: info@wildacresleadership.org
Web Page: www.wildacresleadership.org

February 2, 2007

Ms. Bertha Todd
114 Mercer Avenue
Wilmington, NC 28403

Dear Ms. Todd,

Thank you for agreeing to speak with the 2006-2008 William C. Friday Fellows for Human Relations during their seminar on Leading in an Ever Changing World.

Your session will take place on Saturday, February 10th from 12:15-2:15 pm at Thailian Hall and we'd very much like you to join us for lunch from 11:30 am-12:15 pm prior to this. Your session is entitled *Leadership Converstation: Wilmington Leaders Facing Adaptive Challenges* and a design for the session with an indication of objectives, audience, structure and opening questions is attached. Your colleagues on the panel are listed there as well.

A couple of pieces of information that will be helpful for your planning are here, including:
* the guidelines for dialogue utilized by the group in doing our work together;
* brief biographical information on the eighteen 2006-2008 Friday Fellows.

We are grateful for your willingness to give your time to this effort. It is important that the Fellows know about your efforts in Wilmington and learn from your leadership journeys.

If you have any questions or concerns, please contact me at 919-286-7186 or kathleen@wildacresleadership.org. In the event you need to reach me on February 10th, my cell number is 919-423-4925 and my colleague Sterling's is 919-819-0910.

With regards,

Kathleen C. Clark
Program Director

Appendix B

The following pictures represent various periods of activity and programs in my life. A bit restless or energetic? The answer will be left up to the reader.

Mary Lillie Lofton (former educator and member of Chestnut Street Presbyterian Church (USA)) and Bertha B. Todd. For several years, Alpha Psi Omega Chapter of Alpha Kappa Alpha Sorority, Incorporated sponsored a program recognizing senior citizens. Ms. Lofton was one of the seniors I sponsored when the proogram was held at St. Stephen AME Church. Picture by John Davis.

For a number of years, I was a very active member of Church Women United. This picture is an example of my participation in a drama involving a diverse group of women. My assignment was to dress as a Native American. Well, I did my best!

During the seventeen years I served as an assistant principal at J.T. Hoggard High School, I wrote proposals for several school programs and activities. I also spent a quite a bit of time writing rebuttals regarding something that may have occurred at Hoggard.

Receiving the Honorary Doctorate of Humanities in August of 2000 from the University of North Carolina at Wilmington. Dr. Cavanaugh is at the podium as Dr. James Leutze, who was chancellor at the time, looks on.

My sister, Ida Boykin Cooper (deceased), was an accomplished pianist and organist. When she passed in June of 1995, a group of adults (initiated by yours truly) organized a special music group – "The Special Piano Pupils". One of the criterion, was and still is, members must make mistakes while performing. The primary goal – to motivate us to practice AT LEAST twice a year. Both recitals, fall and spring, are always held in a private home.

Talking with a group of teens in a gym.

Serving as mistress of ceremonies in Raleigh, NC while serving on Governor James Hunt's North Carolina Human Relations Council.

In 1955, The Wilmington, NC Chapter of The Links, Incorporated sponsored a masquerade ball at the Community Boys' Club (now the Community Boys' and Girls' Club). The person who was to serve as the mistress of ceremonies during intermission did not appear. The more experienced members coerced me into serving as mistress of ceremonies for the program. Mistress of ceremonies by default!!! Picture taken by Dr. Hubert A. Eaton, Sr.

My twin sister, Myrtle, and her spouse, Dr. Robert R. Sampson, celebrating their 50th wedding anniversary.

One of the highlights of my college years was singing, traveling, and performing with the college choir. We would always sing and visit several states. This picture was taken by a New York photographer who gave us all a huge discount!

This photo represents The Links', Incorporated Southern Area Conference Reception held at the Blockage Runner Hotel at Wrightsville Beach, NC in 1967. The Wilmington, NC Chapter of The Links', Incorporated organized this international meeting. The Southern Area encompasses seven states (Alabama, Florida, Georgia, Louisiana, Mississippi, North Carolina and South Carolina) and the Bahamas. In the center of the picture are Dr. and Mrs. Hubert A. Eaton, Sr. Celeste Burnett Eaton was responsible for chartering the Wilmington Chapter for this premier organization. My spouse and I are center right in the photograph.

Suggested Readings

Bellamy, R. and Cantwell, Si (Eds.) 2008. <u>Moving Forward Together: A Community Remembers 1898</u>. Wilmington, NC: The 1898 Foundation.

Brunson, Deborah A., Linda L. Lampl, Felecia F. Jordan – <u>Jackson Interracial Communication: Contexts, Communities, and Choices</u>. Dubuque, IA: Kendall Hunt Publishing Company.

Eaton, H. (1984). <u>Every Man Should Try</u>. Wilmington, NC: Bonaparte Press.

McLaurin, Melton, A. (1987). <u>Separate Pasts: Growing Up White in the Segregated South</u>. Athens, GA: University of Georga Press.

Prather, Sr., H.L. (1984). <u>We Have Taken a City: Wilmington Racial Massacre and Coup of 1898</u>. Rutherford, NJ: Fairleigh Dickinson University Press.

Sampson, Myrtle Boykin (2010). Crazy Lady: Achievement Against The Odds. Greensboro, NC: Lulu Publishers.

Truman, Karol K. (2003). Feelings Buried Alive Never Die... St. George, Utah: Olympus Distributing.

Index

"C"

"F"

"N"

"O"

"P"

"T"

"Y"

"Z"